Smartphone Cultures

Smartphone Cultures explores emerging questions about the ways in which this mobile technology and its apps have been produced, represented, regulated and incorporated into everyday social practices. The various authors in this volume each locate their contributions within the circuit of culture model.

More specifically, this book engages with issues of production and regulation in the case of the electrical infrastructure supporting smartphones and the development of mobile social gambling apps. It examines issues of consumption through looking at parental practices relating to children's smartphone use, children's experience of the regulation of this technology, both in the home and in school, how they cope with the mass of communications via the smartphone and the nature of their attachment to the device. Other chapters cover the engagement of older people with smartphones, as well as how different cultural norms of sociability have a bearing on how the technology is consumed. The smartphone's implications for other theoretical frameworks is illustrated through examining ramifications for domestication, and the sometimes-limited place of smartphones in certain aspects of life is examined through its role in the practices of reading and writing. *Smartphone Cultures* presents the latest international research from scholars located in the UK, Europe, the US and Australia and will appeal to scholars and students of media and cultural studies, communication studies and sociologists with interests in technology and social practices.

Jane Vincent is Senior Researcher and Visiting Fellow in the Department of Media and Communications at the London School of Economics and Political Science and member of EU COST Actions examining print and digital media, and media issues in ageism. Jane is co-editor of publications including *Social Robots from a Human Perspective*, *Migration, Diaspora and Information Technology from a Global Perspective* and *Electronic Emotions, The Mediation of Emotions via Information and Communication Technologies.*

Leslie Haddon is Senior Researcher and Visiting Lecturer in the Department of Media and Communications at the London School of Economics and Political Science, UK. He is the author of *Information and Communication Technologies in Everyday Life*, co-author of *The Shape of Things to Consume* and *Mobile Communications: An Introduction to New Media*, editor of *The Contemporary Internet* and co-editor of *Everyday Innovators, The Social Dynamics of Information and Communication Technology, Generational Use of New Media, Kids Online* and *Kids Risk and Safety Online.*

Smartphone Cultures

**Edited by Jane Vincent and
Leslie Haddon**

Routledge
Taylor & Francis Group

LONDON AND NEW YORK

First published 2018
by Routledge

2 Park Square, Milton Park, Abingdon, Oxfordshire OX14 4RN
52 Vanderbilt Avenue, New York, NY 10017

Routledge is an imprint of the Taylor & Francis Group, an informa business

First issued in paperback 2019

British Library Cataloguing in Publication Data
A catalogue record for this book is available from the British Library

Library of Congress Cataloging in Publication Data
A catalog record for this book has been requested

ISBN: 978-1-138-23438-3 (hbk)
ISBN: 978-0-367-33299-0 (pbk)

Typeset in Times New Roman
by Wearset Ltd, Boldon, Tyne and Wear

Contents

Conclusion 177

Illustrations

Figures

Tables

Contributors

César Albarrán-Torres is Lecturer in Media and Communication at Swinburne University of Technology. He is widely published in academic and non-academic outlets as a researcher, writer and film critic. His research focuses on digital gambling platforms, political activism and mobile media in Mexico and film.

Naomi S. Baron is the Executive Director of the Center for Teaching, Research and Learning and Professor of Linguistics at American University in Washington, DC. Her research interests include electronically mediated communication, writing and technology, the history of English, and higher education. A former Guggenheim Fellow and Fulbright Fellow, she has published eight books. *Always On: Language in an Online and Mobile World* won the English-Speaking Union's Duke of Edinburgh English Language Book Award for 2008. Her newest book (2015) is *Words Onscreen: The Fate of Reading in a Digital World*. She taught at Brown University, Emory University and Southwestern University before coming to American University, where she has served as Associate Dean in the College of Arts and Sciences, Chair of the Department of Language and Foreign Studies, and Director of the TESOL Program.

Carla Barros is Professor at the Department of Media and Cultural Studies and at the Graduate Program (MA and PhD) in Communication of the Fluminense Federal University (UFF), Rio de Janeiro, Brazil. PhD in Business Administration, Post-Graduate in Anthropology at Federal University of Rio de Janeiro (UFRJ). Her research focuses on anthropology of consumption and anthropology of communication, working mainly with low-income groups. She is coordinator of the research group Núcleo de Estudos em Comunicação de Massa e Consumo – NEMACS (Studies in Mass Communication and Consumption), connected to CNPq (National Counsel of Technological and Scientific Development). She is co-author of the book *Cultura e experiência midiática (Culture and Media Experience)* (Ed. Mauad, 2014) and has published several essays and texts in various journals and collections.

Manuela Farinosi is Post-doctoral Researcher in Sociology of Communication in the Department of Humanities and Cultural Heritage at the University of Udine, Italy.

Troels Fibæk Bertel is Assistant Professor of Communication Studies at Roskilde University. His work centres on the use and social consequences of media and communication in everyday life and his research interests include mobile media and communication, domestication theory and everyday civic engagement of vulnerable groups in social media.

Miguel Angel Casado del Río is Lecturer at the Department of Audiovisual Communication and Advertising at the University of the Basque Country. His research interests include cultural industry economics, public media systems and children and new media. He is a member of the European research network funded by the European Commission EU Kids Online.

Mireia Fernández-Ardèvol is Senior Researcher at the Internet Interdisciplinary Institute (IN3) at the Universitat Oberta de Catalunya (UOC) within the research group Communication Networks and Social Change. Mobile communication has been one of her main areas of study since 2003, with a combined sociological and economic focus. She develops this interest from three perspectives. First, focused in Latin America, the analysis of the contribution of mobile communication to development and poverty reduction; second, the role of mobile communication in social networked movements; and third, the analysis of how mobile communication is incorporated among older individuals in different countries. Regarding the transition towards aged networked societies, she is responsible for the area Telecommunication Technologies of the Ageing + Communication + Technologies project (http:\\actproject.cat) and is active member of the EU COST network on Ageism.

Maialen Garmendia is Senior Lecturer at the Sociology and Social Work Department at the University of the Basque Country. Her research interests include media and everyday life and children and digital technologies. She is a member of the European research network funded by the European Commission EU Kids Online.

Gerard Goggin is Professor of Media and Communications at the University of Sydney. He is also an Australian Research Council Future Fellow, studying disability, digital technology, and human rights. Gerard is widely published on mobile media and communications, with key books including *Locative Media* (2015), *Routledge Companion to Mobile Media* (2014), *Mobile Technology and Place* (2012), *Global Mobile Media* (2011) and *Cell Phone Culture* (2006). He is currently working on a book on disability and the mobile phone.

Leslie Haddon is Senior Researcher and Visiting Lecturer in the Department of Media and Communications at the London School of Economics. His research over the three past decades has focused on the social shaping and consumption of ICTs, especially in studies of domestication. He has authored, co-authored, edited and co-edited eight books in this field and was series editor for the Berg New Media series. More recently he helped to coordinate the EU Kids Online project and participated in the Net Children Go Mobile project

Maren Hartmann is Professor of Communication and Media Sociology at the University of the Arts in Berlin. She has taught and researched at several other universities in the past, in Germany, Belgium, the UK and Denmark. Her PhD (University of Westminster) was published as 'Technologies and Utopias: the cyberflâneur and the experience of being online' in 2004. Most recently, she published a book on domestication (in German) and began a research project on the question of time and mobile media use, funded by the German funding association (DFG). She has been involved in European research projects (EMTEL I & II) as well as the European (ECREA) and the German communication association (DGPuK). Her research fields cover mobile media and mobility, cyberculture, media sociology as well as the question of creative research methods.

Estefanía Jimenez is Lecturer in Media Studies at the School of Social Sciences and Communication of the University of the Basque Country She has been a member of the EU Kids Online network since 2012 and also participated in the Net Children Go Mobile project as the Spanish representative. She works on media literacy, audience research and usage of SNS.

Claudia Lampert has been working as Senior Researcher at the Hans-Bredow-Institut of Media and Communication Research since 2006. One of her particular research interests and emphases is in the area of media socialisation and media education. In the context of various projects, she is currently working on the role of digital media in the everyday lives of children and adolescents. From 2012–2013 she was involved in a study on media education strategies in families, funded by the Media Authority North Rhine-Westphalia (Wagner, Gebel, Lampert 2013). Furthermore, she is the German contact in the EU Kids Online and the Net Children Go Mobile project, and also member in the COST Action 'The Digital Literacy and Multimodal Practices of Young Children' (IS1410).

Christopher Lim is Programme Director for product design at the Duncan and Jordanstone College of Art and Design, University of Dundee with research interests in the area of design for aging population, particularly in the relationship between interaction design and prior generational technological experience; personalized 3D printing for healthcare sector and the investigation of co-design practice as a process for novel technological products creation.

Giovanna Mascheroni is Senior Lecturer in Sociology of Communication and Culture in the Department of Sociology, Università Cattolica of Milan, and a Visiting Fellow at the Department of Media and Communications, LSE. She coordinated the Net Children Go Mobile project and is part of the management group of EU Kids Online.

Marije Nouwen holds a professional BA in Communication Management, a MA in Social and Cultural Anthropology and a certificate in Human Centered Design. She has been working as a researcher on children and digital media at the Meaningful Interactions Lab (Mintlab, KU Leuven – imec) since 2013. Her research includes parental mediation of young children's digital media use, the multi-stakeholder perspectives regarding digital media at school and children's motivations in music learning.

John O'Sullivan lectures in journalism and new media at Dublin City University, where he has chaired the MA in Journalism. As a print journalist, he covered technology and society. His research has focused on professional values and the Internet, and on the role of print and digital formats in news.

Sora Park is Associate Professor of Communication and Senior Research Fellow at the News & Media Research Centre, University of Canberra. Her research focuses on digital media users, media markets and media policy and she has written widely on the economics of television, newspaper markets and other information industries. She has extensive experience in policy research and consultancy regarding digital media in South Korea. Her previous positions include Research Fellow at Korea Press Foundation, Director of the Interdisciplinary Program of Women's Studies at Hanyang University, Chair of the School of Communication Arts at Kwangwoon University and Research Fellow at the Korea Press Foundation. She received her PhD in Communication Studies from Northwestern University.

Cristina Ponte is an Associate Professor of Communication Sciences and a member of CICS.NOVA research centre, at Faculdade de Ciências Sociais e Humanas, Universidade Nova de Lisboa (FCSH/NOVA), Portugal. With a background in Communication and Education, her research examines children, youth and media; media and generations, with a focus on the family; digital inclusion, media, journalism and society. Coordinating the Portuguese team in the EU Kids Online Project since 2006, she has wide experience in leading international and large teams of researchers, including the Working Group on Social Integration in the COST Action *Transforming Audiences, Transforming Societies* (2010–2014), and the funded FCT projects *Children and Young People in the News* (2005–2007) and *Digital Inclusion and Participation* (2009–2011), the latter with the University of Texas at Austin. She is the author/editor of 12 books and she has published several articles in Portuguese and English.

Andrea Rosales is Post-doctoral Researcher at the Communication Networks and Social Change group, of the Internet Interdisciplinary Institute (IN3) at the Universitat Oberta de Catalunya (UOC). With a PhD in Human Computer Interaction, an MA in and a BA in Journalism she researches from an interdisciplinary perspective. She conducts user studies related to ICTs, especially with children and older people. Her activities include ethnographic explorations, co-design studies, prototyping, evaluation processes and data analysis.

She also developed wearable systems for playful and educative purposes. Her current research focuses on seniors and playful interactions with mobile technologies and especially wearable technologies. How do seniors use mobile technologies? How does this differ from younger adults? How do older people learn to use technologies? And, what new technologies do they imagine would be useful in their lives?

José Alberto Simões holds a PhD in Sociology from Faculdade de Ciências Sociais e Humanas, Universidade Nova de Lisboa (FCSH-UNL), where he is Assistant Professor in the Department of Sociology. He is also a researcher at CICS.NOVA (Interdisciplinary Centre of Social Sciences), a research unit of FCSH-UNL. He has participated in several research projects (both national and international) in the areas of sociology of culture, youth cultures, and communication and digital media. He has been a Member of EU Kids Online network since 2006 and a national contact of Net Children Go Mobile project. Until recently he coordinated *Networked Youth Activism: Digital Media, Social Movements and Participatory Culture among Young Activists*, funded by the Portuguese Foundation for Science and Technology.

Sofie Vandoninck has an MA in Communication Sciences from KU Leuven in 2005. She first worked as research assistant. In 2011 she started a PhD at the Institute for Media Studies (KU Leuven), which she defended in March 2016. Her PhD project focuses on identifying vulnerable children's coping strategies, and why some children are resilient while others are not. She investigates how children's individual and social contexts play a role in their exposure to online risks and opportunities, the development of online resilience and use of coping strategies. She has been actively involved in the EU Kids Online project since 2009. Within EU Kids Online, she mainly focuses on coping with online risks and the development of (online) resilience. From September to December 2013, she worked with the EU Kids Online team on the qualitative analysis of the EU Kids interviews and focus groups at Masaryk University in Brno. In 2014, she actively cooperated in the Net Children Go Mobile project, collecting and analysing data for Belgium.

Anca Velicu, PhD, is Senior Researcher at the Institute of Sociology (Sociology of Communication and Public Space Laboratory) within the Romanian Academy. Her main research interests include the sociology of the media, children's use of Internet and mobile Internet, young children and digital technologies, and media violence. Some of the research projects in which she was involved are: from 2009–2012 she was director of the project *The Impact of Media Violence on Romanian Children. An Analysis of the Civic, Ethical and Aesthetical Dimensions* (funded by National Agency for Research), since 2009 she has been member of the Romanian team of EU Kids Online project and between 2012–2014 she was involved, as national contact, in the Net Children Go Mobile project.

Jane Vincent is Senior Researcher, Visiting Fellow and Guest Teacher with the Department of Media and Communications, London School of Economics and Political Science. Her research interests focus on the social practices of information and communication technology users of all ages and particularly mobile communications experiences of children and the very old. A member of several EU COST Actions since 2004, including FP1104 on Print and Paper and IS 1402 on Ageism, she has edited and contributed to numerous publications.

Bieke Zaman is Assistant Professor in Human-Media Interaction/Digital Humanities at Mintlab, part of the Institute of Media Studies (KU Leuven – imec), Belgium. She graduated from the KU Leuven in 2004 as a master in Communication Sciences (summa cum laude), obtained post academic degrees in Usability Design (2005) and Web Development (2007), and a doctoral degree in social sciences (2011, KU Leuven). Working on the tech side of social, and on the social side of tech, Zaman pursues research programmes on Children, Digital Media and Design, and Games and Learning. She is member of several academic editorial boards (e.g. *International Journal of Child-Computer Interaction*), international conference committees (e.g. ECREA, CHI Play, Interaction Design and Children) and international networks (e.g. EU COST Action IS1410 DigiLitEY).

Acknowledgements

The authors of Chapters 1, 4, 6, 9 and 10 of this volume draw on the work of the 'EU Kids Online' network funded by the EC (DG Information Society) Safer Internet Programme (SI-2010-TN-4201001); see www.eukidsonline.net.

The authors of Chapters 1, 4, 6, 9, 10 and 11 of this volume draw on the work of the 'Net Children Go Mobile' project; see www.netchildrengomobile.eu.

The editors thank Bob Bradshaw for his assistance with the reproduction quality of the figures.

1 Introducing smartphone cultures

Jane Vincent and Leslie Haddon

Smartphone Cultures aims to explore emerging questions about the ways that this mobile device technology has been appropriated and incorporated into everyday social practices. We have allowed some years for the smartphone to become embedded globally in the mobile communications market and for the apps market to mature before proposing this volume, during which time various authors have begun to construct a smartphone literature that first examined what people are doing with these devices (Chen 2011; Berry and Schleser 2014) and are now beginning to look more deeply at the cultural impact of these behaviours and activities (du Gay *et al*. 2013; Miller 2014; Donner 2015; Kobyashi *et al*. 2015). The volume covers a variety of different uses and experiences, in the hands of different users living in different contexts to see not only their practices, but what the smartphone technology means to them. We look at what the smartphone enables and some challenges it presents, and, indeed, at the aspects of life where it actually has little impact. We also examine the various attempts at institutional and individual levels to keep control of the technology, either because of general worries about the changes that it threatens, or as a way of dealing with the more mundane problems that the use of the smartphone can throw up in everyday life. No one volume can exhaustively cover a device that has such diverse potential, both in what it can do or support and by virtue of that, how it can be represented and evaluated. However, this book can and does aim to capture the multifaceted nature of the smartphone phenomenon, the different ways it can be analysed, how it can be framed, and identifies research questions for the future.

To bring some structure to this diversity, and have one overarching framework for the book, we specifically asked the authors to frame their work in terms of the cultural processes identified within the circuit of culture (Johnson 1986; du Gay *et al*. 1997).

In his book chapter, Johnson originally used this circuit, Figure 1.1, to identify the key types of cultural process studied in the relatively new subject of cultural studies and how these interlinked. To illustrate this Johnson provided the brief worked example of the Mini Metro car. He identified the 'moment' of 'production', which entailed not only the making of a material object, the car, but the making of meanings, what the car stood for. Once produced, as a 'text',

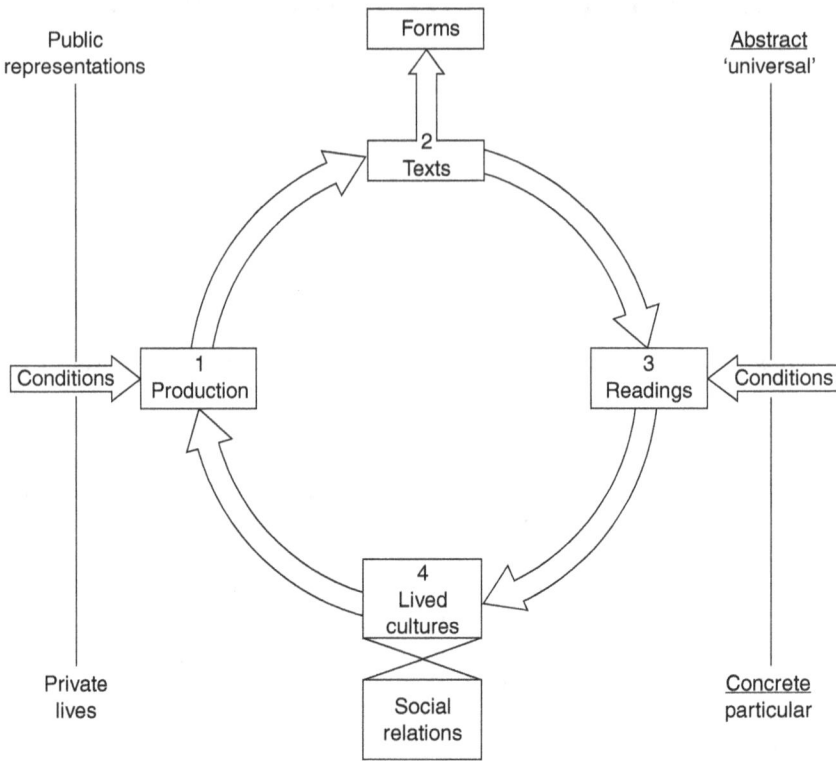

Figure 1.1 Circuit of culture.

Source: Johnson 1986, p. 284.

Note
Pearson Education Limited Copyright. Reproduced with permission from the publisher.

it was open to further 'readings', further interpretations, where not only other commentators but 'ordinary readers', such as those who used the cars, could see the car in terms of the role it played in their lives, in their 'lived culture'. Although not developed in Johnson's text, we can take the example further noting how people used the car, and how they felt about it, could in principle be picked up in the next round of production, be that in terms of alterations to design or advertising copy. It is worth emphasising that this model was not about theorising a technology – this car was only a particular example of a 'cultural form'. But the framework, that was really highlighting the questions that a researcher might ask, could equally apply to other cultural forms such as, citing Johnson's own examples, a book, a television series or a public ritual.

Some years later du Gay *et al.* (1997) drew on this approach using a variant of the original circuit, Figure 1.2, when exploring the 'Story of the Walkman'.

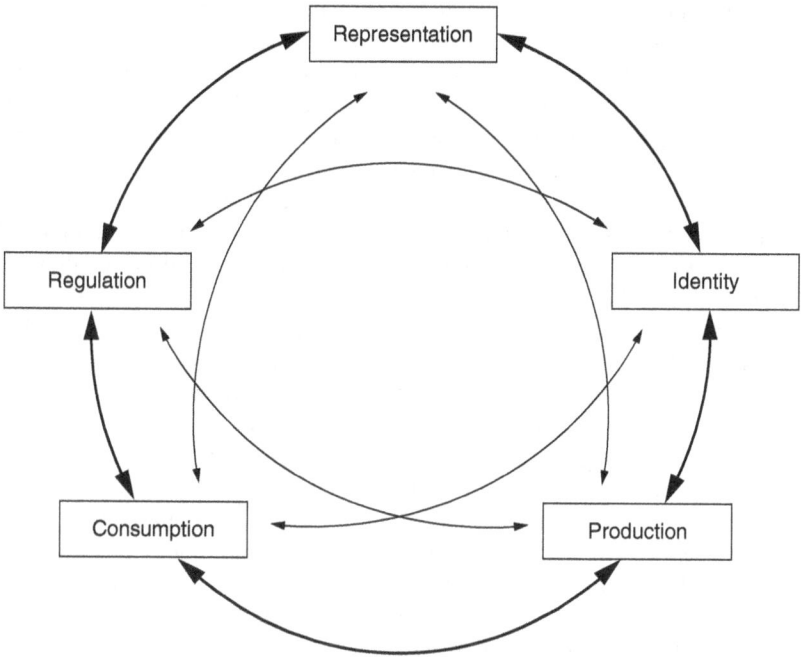

Figure 1.2 Circuit of culture.

Source: Du Gay *et al.* 2013 p. xxxi [1997].

Note
Reproduced with permission from the publisher.

This new portable music playing device that appeared to be having a significant impact on society, for example raising new questions about the nature of privacy in public spaces long before the mobile phone was to do so.[1] In their textbook aimed at UK Open University students du Gay *et al.* were, again, demonstrating the main types of cultural studies analysis that one could conduct using the worked example of the Walkman as a cultural form, as they clarified further in the second edition of the book (2013). But while they used the principle of the circuit, some of their terms and moments were slightly different. 'Production', somewhat similar to the Johnson version, remained, but the authors added 'representations' of the Walkman and 'identity' (here both in the sense of identifying with the product and the identity of the company producing the Walkman). Finally, in this version of the circuit we have 'consumption', covering the experience of the Walkman and what that can mean and symbolise for users and others, and 'regulation', the attempts to control usage of the technology because of the threats to social life that it represented. Du Gay *et al.* stressed that the original aim of their book was purely pedagogical, but acknowledged that it was in practice taken up across a variety of disciplines as a 'research text' (2013, p. xvi). We still find it useful for stimulating research questions.

The general nature of the circuit model, either version, means that it is flexible enough to provide a framework for locating contemporary studies despite being designed nearly three decades ago. For example, under 'production' (which would draw on writers describing the industry such as Woyke 2014) we would also now have to take into account contemporary discussions of 'prosumption', and in the case of the smartphone the development of apps. Meanwhile the vision of Snickars and Vonderau (2012) would be an example of representations of what the smartphone means for society. Following Johnson, and du Gay *et al.*, then, we will be using this model in the present volume to frame smartphone cultures, first to locate the chapters in this volume within existing smartphone studies but second, where possible, to use the framework as an aid to exploring what cultural processes could be researched in the future.

While smartphones might be in some sense 'new', which in turn makes the novelty of the technology attractive, the social and communicative affordances of the devices are themselves built on the back of previous products and user experiences. Hence, in addition to the circuit of culture, the smartphone would also have to be located historically and in this regard smartphones, and certainly the exponential growth in consumer demand for smartphones, even took industry by surprise. The adoption of its precursor, the mobile phone, was already growing globally at a phenomenal rate (Kakihara 2014) but the smartphone, with its access to the internet and thus much more information, communication and vastly greater multifunctionality, seemed to provide the foundation for potential cultural shifts that we are exploring in this volume. This very rapid and high-profile development itself led to some of the representations of the societal meaning of smartphones noted earlier. Yet, to put this technology into perspective, we also need to appreciate the smartphone is, in many respects, just one of the latest developments in a family of products or services which combine to deliver media and communications for consumers.

Then we have to consider the role of users in this historical process. Technology and industry-led developments in mobile communications delivered via increasingly sophisticated devices have contributed to the shaping of modes of social interaction, such as the mobile communication via social media applications. However, it is worth noting that innovations in this field have by no means followed a wholly industry-determined path. Indeed, in their choice of which information and communication products and services to adopt and adapt, users have already exerted some influence on the evolution of this field. For example, not all products in the run up to the smartphone have been successful, such as wireless application protocol (WAP) that aimed to deliver an early version of internet surfing. In contrast, and contrary to industry expectations, early innovations like Short Message Service, and Pay as You Go on mobile phones were pulled into the market by the degree of unanticipated consumer interest (Taylor and Vincent 2005). In this way users helped to shape future products, albeit while industry monitored the trends among and actions of their consumers and responded with new products. For example, teenage girls painting the back of phones in Finland led to coloured devices and decorated handset covers, or, personalised ring tones that in the early days of mobile phones were downloaded from a music library at Nokia HQ bespoke for each customer (Halper 2004) later became more standard mobile phone options. Thus, in this volume we would have to ask how user agency is now being expressed in relation to smartphones and how producers respond to this.

In order to understand some of the experiences, more particularly in our framework the 'readings', of this technology we also need to consider a different type of history. Accounts of the introduction of new technologies in the past (such as the telephone) highlighted the common occurrence of negative responses and even moral panics (Marvin 1990; Lasen 2005) sometimes entailing initial resistance to the threat of this 'newness'. Hence it is important to appreciate a history of perceptions, or concerns, that underlie such reactions. For example, in this volume we capture how parental concerns about their children's smartphone use do not only reflect a moral panic about online risks but also a long-standing discomfort – previously felt in relation to television, computers and electronic games – about the balance in their children's lives being upset by the threat of too much screen time. Meanwhile one recurrent theme in recent generations has been that parents often feel less technologically expert than their children (Haddon and Vincent 2015).

Framed in terms of the 'prosumers' of this technology in the spirit of Toffler (1980), some analysts stress how a smartphone user is now able to combine and condense an exponential increase in multimodal social relations and media consumption. More celebratory accounts would argue that never before has *anytime, anywhere, always on* connectivity been more apposite for describing the opportunities for staying in touch, finding information, enjoying media and having instant connectivity. While there might be some truth in this compared to the era when PC access to the internet dominated, as well as exploring the agency of users, we would also need to explore the constraints on their experience of this technology, as will be particularly well demonstrated in this book in relation to children's use.

In sum, in this volume we aim to provide a strategic assessment of smartphone use to unpack and explore its cultural impact on society and on individual users. Here the contributors have addressed smartphone culture not from the perspective of the technology's potential but rather from the point of view of the actual influence of the affordances of smartphones and through the experiences, aspirations and concerns of or about its users. For example, we cover such dimensions as the ways in which people use or do not use smartphones for particular purposes because of how they want to represent themselves, or how parents sometimes restrict their children's use because of fears about how the devices might affect their lives. Similarly, when discussing production we would want to think about how actual and anticipated practices of users are in turn incorporated by industry into the design of smartphone apps.

While as a personal device the smartphone has individualised and personalised qualities and functionality that differ from user to user, how it is used *en masse* in the day to day activities of contemporary society is examined in this book through the lens of various shared social practices of its users. This nuanced and often intimate approach demands an openness to theoretical/conceptual contributions that are flexible and broad enough to encompass the multitude of facets and interactions that using a smartphone entails. Also popular are theories of the presentation of self (Goffman 1959; Ling 2004) and domestication (Silverstone and Haddon 1996) that have been applied to previous studies of mobile communications; the social shaping of technology and users (MacKenzie and Wacjman 1999; Lasen 2005; Vincent 2006); the exploration of the affordances of devices (Gibson 1977; Goggin 2006; Schrock 2015), and mediatisation, which shows how aspects of society are intertwined with technological processes and the texture of social life (Harper 2010; Jansson 2013).

The studies explored in this volume draw on these and other frameworks but also look beyond how smartphones and tablets are used to consider what impact these devices are having on society and even the environment.

Looked at from an industry perspective, and similar to the introduction of the Walkman, smartphones and tablets have been seen or 'represented' as 'disruptive technologies' (Christensen 2005). From this perspective, these new technologies offer alternative interfaces for human/machine interaction that cut through previous media and information practices delivering content and communication in new ways. In fact, in their examination of disruptive technologies, McKinsey MIG (Manyika *et al.* 2013) specifically highlight the significance of smartphones in a technology future encompassing mobile internet, the internet of things and the cloud. Indeed, of the 12 disruptive technologies they identify, four make mention of smartphones – including the issue of battery and electricity supply and consumption to be discussed in this volume. Hence it is important to assess whether this is just another representation of the future of smartphones, whether this is the 'reading' agreed to by users or whether this is providing some insight into how smartphones are changing everyday practices.

As we explore the evolution of smartphones in this volume we anticipate there will be many factors influencing and shaping user experience and industry developments. Smartphones have developed so we now have 'all in one' devices analysed according to the different and innovative things people can do with them (Berry and Schleser 2014). Thus rather than exploring only the social practices of mobile phone users (Ling 2004; Katz 2005), we are now asking questions about how the smartphone has impacted social relations in contemporary society and about the readings of differing forms of the cultural representation of smartphones.

From a social researcher's perspective, the very multifunctionality of smartphones, partly enabled by these diverse apps, has to some extent led to some fragmentation of research, separating out user experiences according to what they do with or access by their smartphones or what different social issues particular uses of smartphones raise. This volume views such diverse research as capturing a plurality of smartphone cultures, which collectively help to convey a sense of the place of the smartphone in contemporary life. These issues are examined in 12 chapters presented within five themes as set out below.

Note

1 It is noted here that the authors recently updated their text to take account of issues raised by the new technologies that have emerged since the Walkman, including smartphones and tablets (du Gay *et al.* 2013).

Bibliography

Berry, M. and Schleser, M. (ed.) (2014) *Mobile media making in an age of smartphones*, New York, Palgrave Macmillan.

Chen, B. X. (2011) *Always on: How the iPhone unlocked the anything-anytime-anywhere future – and locked us in*, Philadelphia, De Capo Press.

Christensen, C. M. (2005) *The innovator's dilemma. When new technologies cause great firms to fail*, Cambridge, Mass, Harvard Business School Press.

Donner, J. (2015) *After access inclusion development and a more mobile internet*, Harvard, MIT Press.

Du Gay, P., Hall, S., Janes, L., Mackay, H. and Negus, K. (1997) *Doing cultural studies: The story of the Sony Walkman*, London, Thousand Oaks, Sage.

Du Gay, P., Hall, S., Janes, L., Koed Madsen, A., Mackay, H. and Negus, K. (2013) (Second edition) *Doing cultural studies: The story of the Sony Walkman*, London, Thousand Oaks, Sage.

Gibson J. J. (1977) The theory of affordances, in Shaw, R. and Bransford, J. (eds) *Perceiving, acting, and knowing: Toward an ecological psychology*, New York, Laurence Erlbaum Associates.

Goffman, E. (1959) *The presentation of self in everyday life*, Harmondsworth, Penguin Books.

Goggin, G. (2006) *Cell phone culture mobile technology in everyday life*, Abingdon. Routledge.

Haddon, L. and Vincent, J. (2015) *UK children's experience of smartphones, and tablets; perspective from children, parents and teachers* LSE, London, Net Children Go Mobile.

Halper, M. (2004) The sweet sound of success in *Time*, 8 August 2004. http://content.time.com/time/magazine/article/0,9171,901040816-678568,00.html (last accessed 10 April 2017).

Harper, R. H. (2010) *Texture: Human expression in an age of communications overload*, Harvard, MIT Press.

Horst, H. A. (2013) The infrastructures of mobile media: Towards a future research agenda, *Mobile Media & Communication* 1 (1): 147–152.

Jansson, A. (2013) Mediatization and social space: Reconstructing media for the transmedia age, *Communication Theory* 23 (3): 270–296.

Johnson, R. (1986) The story so far: And further transformations? in Punter, D. (ed.) *Introduction to contemporary cultural studies*, pp. 277–313, London, Longman Group.

Kakihara, M. (2014) Grasping a global view of smartphone diffusion: An analysis from a global smartphone study', *2014 International Conference on Mobile Business*. Paper 11. http://aisel.aisnet.org/icmb2014/11.

Katz, J. E. (2005) *Magic in the air: Mobile communication and the transformation of social life*, Piscataway, Transaction Publishers.

Lasen, A. (2005) History repeating? A comparison of the launch and uses of fixed and mobile phones, in Hamill, L. and Lasen, A. (eds) *Mobile world. Past, present and future*, pp. 29–60, Dordrecht, Springer.

Ling, R. (2004) *The mobile connection. The cellphone's impact on society*, Amsterdam, Morgan Kaufmanm.

Kobayashi, T., Boase, J., Suzuki, T. and Suzuki, T. (2015) Emerging from the cocoon? Revisiting the tele-cacooning hypothesis in the smartphone era, *Journal of Computer Mediated Communication* 20: 330–345.

Mackenzie, D. and Wacjman, J. (eds) (1999) (Second edition), *The social shaping of technology*, Milton Keynes, Open University Press.

Manyika J., Chui, M., Bughin, J., Dobbs, R., Bisson, P. and Marrs, A. (2013) *Disruptive technologies: Advances that will transform life, business, and the global economy*, McKinsey Global Institute. www.mckinsey.com/insights/business_technology/disruptive_technologies (accessed 1 June 2015).

Marvin, C. (1990) *When old technologies were new; Thinking about electric communication in the late nineteenth century*, Oxford, Oxford University Press.

Miller, J. (2014) The fourth screen: Mediatization and the smartphone, *Mobile media and Society* 2 (2): 209–226.

Morley, D. (2009) For a materialist, non-media-centric media studies, *Television & New Media* 10 (1): 114–116.

Schrock, A. (2015) Communicative affordances of mobile media: Portability, availability, locatability, and multimediality, *International Journal of Communication* 9, 1229–1246ß.

Silverstone, R. and Haddon, L. (1996) Design and the domestication of information and communication technologies: Technical change and everyday life, in Silverstone, R. and Mansell, R. (eds) *Communication by design. The politics of information and communication technologies*, pp. 44–74, Oxford, Oxford University Press.

Snickars, P. and Vonderau, P. (eds) (2012) *Moving data: The iPhone and the future of media*, New York, Columbia University.

Taylor A. S. and Vincent J. (2005) An SMS history, in Hamill, L. and Lasen, A. (eds) *Mobile world past, present and future*, pp. 75–92, Dordrecht, Springer.

Toffler, A. (1980) *The third wave*, New York, Bantam Books.

Vincent, J. (2006) Emotional attachment and mobile phones, *Knowledge Technology and Policy* 19 (1): 18–206.

Woyke, E. (2014) *The smartphone anatomy of an industry*, New York, The New Press.

Part I

Infrastructure and applications

2 Circuit(s) of affective infrastructuring

Smartphones and electricity

Maren Hartmann

Introduction

I woke up this morning to the sound of my smartphone alarm clock. I then unplugged the smartphone from its electrical cord, ending its nightly loading routine. Before getting up, I quickly checked the weather through the weather app and additionally checked whether I had any WhatsApp messages, since my husband is spending a few days in the US and I wanted to see what he might have written during his day, which is currently my night. I then put the phone away in order to begin my day. All these are routines that are well known to many of 'us'. And while they are by no means practised everywhere and by everyone, they are taken for granted by many others. These mundane activities represent important elements of smartphone cultures and therefore feature in much of the research.

Studies of smartphone cultures often focus on the ways that smartphones are used and how this use shapes everyday lives. The appropriation and incorporation of this technology and its impact on social relations are key concerns as are the cultural representations thereof (see the introduction to this book). Research might also consider smartphone regulation or the blurring of boundaries between private and other spheres of life. In practice, the mobile phone has been researched more recently in terms of how its 'smartness' changes our interactions with the 'beast'. But what research rarely considers – especially from a media and communication studies perspective – is an even more basic part of the smartphone. What is missing is something that does not feature prominently in my list of routine morning activities either: the infrastructure underlying and supporting all these activities. What would the smartphone be without electricity and without the providers' networks, the Wi-Fi it connects to and all the systems supporting these? These basics are the focus of this contribution.

In this chapter, I use this banal starting point to develop an appeal for the study of these quotidian infrastructures – or, as Susan Leigh Star put it, I would like to encourage us to study boring things more explicitly (Star, 2002). This is despite the fact that a 'dramatic increase in the study of infrastructure has occurred in the social sciences and humanities' (Howe *et al.*, 2015: 1) in recent years. Media and communication studies, especially mobile media studies, have not been part of this trend, although they should be. One of the exceptions is Lisa Parks, who argues that:

> since infrastructures cannot be captured in a single frame, we must read media with an *infrastructural disposition* – that is, when viewing/consuming media we must think not only about what they represent and how they relate to a history of style, genre, or meaning but also think more *elementally* about what they are made of and how they arrived.
>
> (Parks, 2015: 357; italics in the original)

This chapter therefore combines an emphasis on infrastructures and media use in everyday life. This can include the elements that the infrastructures are made of (where do they come from, how are they produced and re-worked, who installs them, how are they maintained, developed, etc.), but also the performative work needed to establish and uphold infrastructure (see Marvin, 1988) and its possible appearance and use in everyday life. For the purposes of this chapter, not all of these can be covered. Instead, electricity (at least some aspects of it) will be the empirical focus here. Nonetheless, the contribution will begin with an argument for the need, at least theoretically, to consider the whole *circuit of infrastructuring*. Following this, further theoretical foci in the analysis of infrastructuring will be added. This framework will then be briefly applied to the electricity example. As a first step, however, the background to the contribution is briefly explored.

The overall aim herein is to begin to open up this (infrastructure) black box from the perspective of the ordinary user. This move is meant to bring this (seemingly) invisible and mundane aspect of mobile media and smartphone use to the forefront. It aims to do so through the theoretical and empirical elements just mentioned. The approach entails a literature overview concerning both supply and use that is then used to structure the research field into a more coherent whole, identifying necessary future research on the one hand and the particular contribution of communication and media studies on the other. This is in line with the move to a 'materialist, non-media-centric media studies' (Morley, 2009). It also follows the call to study infrastructures as 'much more than the cords, wires and material objects ... [but also] the sociopolitical dimensions of infrastructure and the experience of infrastructures' (Horst, 2013: 148). The whole point is to make the seemingly immaterial slightly more visible.

Background

The background to this question is that electronic media – as the name already suggests – have always relied on electricity as an easily and cheaply available resource, but this has become a slightly more public (and problematic) issue ever since media have become more mobile. An increase in battery power has been accompanied by ever more 'demanding' programmes (as both soft and hardware have gained in complexity and hence have an increasing need for energy), wherefore the need to 'recharge' continues to be an issue. Just as the media have become more public, recharging has become a public issue as well. At the same time, resources (such as those needed to generate electricity) and their ecological consequences have generally become a more widely discussed issue. Moreover, the expectation is still one of constant – and potentially invisible – supply. One area where this conflict has begun to be played out is Wi-Fi cafés: with some owners beginning to close down electricity outlets, for example, users were soon fighting back with maps of available plugs or of cafés with better service. At the same time, wireless electricity has been introduced in some places, with a fight for the standard in the technological set-up going on behind the scenes (Qi vs. PMA). These – again rather mundane – examples simply serve to underline the necessity to broaden our current analysis of smartphone cultures.

The circuit of (smartphone) infrastructuring

The circuit of culture (Johnson, 1986; Du Gay *et al.*, 2013) has often been quoted and also productively applied, underlining how a cultural analysis can become inclusive or even holistic. Building on the work of Johnson (which provided a more complex model), Du Gay and his colleagues developed a framework to study culture in all its diverse aspects, exemplified in the case study of the Sony Walkman. Their circuit therefore includes production, consumption, identity, regulation and signification. *Doing cultural studies* (the title of the book) would ideally imply taking all the different perspectives into consideration, as the book exemplifies. In an academic culture of individualistic research projects, the stakes are fairly high for a replication of such a holistic approach. Nonetheless, it has been successfully performed in many diverse fields (ranging from public relations to smartphone uses). While criticism concerning the nature of culture postulated in the model has been uttered (e.g. Finc, 2002), little attention has been given to the infrastructures underlying the different nodes within the circuit.

What is being suggested here is that the circuit of culture needs a slight extension into these infrastructural dimensions. Additionally, it should not be infrastructures, but the process of infrastructuring (see Pipek and Wulf, 2009), since it is a constant negotiation, a process of meaning construction, not only a materiality 'set in stone'. The claim is that the original circuit of culture never fully ignored the infrastructural aspects (its emphasis on materialities is very clear), but it nonetheless did not put an explicit emphasis thereon. With smartphones and similar technologies, it seems impossible to still consider infrastructure a background feature, i.e. an additional to the original circuit makes sense. The circuit would then include production, consumption, identity, regulation, signification and infrastructuring. Our next step is to explore what the latter could imply.

Infrastructure

What are infrastructures? They have been defined as 'the systems that enable circulation of goods, knowledge, meaning, people, and power' (Lockrem and

Lugo, 2016) or as 'a dense interwoven fabric that is, at the same time, dynamic, thoroughly ecological, even fragile' (Bucciarelli in Star, 1999: 377). Brian Larkin, an infrastructure researcher whose work focuses mostly on media and media infrastructures in Nigeria, begins with a similar idea of circulation, but broadens the view to include the everyday:

> Infrastructures are built networks that facilitate the flow of goods, people, or ideas and allow for their exchange over space. As physical forms they shape the nature of a network, the speed and direction of its movement, its temporalities, and its vulnerability to breakdown. They comprise the architecture for circulation, literally providing the undergirding of modern societies, and they generate the ambient environment of everyday life.
>
> (Larkin, 2013: 328)

This architecture for circulation obviously has potential consequences. This is best reflected in one further definition of infrastructure as 'pervasive enabling resources in network form' (Bowker *et al.*, 2010: 98). This builds on Susan Leigh Star's work on infrastructures, as one of the most prominent social science infrastructure researchers. In her seminal text on the ethnography of infrastructure (Star, 1999) Star not only presented a stark reminder that infrastructures tended to be overlooked in research (at that time), but also defined an actual basis for the definition of infrastructures as those just mentioned. Overall, Star identifies the following properties of infrastructure:

a   embeddedness
b   transparency
c   reach or scope
d   learned as part of membership
e   links with conventions of practice
f   embodiment of standards
g   built on an installed base
h   becomes visible upon breakdown
i   is fixed in modular increments, not all at once or globally (see Star, 1999: 381–382).

Hence, these circulation systems tend to be invisible and almost natural, they are mostly part of a larger network of other infrastructures (but then always have points of outlet), and they are linked to conventions, rules, etc. that need to be learned. At the same time, infrastructures are relational (meaning different things to different people) and ecological (they are part of the built environment, i.e. located in other systems and infrastructures that define their possibilities). They are both thoroughly embedded (physically, but also culturally and historically) and at the same time they are the basis for many other things and actions. Their embedded nature is regulated through standards in order to make an exchange between systems possible. Since infrastructures are mostly taken for granted (cf. Star and Ruhleder, 1994) it is one of the tasks of research to question this taken-for-grantedness.

Star also identifies areas that could be analysed or searched for in the study of infrastructure: (1) the master narrative; (2) surfacing invisible work; and (3) the paradoxes of infrastructure (Star, 1999 – we will return to the master narrative below). Her own work that formed the basis for these claims was a study on biologists and their work practices, particularly in relation to the implementation of a new electronic shared laboratory (ibid.: 380). She did not begin her work with infrastructure then, but discovered its importance when looking at something else (the failure to implement a planned system). This moment of (non-) change, of the attempt to implement a new system, is a particularly good one for studying such processes. Hence, Star was particularly interested in the way that infrastructures shape practices. It is therefore not surprising that she quotes Langdon Winner's often quoted (and also controversial) study of bridges to show how embedded these are in social and cultural structures (Winner, 1986). Winner claimed that the bridges built over the new expressways around Long Island in the 1930s were built so low that no public buses could pass. This, however, supposedly prevented lower class people from going to the beachfront. The wider argument is that material objects, in this case built objects, have concrete political and therefore social consequences. However, what Star does not actually look at are everyday lives outside of specific contexts such as biology labs etc. The question for this contribution, however, is, how far the properties that Star develops, the areas she identifies, could also be applied when studying the infrastructures shaping quotidian smartphone cultures.

When turning to the latter, it seems useful not only to broaden the discussion of infrastructure to include the process of infrastructuring, but also to look more specifically at whether media infrastructures provide any distinctive features. Star herself did not differentiate these, although she studies (among others) information communication technology (ICT) infrastructures. For her, these more technical specificities are not central. Lisa Parks, on the other hand, another prominent infrastructure researcher and one of the few with an explicit media studies focus, does differentiate. This can be found in her definition of infrastructure:

> First the term infrastructure emphasizes materiality and physicality and as such challenges us to consider the specific locations, installations, hardware, and processes through which audiovisual signals are trafficked. Second, the term infrastructure helps to foreground processes of distribution that have taken a back seat in much humanities research on contemporary culture, which has tended to prioritize processes of production and consumption....
>
> (Parks, 2015: 356)

Hence we can take an emphasis on materiality and physicality (embedded again) from Parks, plus an emphasis on distribution, i.e. the general question of how something (signal, code, but also content) spreads and how this spread is organized, both physically and organizationally. The limitation in terms of audiovisual signals, however, does not apply to our smartphone example. As outlined above, it is the combination of electricity, the provider's network, the Wi-Fi as well as possible audiovisual signals transmitted through these combined infrastructures that make up the smartphone focus. In a more comprehensive study of media infrastructuring processes, i.e. the circuit of infrastructuring, it would be crucial to include these. For the time being, we remain with our electricity focus, since this seems even less visible and therefore even more taken-for-granted. Before entering this concrete field, we first need to define the infrastructuring process.

Infrastructuring

The term infrastructuring has not yet been widely adopted. Or rather, it has begun to appear in the design research context, partly referring to Star's work, but not elsewhere. Within the (information system) design context, Pipek and Wulf 'will subsume all activities that contribute to a successful establishment of usages under the term "infrastructuring" to avoid confusion with classic notions of 'design' as design-before-use performed by professional designers' (Pipek and Wulf, 2009: 7). Apart from the establishment of uses, the long-term anticipation process, i.e. the process of imagining what future uses might look like (ibid.; Björgvinsson, Ehn and Hillgren, 2010), is also referred to as infrastructuring. It is hence a long-term process that involves anticipation, the design phase, but also the processes of appropriation and use after that (in that sense it is very similar to the broad understanding of domestication – see Silverstone and Haddon, 1996). This perspective provides an emphasis on the users' adoption and adaptation of the infrastructure, its implementation in everyday life routines, both time- and space-based. The inclusion of imagining future use is an extension in the timeline, but also in the breadth of uses – uses that were not anticipated or planned are all seen to be part of infrastructuring.

> Infrastructuring entangles and intertwines potentially controversial 'a priori infrastructure activities' (like selection, design, development, deployment, and enactment), with 'everyday design activities in actual use' (like mediation, interpretation and articulation), as well as 'design in use' (like adaptation, appropriation, tailoring, re-design and maintenance)....
>
> (Björgvinsson, Ehn and Hillgren, 2010: 43)

This is combined with an emphasis on the discursive entanglements that infrastructuring processes are based in, but equally also shape. Discursive entanglements emphasize the language used to describe infrastructures and infrastructuring, as well as the general societal discourses that this language use is embedded in. Both play a major role in the way that infrastructures can be imagined (or not), will be supported (or not) and will be ultimately dealt with. Hence, Star and Bowker emphasize the importance of metaphors in both enabling and restraining possible developments of infrastructure (2002: 155), while the anthropologist Brian Larkin describes 'the act of defining an infrastructure' (in research) as 'a categorizing moment' (Larkin, 2013: 330). It is a selection process that defines which aspect of the multilevel (meaning) structure will be regarded and which not, since 'infrastructures are not, in any positivist sense, simply "out there." ' (ibid.). Star and Ruhleder (1994) and Star and Bowker (2002), on the other hand, do not use the term infrastructuring, but instead describe a process of learning what the use of infrastructures can imply and how they 'happen' or rather become.

Part of this learning process is the acquisition of knowledge of the master narratives surrounding the infrastructures, which Star asked us to analyse. Some infrastructures might indeed be less clearly embedded in master narratives, but consist of several discursive entanglements (and are therefore easier to shape), while others do indeed carry a slightly heavier baggage. In terms of wireless communication, there appears to be a master narrative that implies mobile, free, seamless and effortless communication, embedded in similar lifestyles. It is an individualistic master narrative that does not fit too well with the master narratives of electricity, which are much more about political efforts, great inventors, etc. (see Hughes, 1983). This tension potentially explains why electricity is more in the background.

The practices of infrastructuring hence put an emphasis somehow on the traditional human actor, but their analysis tries to uncover the relationship to other, material, symbolic, political structures, once again supporting the claim that infrastructure is relational. Everyday uses are defined as important for our understanding of infrastructuring, despite its invisibility. Hence the claim that 'working infrastructures standardize both people and machines' (Star and Bowker, 2002: 154) moves to the forefront. This standardisation stems from the routines and practices that are built around working infrastructures. The infrastructure machines themselves as well as those attached in one way or another to the infrastructure only need to be shaped and adapted in the beginning. As soon as these are operational, the working structures, machines and routines will form a standardised setting that is usually only challenged when either something goes wrong or something new is introduced.

The circuit of infrastructuring simply re-emphasises the importance of taking into account these diverse practices, materialities, narratives, etc. That regulation and standardisation are crucial to infrastructures is widely accepted (see e.g. Star, 2002). Production of infrastructure is also a widely understood to be part of the process. The consumption dimension, however, which emerges as highly important in the design research references given above, was not present in older writings on infrastructures. The addition of discursive entanglements and narratives could be seen to add to the question of how infrastructuring processes help shape identities (or at least identification) – another crucial aspect of the circuit of infrastructuring. Within the move to broaden infrastructure studies, in which Star especially has been involved, this is already implied. Since infrastructure is less obvious than in other cultural studies contexts, however (partly thanks to the invisibility), it needs to be more explicitly researched. Broadening overall implies the emphasis on the relational and ecological, as shown above. Let me now turn to my small example to exemplify the points made above.

Wi-Fi cafés and electricity

The background to the following observations is an older (and smaller) research project of mine, in which I studied the adoption and appropriation processes of Wi-Fi use in Wi-Fi cafés. It started with the first wave of free Wi-Fi access in selected cafés in Berlin and ended when this had become a rather widespread norm (2005 until 2009). One of the unexpected results of the observations that were part of the project was the importance of electricity in these places. While the Wi-Fi signal was also obviously crucial in the appropriation processes, electricity turned out to be an even more scarce resource. While this did not matter as long as the battery was charged, it became crucial as soon as this was not the case. The lack of electricity outlets in the two cafés I studied caused irritation, often communication (about sharing the scarce resources), but sometimes also limited use, i.e. people left the café. The cafés reacted rather differently. The first one did not make any changes, limiting access to the few sockets. The other one, however, increased the number of plugs after it discovered that there were simply not enough to get everyone connected (this happened after my main fieldwork). Rather than extensively rewiring the whole place though, they simply offered extension cords. Quite a few now litter the place. Overall, trying to regulate use was an important issue in the café that made no changes, hence the outlets were one of the 'invisible' elements of regulation (more visible forms included a minimal charge; specific times for Wi-Fi use; a limitation to specific tables).

Even more openly, some Starbucks cafés caused an uproar in 2011, when they began to explicitly cover up power outlets to prevent their use. Starbucks had originally been one of the first – as early as in 2001 – to install Wi-Fi in its cafés. It then began to offer free Wi-Fi in the US in 2010 (2 hours free with prior log-in). While many users protested against the covering of outlets, there were other users who clearly stated at least an understanding:

> If you are one of those people who uses Starbucks as their office, sits in a store for 8+ hours a day, putting all your files on a table, using a separate chair for your laptop case/suitcase enjoying unlimited free refills with your Starbucks card, asking for cups of water and refusing to move until you are good and ready all for the $1.85 you pay as 'rent,' then perhaps your actions will answer your questions [about covering the outlets].
> (http://starbucksgossip.typepad.com/_/2011/08/should-starbucks-stores-cover-power-outlets-when-computer-parking-gets-out-of-hand.html)

The idea of covering up sockets did not spread – instead, Starbucks once again refocussed on these customers and began instead to offer wireless power charging facilities in at least some of the US cafés. This again is connected to yet another important element of infrastructuring: the question of standards (see above):

> Standards are ultimately set in a coffee shop, not in a conference room.
> (Schreiber quoted in Hollister, 2013)

Daniel Schreiber is president of Powermat (PMA) and a member on its Board. PMA and WPC (Qi) are the two standards group for wireless charging currently in competition. Hence while the quote might sound slightly tongue-in-cheek, in terms of the standards for wireless charging, the suggestion is not far-fetched. Starbucks was crucial in bringing Wi-Fi into everyday life, introducing it as a standard feature first for early adopters, letting it spread to others users eventually. Similarly, wireless charging will not become a household standard before it is introduced elsewhere. In fact, cafés and similar places will become the battleground for which standard will succeed. Hence, Starbucks' adoption of the Powermat and its decision to offer it nationwide in the US (before extending the offer in Europe and Asia) is one important step in this battle.

It shows many of the key elements of infrastructure mentioned above: it becomes fixed in modular increments, is built on an installed base (here a coffee chain plus their expertise in Wi-Fi), it embodies standards (albeit still in flux), it links with conventions of practice (people are already using the coffee chain for brief breaks in connection with upholding a mobile lifestyle), and its use is learned as part of membership of a community of users (through explanatory bits in the café, through copying use in action, etc.). The embedded nature of the existing infrastructure that supports this innovation is particularly clear when it comes to wireless charging, since the use of electricity sockets has been around for much more than 100 years. And the desperation experienced upon breakdown is partly addressed in how wireless charging is marketed (when you desperately need to recharge, you only need to enter the next Starbucks café). When the charging, however, does not work, one's dependence becomes even more apparent.

At the same time, wireless charging is entering our lives in other spheres as well, thus underlining its infrastructuring has entered yet another level. In this case, IKEA is the marker of its move into everyday life. The company began to offer furniture that enables wireless charging in the US and the UK in 2015 (they, however, use the Qi standard). It does, however, clearly build on the existing, older infrastructure, i.e. the wireless recharging facility could not work without the electricity outlet into which the charger or table is plugged.

Affective infrastructuring

In the following, I would like to extend the circuit of infrastructuring even further, albeit slightly more speculatively. This is meant to be an extension of the identity dimension of the circuit, but also the consumption aspect. For both, it is considered useful to use Parks' turn to affects:

> My general argument is that there is a need, on the one hand, for a broader imagining of *infrastructural affects* – experiences, sensations, structures of feeling – generated through peoples' material encounters with media infrastructures (not just interfaces but physical sites, installations, facilities, hardware), while, on the other hand, there is a need for an ongoing critique of

the ways in which affect continues to serve as part of the base of media infrastructural operations.

(Parks, 2015: 2–3)

I would like to use Parks' stress on infrastructural affects to extend the study of infrastructuring to include the affective dimension i.e. how people feel about it, react to it without reflection. The reasons are manifold: first of all, it takes the infrastructuring idea seriously, which includes those uses that are not necessarily designed in a traditional way. Such uses, however, often stem from the quotidian experiences of something or the immediate, unconscious structures of feelings that emerge when encountering or using infrastructures. On the other hand, the question remains as to whether this aspect is indeed as important as just suggested – or whether infrastructures (such as electricity) do not offer such great affectual potential.

In many ways the focus on contingency already implies, at least in principle, a way to explore the emotional involvement in our encounter with infrastructures, or more often, in the examples given above, when they are found to be lacking. This is, as Parks repeatedly showed, a chance to address the question of the materiality and our encounter therewith. In the example mentioned above, the affective dimension of infrastructuring was definitely visible in those moments when it (the plug) became the desirable object, since the opportunities it offered (charging) provided the necessary basis for other forms of practice (communication, production, etc.). The lack of sufficient plugs became an issue of frustration, sometimes of exhilaration (upon finding a plug unexpectedly or of having encountered someone who was willing to share), often of feigned indifference. The taken for granted nature of electricity especially (in contrast to Wi-Fi) often makes it generally less easy to show the affect it induces. In contrast to a home, however, this semi-public space of the café provides an environment where the lack of electricity infrastructure becomes more visible and therefore produces higher affective infrastructuring since the emotions people feel is connected to their practices.

My own involvement with electricity has become more affect-led over the time I have been thinking about this chapter. Electricity is increasingly becoming fragile and thereby more limited. While watching video clips about electricity production (in the hope of gaining insights into infrastructural imaginings as Parks suggests), I was reminded of the 'natural nature' of electricity, i.e. the fact that we gain it from natural elements. This adds the dimension of sustainability to our emotions – the question of the long-term consequences of our electricity use. There is a tension between this and our constant expectation of electricity simply 'being there'.[1] Additionally, our increasing dependence on electricity thanks to our reliance on computers of all kinds, hints at a growing importance of these questions – and the related affects.

Yet another layer of affectual infrastructuring can be explored with the help of Larkin, who describes a more historically based affectual engagement. He speaks of the 'sedimented history and our belief that, by promoting circulation, infrastructures bring about change, and through change they enact progress, and through progress we gain freedom' and refers to the 'enthusiasm of the imagination' as developed by Mrazek (Larkin, 2013: 332). Larkin thereby returns us to the early days of electricity (when cities like Berlin became an 'electropolis') that still continues today. It is the master narrative interwoven with affect. However, the enthusiasm of the imagination – at least when we add the question of freedom – can nowadays more easily be stimulated by the internet and related services than by electricity (although this might be playing out differently in different parts of the world). When focusing this general discourse onto smartphones and related technologies, their personal and portable nature suggest a freedom of movement and of individual choice. This freedom is partly material – only once in a while does the smartphone need to be plugged in to the good old network set in stone. At the moment, the power infrastructure need to support smartphones is more mundane, less fascinating than other, new infrastructures and therefore the imagination of electricity infrastructuring is more limited. This is also expressed in moving it even further into the background by making it wireless. Since, however, this infrastructure will become even more crucial in the days to come, that imagination of plugging in, of gaining power, of connecting to yet another network, of being without borders, might need to be stirred more actively.

Not really an end …

> Electricity may be the most obvious substratum that allows the computer to operate. But, as Edwards (1998) notes, although electricity is the infrastructure of the computer, the computer is the infrastructure of electricity supply, as the entire transmission industry is regulated by computers. Electricity, in turn, has other infrastructures, which can include oil production … financial mechanisms innovated in the wake of decentralization that allow electricity to be sold on an open market, or the labour networks necessary to produce and transmit power.
>
> (Larkin, 2013: 329)

As Larkin rightly points out, separating out electricity as the infrastructure is neither properly possible nor adequate, given the basic assumptions of the theoretical framework developed around the idea of infrastructures and infrastructuring. On the other hand, one needs to start somewhere. In the context of communication and media studies, the most overlooked, but nonetheless constantly present version of infrastructure is electricity. It is taken for granted and to a great extent invisible, but constantly also lacking.[2] What do we know about the infrastructure behind all these 'things' and services we use every day and what about the quotidian experience thereof? Do we actually think about the infrastructure? And if yes – when and how do we do so? To take this into consideration more, maybe only as an additional point in other research projects around smartphone cultures, would enable a better understanding of what underlies much of what we do a lot of the time. We should increase, as Parks (2015) puts it, the infrastructural intelligibility. It would enable us to perform a materialist, non media-centric kind of media studies that also begins to intervene via design processes.

One should also not forget that electricity is also a highly unevenly distributed infrastructure – 25 per cent of the world's population are without access to it (Sparks in Watson and Hill, 2012: 115). Hence, infrastructuring takes on an entirely different meaning in these contexts. We need to be aware of these limitations of our framework (of our limited perspective), when we develop it further and especially when we begin to apply it in empirical projects. Another point to at least consider pops up when we return to the wider framework of media networks: datacentres are of huge importance when it comes to energy consumption on the one hand and increasing infrastructural reliance on the other. After all, the smartphone content is often stored and distributed from there. They provide the connections between different providers, servers, etc. They are those hubs that the networks rely on, albeit often located in far-away places. These datacentres, too, are highly dependent on electricity.[3] These tensions – between non-existent electricity grids (and other infrastructure gaps) and the growth of new infrastructures elsewhere – present just glimpses of the framework that infrastructure questions and future uses are embedded in. In a circuit of infrastructuring, they are important aspects.

For the purpose of this chapter, however, the user and affective involvements were more prominent. Overall, they were meant to underline the importance of infrastructure in any cultural analysis of smartphone cultures. They can be addressed, as is increasingly the case, on the level of the actual material infrastructural roots – or also, slightly more removed, in the infrastructural experience within quotidian culture and its related imaginaries and affects. But before my power metre will now get too low, I will have to plug my machine (and myself?) into 'the grid'.

Notes

1 I am grateful for Leslie Haddon for pointing this out as well as other helpful hints given in the review process.
2 As Leslie Haddon rightly noted, not all infrastructure is invisible all of the time. Large electricty poles in the countryside are one obvious example.
3   Datacentre energy requirements have grown massively in the past 12 months, suggesting that rising energy costs and stricter regulations are not helping to limit datacentre power use and cut carbon emissions. Between 2011 and 2012, power requirements grew by 63% globally…. However, outsourcing, cloud and virtualization developments and the use of more efficient design methodologies would keep the power requirements low, the study estimated.
        (Article in *Computer Weekly* referring to the DatacenterDynamics 2012 Global Census)

References

Björgvinsson, E., Ehn, P. and Hillgren, P. A. (2010) Participatory design and 'democratizing innovation', in: PDC '10, Proceedings of the 11th biennial participatory design conference, Sydney, Australia, 29 November–3 December 2010 New York, ACM Press, pp. 41–50.

Bowker, G. C., Baker, K., Millerand, F. and Ribes, D. (2010) Toward information infrastructure studies: Ways of knowing in a networked environment, in Hunsinger, J., Klastrup, L. and Allen, M. M. (eds) *International handbook of internet research*, Dordrecht, Springer, pp. 97–117.

Du Gay, P., Hall, S., Janes, L., Madsen, A. K., McKay, H. and Negus, K. (2013) *Doing cultural studies: The story of the Sony Walkman*, 2nd edn. London, Sage.

Fine, B. (2002) *The world of consumption: The material and cultural revisited*, London and New York: Routledge.

Hollister, S. (2013) Did the future of wireless charging get decided by a coffee cup? *The Verge* 8 May 2013.

Howe, C., Lockrem, J., Appel, H., Hackett, E., Boyer, D., Hall, R., Schneider-Mayerson, M., Pope, A., Gupta, A., Rodwell, E., Ballestero, A., Durbin,T., el-Dahdah, F., Long, E., Mody, C. (2015) Paradoxical infrastructures: Ruins, retrofit, and risk, *Science, Technology & Human Values*, 1–19. doi: 10.1177/0162243915620017.

Horst, H. A. (2013) The infrastructures of mobile media: Towards a future research agenda, *Mobile Media & Communication*, 1 (1): 147–152.

Hughes, T. P. (1983) *Networks of power. Electrification in western society, 1880–1930*, Baltimore and London, The Johns Hopkins University Press.

Johnson, R. (1986) What is cultural studies anyway? *Social Text*, (16): 38–80.

Larkin, B. (2013) The politics and poetics of infrastructure, *Annual Review of Anthropology*, 42: 327–343.

Lockrem, J. and Lugo, A. (2016) Infrastructure. www.culanth.org/curatedcollections/11-infrastructure (accessed 6 April 2016).

Marvin, C. (1988) *When old technologies were new: Thinking about electric communication in the late nineteenth century*, New York and Oxford, Oxford University Press.

Morley, D. (2009) For a materialist, non-media-centric media studies, *Television & New Media*, 10 (1): 114–116.

Parks, L. (2015) 'Stuff you can kick': Toward a theory of media infrastructures, in Svensson, P. and Goldberg, D. T. (eds) *Between humanities and the digital*, Cambridge, Mass. and London, MIT Press, pp. 355–374.

Parks, L. and Starosielski, N. (2015) *Signal traffic: Critical studies of media infrastructures*, Champaign, University of Illinois Press.

Pipek, V. and Wulf, V. (2009) Infrastructuring: Towards an integrated perspective on the design and use of information technology, *Journal of the Association of Information Systems (JAIS)*, 10 (5): 306–332.

Silverstone, R. and Haddon, L. (1996) Design and the domestication of information and communication technologies: Technical change and everyday life, in Silverstone, R. and Mansell, R. (eds) *Communication by design. The politics of information and communication technologies*, Oxford, Oxford University Press, pp. 44–74.

Star, S. L. (1999) The ethnography of infrastructure, *American Behavioral Scientist*, 43 (3): 377–391.

Star, S. L. (2002) Got infrastructure? How standards, categories and other aspects of infrastructure influence communication, Paper presented at the 2nd Social Study of IT workshop at the LSE – ICT and Globalization. 22–23 April 2002.

Star, S. L. and Bowker, G. C. (2002) How to infrastructure, in Lievrouw, L. A. and Livingstone, S. (eds) *Handbook of new media – social shaping and consequences of ICTs*, London, Sage, pp. 151–162.

Star, S. L. and Ruhleder, K. (1994) Steps towards an ecology of infrastructure: Complex problems in design and access for large-scale collaborative systems. Proceedings of the Conference on Computer Supported Cooperative Work (CSCW 94 – Transcending Boundaries, October 22–26, Chapel Hill, NC). New York: ACM Press, pp. 253–264.

Watson, J. and Hill, A. (2012) *Dictionary of media and communication studies*, 8th edn. London: Bloomsbury.

Winner, L. (1986): Do artifacts have politics? in Wacjman, J. and Mackenzie, D. (eds) *The social shaping of technology: How the refrigerator got its hum*, Milton Keynes: Open University Press, pp. 26–37.

3 Mobile betting apps

Odds on the social

César Albarrán-Torres and Gerard Goggin

Introduction

For centuries, betting on sports, elections, future life events and so on, has been a common, de-institutionalised, everyday practice for millions of individuals around the world. Betting can be defined as an agreement between two or more parties in which the party that makes an incorrect prediction on an uncertain event has to make a previously stipulated payment to the winner. Betting has been present across the ages and in different parts of the world (Binde 2005b), and worked as a mechanism for socialising and, in some cases, for the redistribution of wealth (Binde 2005b; Reith 2007). Betting has become entrenched in various social spheres and cultural practices (De Goede 2005; Nicoll 2013). Offline social betting is generally conducted in an informal way in public and domestic environments and wagers are sealed with a handshake and guaranteed by mutual trust. In contrast to most forms of gambling, including commercial sports betting, there is generally no 'house' to oversee and regulate transactions. Up until the recent popularisation of smartphones, technological change had not played a significant role in the development of the cultural practices associated with casual betting.

Similarly to other forms of gambling such as poker (Albarrán-Torres and Goggin 2014), roulette or slot machines (Albarrán-Torres 2016), formal and informal betting has been reframed with its translation onto mobile devices. In the late 2010s, a decade after the epochal arrival of the smartphone in the form of the iPhone in 2007, gambling via mobile devices, apps and platforms is increasingly well entrenched. It is now common for betting and wagers to occur on mobile devices, as part of the broader ecologies of digital culture and gambling. Horse race betting, for instance, is now deeply influenced by expanding infrastructural and social networks that rely on digital information (Kruse 2016). As Kruse notes, horse racing has witnessed pioneering developments in computer networks, first with mechanic totalisator machines, followed by electronic, then digital technology, supporting the calculation of odds and taking of bets (Kruse 2016: 5). For their part, social media have become integrated into such sporting and wagering events, allowing punters to interact via their private screens with each other, as well as with public screens and betting systems

(Gainsbury *et al.* 2015). The immediacy of mobile betting has seen operators offering wagering opportunities during sporting events, allowing punters to place bets on minuscule details during a game, lessening the stigma associated with gambling:

> It's not like going and sitting in the smoky old TAB with all the old beer and the stale piss smell. It's the new Facebook of betting or something.
>
> (Jane, 18–29, interviewee quoted in Hing *et al.* 2014)

The provision of mobile gambling apps is dominated by the established gambling enterprises, including those backed, licensed or regulated by the state. Amid these new patterns of provision, there are also clear signs of 'disintermediation' betting and gambling, where intermediaries between gamblers and gambling businesses are reduced with the entry into the market of new entrepreneurs, firms and enterprises. These developments include the widespread proliferation of casinos and bookmakers that deal in the cryptocurrency Bitcoin (Adams 2013). Bitcoin is but one facet of a wide range of mooted and experimental gambling developments underway using the underlying Blockchain technology – a digital data technology that allows 'blocks' of data to be stored in a chain, and kept track of in a distributed ledger. Blockchain makes possible the circulation and value assurance of digital currencies like Bitcoin, allowing gambling to spread globally beyond the regulation of traditional banks, finance institutions and governments (Huber 2016).

Another marker of the disintermediation of traditional gambling technologies and the appearance of new mediations is the emergence of social betting apps – the focus of this chapter. Our argument is that social betting apps gather together and extend various aspects of contemporary gambling (especially online and mobile gambling) fused together with key elements of smartphone culture. In what follows, first, we outline our framework for understanding smartphone culture as it unfolds with socio-technical practices of gambling. Second, we discuss social betting apps and their cultural innovation. Third, we offer concluding remarks.

Smartphone culture and mobile gambling

The story of the emergence of mobile gambling can be told as part of the more general development of gambling, its social practices and technologies, especially online gambling (Wood and Williams 2007; Albarrán-Torres 2017). The history of online gambling starts in 1994, when the independent Commonwealth country of Antigua and Barbuda passed a *Free Trade & Processing Act* (Franklin 2001). Elsewhere some pioneering programs to conduct gambling transactions online, such as the software CryptoLogic, designed in Canada, were adopted by gambling enterprises in territories with lax regulations such as the Isle of Man. It was not until 1998 that the online gambling industry became a worldwide phenomenon with the establishment of the online casino Planet

Poker, challenged in turn by Paradise Poker in 1999, and then the relentless pro-liferation and fierce competition of desktop-based online casinos began.

Through this early period of online gambling, the internet was emerging as a mainstream media technology. For their part, gambling interests were still inves-tigating and experimenting with other media technologies, such as subscription, cable television to extend gambling's research and markets. Against this back-drop of the development of digital, convergent media, online and mobile gamb-ling can be seen to have some distinctive features and specific histories (King, Delfabbro and Griffiths 2010; Albarrán-Torres and Goggin 2014). One of the earliest uses of mobile phones was in illegal gambling. This is evident in mid-1990s press reports of illegal gambling houses, where mobile phones are often mentioned, in passing, as key communication devices. In various places around the world, for example, mobile phones became a way to by-pass the need to operate a gambling house – as, for instance, in illegal betting on football in Thai-land (Bardacke 1996), or on cricket in India (*Times of India* 1997). We can observe that in the early days of mobile phone adoption ownership by bookmak-ers also figured as the latest signifier of their ostentatious, low-life identity (Reid 1997). This kind of representation of the mobile phone and identity occurs at roughly the same time that industry interests, analysts, business and technical writers, and academic researchers (Griffiths 2007) alike were pointing to online gambling as a likely growth area for emerging mobile web applications (Price 1999). Ironically, the emergence of the mobile internet as a potential platform for betting information and transactions occurred at a time when offshore betting (from locations such as Gibraltar, historically an epicentre of online gambling) was still denied access to new television platforms in national jurisdictions (something which occurred with teletext in the UK) (Reid 1999). UK betting shops such as Chandler, Ladbrokes and William Hill already offered telephone betting, a facility that was being used by keen punters in other countries (such as Hong Kong) where this was banned (Landler 2001).

Mobile gambling was predicted to come into its own with the advent of third generation (3G) mobile phones. The company awarded the licence to run the UK National Lottery, Camelot, launched its main drawcard, Lotto, on the internet in early 2004, followed by interactive television and mobile phones (Carter 2004). Similar plans were hatched by a new company Gamex to partner with China-Lotto, something potentially supported by the Chinese government, keen to stamp out illegal gambling (Blackwell 2006). With the rollout and take up of mobile premium services, leading British mobile phone companies released a code of conduct in 2004 to ward off concerns about children having access to gambling and pornography, among other premium services being offered on 2G and 3G phones (Goggin and Spurgeon 2005). Notably, there were the concerns that potentially unfair competition and gambling-like situations were occurring in the increasingly popular, interactive, mass television formats, where viewers phoned or texted in – for instance, to give answers to a quiz (Bell 2007).

In many ways, mobile gambling was relatively limited – despite the hype, and dizzying rise of online gambling – until the advent of the smartphone. In 2007, for instance, the US company 888 released a mobile casino product as it sought to expand in UK and European markets in the wake of a US crackdown on internet gambling (Killgren 2007). By 2013, the Dublin-based bookmaker Paddy Power credited mobile gambling with a sharp up-tick in its fortunes (Smyth 2013). Mobile gambling was helping grow company revenues, and contribute to state coffers as well as private interests, despite widespread bans. In China, state-run lotteries were the exception to the general illegality of gambling, and their success was particularly fuelled by mobile gambling (Rabinovitch 2013).

As these examples illustrate, the trajectory of mobile gambling has not been straightforward (Cosgrave and Klassen 2001; Reith 2007). It is worth recalling that the availability of official outlets, channels and modes for gambling is recent, relative and differs widely across different countries, as well as social, economic and cultural groups. Woven into this fabric of contemporary gambling are the dynamics at play in mobile gambling that are our focus here: namely, the nature of the 'social', and how it is articulated.

In order to understand how the 'social' of mobile gambling is assembled (Latour 2005; DeLanda 2006), we need a model to understand how smartphones fit into this. Here we turn to the 'circuit of culture' approach, devised by Richard Johnson (Johnson 1986), developed by Paul Gay et al. (Du Gay et al. 2013) and used by one of us for theorising mobile phone culture (Goggin 2006, 2011). In the form proposed by Du Gay and his collaborators, cultural artefacts should be studied by tracing their movement and constitution through five interlocked processes: representation, identity, production, consumption and regulation (Du Gay et al. 2013). Goggin modifies the model by adding technology to the circuit of culture. Some 30 or so years after Johnson's original notion, there is much to be debated about the adequacy of this circuit of culture. The theoretical underpinnings of his conceptualisation can be updated via various efforts to better theorise the distinctive *communicative* dynamics at play in the socio-technical transformations of societies in the twentieth-first century (Dean 2005). With these theoretical extensions, the circuit of culture remains a useful and flexible broad guide to key elements for analysing and researching culture, especially artefacts and technology. As the common reference model of this volume, the circuit of culture approach is especially apposite for mobile betting via smartphones.

To demonstrate the circuit, we will take the example of regulation. Gambling is often – if not typically – approached in two main ways: everyday fun, pleasure and social participation (Nicoll 2008) versus moral torpitude, anxieties, fears and discourses of addiction that are often racially or gendered code (Nicoll 2012), as well as powerful discourses of risk. This kind of threshold fear – often verging onto a full-blown 'moral panic' (Hall et al. 1978/2013) – connects to a reflex response that regulation of various sorts is needed: personal regulation of problematic gambling behaviours; therapeutic or medical intervention for gambling addictions; and law and policy responses to regulate gambling institutions, industries, design of gambling technologies, information and the allowable practices through which gambling occurs. Recall that in the UK, betting shops were legalised in 1991, and that it was only in 1993 that betting shops were able to stay open at night – previously being obliged to close at 6.30 p.m. (Engel 1993). In the US and India, as well as many other jurisdictions, mobile gambling was slow to expand because of proscription and heavy regulation existing alongside big gambling markets (*Times of India* 2010).

Given the constitutive nature of gambling and its mediations, the circuit of culture model is especially useful for approaching and understanding its social dynamics. The circuit of culture approach is also suitable for analysing the mix of representations, identity formations, production and consumption, technology and other aspects that produce the social in relation to digital technology, especially in relation to social media. Consider the now very familiar and powerful kind of 'social imaginary' of digital technology (Mansell 2012) conceived variously by different, though related, concepts of 'participatory culture' (Jenkins 2006), collaborative consumption and production and 'sharing' (O'Hara and Brown 2006; Hamari *et al.* 2015; Meikle 2015; Sundarajan 2016). Products, services and platforms generated and underpinned by these discourses include popular brands such as Tripadvisor, Uber, AirBnB, social media platforms such as Facebook, as well as emergent 'fintech' business. In the present conjuncture, a day does not pass without news of a new start-up aiming to disintermediate existing commercial relationships, providing new mediations and connections among individuals and groups. This is occurring in the digital gambling market also, with an especially interesting case being pioneering social betting apps, to which we now turn.

The cultural innovation of social betting apps

From relatively early in the emergence of mobile gambling, commentators debated its social characteristics and implications compared to other avenues, as evident in these two quotes from a commentary piece in the *Guardian*:

> Mobile betting between friends is more socially stimulating and accessible than the set-top box.
>
> (*Guardian* 2001)

> Today, in a fragmented media universe, the need for togetherness and communication has never been stronger – witness the popularity of messaging and mobile phones. The pleasure of gambling in groups is communal, tribal even.... The British enjoy doing things together.
>
> (*Guardian* 2001)

This sense of *mobile sociality* was something picked up and averred by academic researchers also, as in Mark Griffiths' note that: 'Mobile gambling is also well suited to personal (i.e. one-to-one) gambling, where users bet against each other rather than bookies' (Griffiths 2007: 553). If we move forward a decade, we find this kind of vision being enacted in the form of social betting apps.

As they have emerged in recent years, social betting apps are a new mobile platform that mediates wagering among individuals, presumably close acquaintances, by providing a system through which the parameters of the bet (number of participants, the stake, terms and conditions) are established and a payout guaranteed. The developer generally makes profit by charging a handling fee. Social betting apps operate mainly in the UK and US, and, like other gambling services (Albarrán-Torres 2017) are often hosted by overseas servers. Social betting apps bring an element of locality and immediacy back to betting, which was reconfigured through desktop-based online transactions that exacerbated distance and oftentimes anonymity. These apps have been described as an effort of the gaming and gambling industries to capture new gamblers.

The social betting app category made its debut in October 2013, when the San Francisco-based start-up Social Bet Inc. launched Youbetme for Apple devices during the DEMO new technology conference in Silicon Valley. The beta version was tested by 5,000 users (Bernhard Jr. 2013). Youbetme (www.youbetme.com) is described by its developers as 'the handshake of the future'. In its promotional video, the developers encourage users to bet on things like 'who can drink beer the fastest', as well as sports and predictions on televised contests such as *Dancing with the Stars*. When the app was first released, Jason Neubauer, Social Bet CEO, described the business model as follows:

> People have been wagering since the beginning of time. Our goal is to make betting among friends more fun, easy and social. While we're at it, we aim to capitalise on the $100 billion mobile betting market, along with the booming social network and mobile app economies.
>
> (Quoted in *Innovate Gaming* 2013)

It is important to note that Neubauer's previous venture, the Irish real-money betting site InTrade, was shut down due to financial irregularities (Bernhard Jr. 2013). With Youbetme, Neubauer hoped to avoid 'any handling of money between people who use his site to bet with each other' (Bernhard Jr. 2013). Rather than solely the 'thrill' of gambling, instead the 'social' is privileged right from the inception of this app. For instance, Reed Shaffner, adviser to Social Bet, argues that Youbetme 'uniquely focuses on the social storyline aspect of betting, rather than on the transaction itself, taking betting back to its original purpose of good clean fun' (*Innovate Gaming* 2013). Youbetme incorporates some of the main affordances of social networking sites. It facilitates messaging between participants and has Facebook integration. It also allows users to add 'spectators' to their bet, with the purpose of increasing 'the social quotient' (*Innovate Gaming* 2013) of the game experience. Adding spectators or witnesses to the bet also encourages digital media practices such as showing off and sustaining a public presence (Couldry 2012), which bring betting rituals closer to social networking.

Facebook integration is a key expansion strategy for the broader genre of mobile social games (Goggin 2014), which includes highly popular and profitable titles such as *Candy Crush* and *Clash of Titans* (Hjorth and Richardson 2014; Leaver 2016). Leaver argues that mobile social games constitute a 'social network market' where 'one of the most effective methods of reaching potential players is therefore through the social attention and activity of other players' (Leaver 2016: 214). As one of us has argued elsewhere, in-game socialisation and social media integration in casual gambling apps 'aid in the normalisation of gambling-like procedures, bringing them closer to the realm of casual social gaming' (Albarrán-Torres 2016: 247). In the Youbetme model, betting is framed as a fun activity that is integrated in the user's daily social networking activities. Instead of being framed as a serious and vice-inducing affair, it is presented as a friendly, fun and indeed 'social' way to pass the time.

Similarly, Tedbets (www.tedbets.com) is a platform through which users can customise bets. The company describes its product as 'a peer-to-peer wagering site that allows players to bet their friends on any event, private or public' (Tedbets 2016). In an effort to merge the user's social and gambling networks, signup with Facebook, Twitter and Google+ is encouraged. Like many real-money gambling operations, Tedbets operates out of the Isle of Man. It was established on March 2013 and is bound by the gambling laws and regulations of this self-governing British Crown dependency (Tedbets 2016).

In TedBets, the betting mechanism is quite user-friendly. The player chooses what to bet on, who to bet with among their contacts, the wager and a deadline for the other party to accept. Once the wager is created and agreed upon, Tedbet retains the funds from each participant until a winner emerges. Scott Burton, founder of TedBets, describes his motivation for creating the app: 'The back-and-forth bets I make with friends are social and enjoyable. It's about competition, rather than the amount of money we're winning' (Burton quoted in Marsden 2014). These apps emphasise the sociability inherent in some forms of gambling, such as betting, as well as the competitive nature of this cultural practice. Competition and showing off are two key dynamics of social games (Leaver 2016), and social betting relies on these. These two dynamics produced data that is then used by the 'house' to generate value.

What sorts of value are generated through casual bettors, however, that Tedbet can benefit from? In its Terms and Conditions, the developers specify the information that the user gives up by using the app. User engagement and play is used as valuable data by the company. The contract by which players are bound states that Tedbet 'reserves the right to publish and promote usernames, locations and winning percentages of the users both within the Site and outside for marketing purposes' (Tedbet 2016). Tedbet also collects personal data to validate a player's identity: 'player's home address (including property number, street name, postcode and phone number) are required, so that the player's identity can be protected and validated' (Tedbets 2016).

Youbetme and TedBets are but two examples of social betting apps. Their take up and revenue share to date remains unclear (in fact, other early social betting apps such as Betable and the Czech app BuddyBet have moved on to proven online casino models). Add to which, these social betting apps, if adopted and 'successful', will find their place in a jostling ecology of mobile, social, online and other digital technologies. That said, social betting apps can be seen as a harbinger of a significant change in gambling cultures. As observed sometime ago, while offline betting is deeply embedded in 'social local arrangements' (Woolley and Livingstone 2009: 38) such as attending horse racing tracks or a local betting shop, through the internet 'transactions have hence become less localised and more mobile both socially and spatially' (Woolley and Livingstone 2009: 39). The promise of social betting apps is much more in tune with the imaginaries, affordances and social practices associated with mobile media and communication. That is, the tropes that privilege physical and social proximity, and friendship over gambling with strangers or through a faceless company. Partaking in this cultural remaking of gambling, these mobile social betting apps also domesticate betting by framing it as an everyday, inconsequential activity, which takes games of chance a step closer towards cultural legitimation (Reith 2007).

Further, social betting apps also fall into morally safe territory (Binde 2005a) when compared to more pernicious and less social gambling practices such as slots that have long been legally and socially scrutinised. In identifying the key factors that make commercial gambling appealing and morally acceptable in Western societies, Binde argues that some people engage only in forms of gambling that have a social dimension, to compete with others or, as is the case with sports betting, to enjoy 'an intellectual challenge' (Binde 2005a: 467). Social betting apps appeal to these three factors by exacerbating the mental challenge and the social dimension of betting, rather than monetary gain or risk.

By providing a digital platform through which individuals can bet anywhere at anytime, social betting apps leverage much vaunted affordances of mobile media, such as immediacy and ubiquity. Social betting apps fall into the category of what we have previously termed 'mobile social gambling', an evolving set of techno-social assemblages (DeLanda 2006) and a

> new form of media and cultural practice that fuses gambling (a longstanding social practice), social networking (in both the older pre-internet and newer online forms), and 'social gaming' (the new social media form, popular especially on Facebook), together with the affordances of mobile media devices, networks, applications, and touchscreens.
>
> (Albarrán-Torres and Goggin 2014)

What players look for is not a 'big win' but fun and social capital in the form of reputation; what companies rely upon is not compulsive play, but compulsive communication. Once potential punters are identified, critics argue, operators 'just have to construct a format that hauls them in – one that combines achievement, enjoyment, excitement and sociability' (Marsden 2014). Clearly there is a sense in which such social betting apps are problematic as they profit from the user's social clout and personal information, and from a communicative act that was not previously institutionalised. This perspective is evident if we apply Jodi Dean's widely discussed notion of communicative capitalism (Dean 2005). Social betting apps establish new communicative configurations among gamblers/gamers and between gamblers and companies, offering a privatised space to encapsulate the social exchange inherent in betting. Casual social exchange is thus inserted into the 'profit-driven infrastructure' (Mejias 2012) that are gaming and gambling markets. In this regard, such contradictions of the mobile social as social betting and mobile gambling generally are supported and unfold in new ways by commercial software, platforms and technologies are features of the wider, global environment of smartphones and mobile media (Goggin 2011; Van Dijk 2013; Baym 2015).

Conclusion: implications for smartphone culture

As we have sought to illustrate in this chapter, mobile gambling offers an especially rich perspective on the rise of mobile media and communication. Like many aspects of mobile media, gambling has been a fair while in the making. As we point out, gambling is prominent in the emerging discourses of mobile phone culture, especially with the advent of 2G mobile premium services and 3G networks. However, it took a while for mobile gambling to arrive as a fully-fledged phenomenon. Along the way, there were many colourful and interesting ways in which gambling was woven into the social coordinates and practices, cultures and discourses of gambling, and practical communicative infrastructures that underpin significant extensions of gambling across many global societies.

So, there is a case to be made that there is a significant turn to mobile gambling that occurs with the advent of smartphones and the efforts by the world's largest gambling providers such as Aristocrat (slot machine manufacturer), Caesars Entertainment and World Series of Poker to enter the mobile gambling market. Various things come to fruition, including mobile internet capabilities of smartphones, the associated emergence of 'apps' and apps culture, the important role that smartphones play in consolidating social media, the new ways that the line is blurred between gambling and gaming raising new consumer policy issues (Markou and Riefa 2016), new kinds of mobile and digital money, and the ways that representations and regulation of gambling changes (Morse 2016). This establishment of mobile gambling entails particular histories and local dynamics that make up the larger global internet, mobile media, transnational and global cultures.

In this scene of mobile gambling via smartphones, social betting apps are a relatively new, still small, but revealing case. Social betting apps seek to deliver on the promise of mobile phones providing a privileged purchase on the social nature of gambling, something augered 15 or so years earlier. Social betting apps also draw on the social imaginaries of digital technology in the present conjuncture, where platforms for apparently direct individual and social connection are widely offered by commercial providers (media titans and start-ups alike) and across many areas of everyday life are being widely taken up.

This said, the fate of social betting apps is unclear at this point in time. There is a general predicament for those developing such software, as to whether the innovative features will simply be incorporated, intellectual property law and realpolitik permitting, into other kinds of larger, more comprehensive mobile, social media and online platforms. Or, whether social betting apps will be steam-rollered by the well positioned giants of global gambling. Whatever the future holds, in social betting apps, and mobile gambling generally, smartphones are important elements in this cultural economy.

References

Adams, G. (2013) Gambling on the bitcoin? *IOL*, 15 December, available at: www.iol. co.za/scitech/technology/internet/gambling-on-the-bitcoin-1.1622293#.Uq5VNGQW1vk (accessed 21 November 2016).

Albarrán-Torres, C. (2016) Social casino apps and digital media practices: new paradigms of consumption, in Leaver, T. and Wilson, M. (eds), *Social, Casual and Mobile Games: The Changing Gaming Landscape*, New York and London: Bloomsbury, pp. 243–260.

Albarrán-Torres, C. (2017) Where the stakes are higher: the global south and the history of online casinos, in Goggin, G. and McLelland, M. (eds), *Routledge Companion to Global Internet Histories*, New York: Routledge, pp. 425–435.

Albarrán-Torres, C. and Goggin, G. (2014) Mobile social gambling: poker's next frontier, *Mobile Media & Communication*, 2(1): 94–109.

Bardacke, T. (1996) Thai punters at odds with the law over bets on Euro 96, *Financial Times*, 10 June, 16.

Baym, N. K. (2015) Social media and the struggle for society, *Social Media + Society*, 1(1), doi:10.1177/2056305115580477.

Bell, E. (2007) Quiz con ought to have put ITV in the rogues' gallery, *Guardian*, 29 January.

Bernhard Jr., K. (2013) YouBetMe founder ups the ante despite government intrade shut-down, *Upstart Business Journal*, 11 March, available at: http://upstart.bizjournals. com/companies/startups/2013/03/11/intrades-fate-doesnt-scare-social.html (accessed 15 November 2016).

Binde, P. (2005a) Gambling, exchange systems, and moralities, *Journal of Gambling Studies*, 21(4): 445–479.

Binde, P. (2005b) Gambling across cultures: mapping worldwide occurrence and learning from ethnographic comparison, *International Gambling Studies*, 5(1): 1–27.

Blackwell, D. (2006) Gamex coming to aim en route to China, 27 November, 21.

Carter, M. (2004) A high-stakes gamble: last week Camelot launched lotto on the inter-net, *Guardian*, 5 January, 36.

Cosgrave, J. and Klassen, T. R. (2001) Gambling against the state: the state and the legiti-mation of gambling, *Current Sociology*, 49(5): 1–15.

Couldry, N. (2012) *Media, Society, World: Social Theory and Digital Media Practice*, Cambridge: Polity.

Dean, J. (2005) Communicative capitalism: circulation and the foreclosure of politics, *Cultural Politics*, 1(1): 51–74.

De Goede, M. (2005) *Virtue, Fortune, and Faith: A Geneaology of Finance*, Minneapolis, MN, University of Minnesota Press.

DeLanda, M. (2006) *A New Philosophy of Society: Assemblage Theory and Social Com-plexity*, London, New York: Continuum.

Du Gay, P., Hall, S., Janes, L., Madsen, A. K., McKay, H. and Negus, K. (2013) *Doing Cultural Studies: The Sory of the Sony Walkman*, 2nd edn, London and Thousand Oaks, CA: Sage.

Engel, M. (1993) Gambling – late-night shoppers come under starters orders, *Guardian*, 17 April, 18.

Franklin, C. (2001) Virtual Las Vegas: regulate or prohibit?, *Duke L. & Tech. Rev.*, 21–42.

Gainsbury, S. M., King, D., Delfabbro, P., Hing, N., Russell, A., Blaszczynski, A. and Derevensky, J. (2015) *The Use of Social Media in Gambling*, Gambling Research Australia, July, Melbourne: Gambling Research Australia, available at: www.gambling research.org.au/publications/the-use-of-social-media-in-gambling-2015 (accessed 18 November 2016).

Goggin, G. (2006) *Cell Phone Culture: Mobile Technology in Everyday Life*, London and New York: Routledge.

Goggin, G. (2011) *Global Mobile Media*, London and New York: Routledge.

Goggin, G. (2014) Facebook's mobile career, *New Media & Society*, 16(7): 1068–1086.

Goggin, G. and Spurgeon, C. (2005) Mobile message services and communications policy, *Prometheus: Critical Studies in Innovation*, 23(2): 181–193.

Griffiths, M. (2007) Mobile phone gambling, in D. Taniar (ed.), *Encyclopedia of Mobile Computing and Commerce*, Hersey, PA: IGI Global, pp. 553–556.

Guardian (2001) Take a gamble on digital betting, *Guardian*, 2 April, 54.

Hall, S., Critcher, C., Jefferson, J., Clarke, J. and Roberts, B. (1978/2013) *Policing the Crisis: Mugging, the State, and Law and Order*, 35th anniversary edn, Basingstoke: Palgrave Macmillan.

Hamari, J., Sjöklint, M. and Ukkonen, A. (2015) The sharing economy: why people participate in collaborative consumption, *Journal of the Association for Information Science and Technology*, 67(9): 2047–2059.

Hing, N., Vitartas, P. and Lamont, M. (2014) *Promotion of Gambling and Live Betting Odds during Televised Sport: Influences on Gambling Participation and Problem Gambling*, Lismore, Australia: Southern Cross University, available at: www.research-gate.net/publication/270713930 (accessed 20 November 2016).

Hjorth, L. and Richardson, I. (2014) *Gaming in Social, Locative & Mobile Media*, Basingstoke: Palgrave Macmillan.

Huber, S. (2016) Gambling industry – how blockchain can make it more transparent, *Fintech News*, 10 June, available at http://fintechnews.ch/blockchain_bitcoin/transparent-gambling-blockchain-gambling-industry-how-blockchain-can-make-it-more-transparent/3844/ (accessed 19 December 2016).

Innovate Gaming (2013) Youbetme debuts first mobile-social betting platform, 29 October, *Innovate Gaming*, available at: www.innovategaming.com/m37291 (accessed 21 November 2016).

Jenkins, H. (2006). *Convergence Culture: Where Old and New Media Collide*, New York: New York University Press.

Johnson, R. (1986) The story so far: and further transformations? in Punter, D. (ed.), *Introduction to Contemporary Cultural Studies*, London: Longman, pp. 277–312.

Killgren, L. (2007) 888 highlights impact of US crackdown, *Financial Times*, 14 February.

King, D., Delfabbro, P. and Griffiths, M. J. (2010). The convergence of gambling and digital media: implications for gambling in young people, *Journal of Gambling Studies*, 26(2): 175–187.

Kruse, H. (2016) *Off-track and Online: The Networked Spaces of Horse Racing*, Cambridge, MA: MIT Press.

Landler, M. (2001) Web comes up fast on the outside, *New York Times*, 18 March, 1.

Latour, B. (2005) *Reassembling the Social: An Introduction to Actor-Network-Theory*, Oxford and New York: Oxford University Press.

Leaver, T. (2016) Angry Birds as a social network market, in Leaver, T. and Wilson, M. *Social, Casual and Mobile Games: The Changing Gaming Landscape*, New York: Bloomsbury, pp. 213–224.

Mansell, R. (2012) *Imagining the Internet: Communication, Innovation and Governance*, Oxford: Oxford University Press.

Markou, C. N. and Riefa, C. (2016). App-solutely protected? The protection of consumers using mobile apps in the European Union, in Rothchild, J. A. (ed.), *Research Handbook on Electronic Law*, Cheltenham and Northampton, MA: Edward Elgar, pp. 391–416.

Marsden, R. (2014) 'You Bet Me?' How a new generation of apps are combining social media and gambling, *Independent*, 13 February, available at: www.independent.co.uk/life-style/gadgets-and-tech/gaming/friendly-wagering-online-social-gaming-sites-let-people-gamble-on-everything-from-losing-weight-to-9124682.html (accessed 21 November 2016).

Meikle, G. (2015) *Social Media: Communication, Sharing, and Visibility*, London and New York: Routledge.

Mejias, U. A. (2012) Liberation technology and the Arab Spring: from utopia to atopia and beyond, *Fibreculture Journal*, 20, available at: http://twenty.fibreculturejournal.org/2012/06/20/fcj-147-liberation-technology-and-the-arab-spring-from-utopia-to-atopia-and-beyond/ (accessed 21 November 2016).

Morse, E. A. (2016) Regulation of online gambling, in Rothchild, J. A. (ed.), *Research Handbook on Electronic Law*, Cheltenham and Northampton, MA: Edward Elgar, pp. 449–471.

Nicoll, F. (2008) The problematic joys of gambling: subjects in a state, *New Formations*, 63, 103–120.

Nicoll, F. (2012) Bad habits: discourses of addiction and the racial politics of intervention, *Griffith Law Review*, 21(1), 164–189.

Nicoll, F. (2013) Finopower: governing intersections between gambling and culture, *Communication & Critical/Cultural Studies*, 10(4), 385–405.

O'Hara, K. and Brown, B. (eds) (2006) *Consuming Music Together: Social and Collaborative Aspects of Music Consumption Technologies*, Dordrecht: Springer.

Price, C. (1999) *FT* information technology review – business jolted into action by online wake-up call, *Financial Times*, 2 June, 9.

Rabinovitch, S. (2013) China's lottery boom conceals worry at damage to the vulnerable, *Financial Times*, 23 January, 9.

Reid, J. (1997) Soccer – Tabor stakes claim to a football fortune, *Guardian*, 31 January, 4.

Reid, M. (1999) Chandler battles against the odds, *Guardian*, 13 July, 29.

Reith, G. (2007) Gambling and the contradictions of consumption: a genealogy of the 'pathological' subject, *American Behavioral Scientist*, 51(1): 33–55.

Smyth, J. (2013) Paddy power boosted by online trading, *Financial Times*, 5 March.

Sundarajan, A. (2016) *The Sharing Economy: The End of Employment and the Rise of Crowd-based Capitalism*, Cambridge, MA: MIT Press.

Tedbets (2016) Terms and conditions. *Tedbets*, available at: www.tedbets.com/info/terms_and_conditions (accessed 4 December 2016).

Times of India (1997) Five held for betting activities in the city, *Times of India*, 24 May.

Times of India (2010) Legalize gambling, subject it to regulation, *Times of India*, 23 April.

Van Dijk, J. (2013) *The Culture of Connectivity: A Critical History of Social Media*, New York: Oxford University Press.

Wood, R. T. and Williams, R. J. (2007) Internet gambling: past, present, and future, in Smith, G., Hodgins, D. and Williams, R. J. (eds), *Research and Measurement Issues in Gambling Studies*, Amsterdam: Elsevier, pp. 492–514.

Woolley, R. and Livingstone, C. (2009) Into the zone: innovating in the Australian poker machine industry, in Kingma, S. F. (ed.), *Global Gambling: Cultural Perspectives on Gambling Organizations*, New York: Routledge, pp. 38–63.

Part II

Understanding family consumption

4 Parental practices in the era of smartphones

Cristina Ponte, Anca Velicu, José Alberto Simões and Claudia Lampert

Introduction

Contemporary relations between adults and children combine elements of nostalgia, anxiety, futurity and self-realization (Lee, 2001; Wyness, 2006), making parental mediation in the digital age a basically emotional project (Clark, 2011b). The scale and the scope of parental obligations are constantly broadening towards 'transcendent parenting' (Lim, 2016) where parents feel they have to constantly manage a complex and diverse multimedia environment in which their children operate, and to model positive behaviour for their children in online and offline social environments, while constantly evaluating the benefits or harm these environments may bring to their children.

Within the circuit of culture framework (Johnson, 1986), the chapter focuses on the dimension of lived cultures, specifically on the ways that parents mediate children's access to and use of smartphones by integrating parents' interviews and children's survey data from the Net Children Go Mobile project.

Parenting and parental mediation in times of smartphones

Researchers on parenting styles (Baumrind, 1991; Darling and Steinberg, 1993) have found that in contemporary societies children have more space to negotiate through an 'ethic of reciprocity' in which authority is earned rather than simply asserted (Thomson and Holland, 2004). In their typology the parental authoritative style, combining high levels of warmth and demands, may be associated with the above mentioned ethic, and contrasts with authoritarian (high demands, low warmth), permissive (low control, high warmth) and neglect (low control, low warmth) ones. This helps to situate family dynamics and identities along both spectra of demands and warmth.

While the parenting styles mentioned above were developed within a pedagogical tradition, the research on parental mediation has its roots in psychology and communication science (Wagner *et al.*, 2013). Parental mediation involves the more intentional efforts made by caregivers to mitigate, regulate or generally shape the way children use and respond to media. Three mediation styles have been differentiated relating to TV and videogames: active mediation (endorsement of media use, explanation of media content, etc.); co-use of media as a passive form of mediation; and restrictive mediation (rules about temporal use, spatial use and content) (Austin, 1993). When parental mediation was examined in relation to the internet, studies considered other elements such as monitoring strategies, e.g. checking the websites visited by the child or his or her social media profile (Livingstone *et al.*, 2011). Consequently, newer approaches to internet mediation have expanded the range of mediation styles, focusing on the evaluation of online content or on the security issues.

Clark (2011a) adds participatory learning to the abovementioned forms of mediation. This refers to parent–child interaction with and through digital media, in the course of negotiating their interpersonal relationship. This type of mediation underlines both parents' emotional and rational motivations and child's role as 'an active participant in learning and relationship-building' (Clark, 2011a, 335). Of particular interest for this chapter, Clark (2011b) also identified four parental concerns and related mediation strategies. The first concern is about children's futures, which parents counteract with a restrictive strategy – when they discussed it in terms of health issues from using screens, time spent online, bad influence of online material, etc. – or with an active strategy – when the concern is framed in terms of improving cognitive development. The second concern relates to family connectedness, which is addressed by using active mediation, co-use and participatory learning. The third concern is about balancing work and family times, which leads parents to use (mobile) media in order to keep in touch with children and keep them busy. And the fourth concern relates to parental self-preservation and self-development, which refers to parents' own needs or interests and not to those of children or families.

While the smartphone raises new issues by virtue of providing online internet access, the literature on its precursor, the mobile phone, also covered a range of parent-child interactions. The issues that mobile phone studies have typically addressed include the relative autonomy and independence of children, the degree of parental supervision and control of children of different ages, questions concerning the ownership of these devices and the strategies that both children and parents use to negotiate with each other (Green and Haddon, 2009). Teenagers' parents are torn between their responsibility for what they perceive as their children's safety and the cultural requirement that parents should allow their children to become independent individuals (Ribak, 2013).

In contrast to a large number of studies on parental mediation related to TV and internet, there are still hardly any studies of smartphone mediation (e.g. Knop *et al.*, 2015). Looking at what little exists, studies of the smartphone also examined the mediation of the use of functions (e.g. special apps) and the situation in which the children are allowed to use the mobile device (Gebel, 2013). Researching mediation practices related to smartphones in the lived cultures of the families has the potential to enlarge the parental mediation agenda still further. For instance, the use of tracking technologies in smartphones that allow parents to locate their kids outside the household implies parental management of children's 'potential space' – the distance that is tolerated or desired between the child and parents (Ribak, 2013) – in relation to their progressive autonomy, privacy and responsibility.

Most research about mobile culture to date – covering both mobiles and smartphones – has focused on teens while explicit research on young children's use remains less common (Ling and Bertel, 2013). A multi-method study from Germany investigating eight to 14-year-old children confirmed the importance of age: the older the children, the more they use the mobile phone to go online and for social purposes, the more concerns parents have and the less influence and control parents expect to exert (Knop *et al.*, 2015).

Finally, one exploratory study of parental visions of children's access to and use of smartphones (Mascheroni, 2014) revealed that these devices are highly charged by optimistic and pessimistic discourses and parental perceptions are primarily shaped by the parents' gender, their own domestication of information communication technologies (ICTs) and the broader discursive environment. While fathers tend to adhere to the enthusiastic imaginary around the internet and aspire to endow their children with the latest technology, mothers are much more likely to justify mobile phones as supports for remote parenting and the micro-coordination of everyday life, noting that their children lack sufficient social or safety skills for using advanced devices such as smartphones.

Research questions and data sources

Before exploring parental mediation questions, it is important to have some base-lines, for example an understanding of the distribution of smartphones among children, and how this varies by country, as well as by such factors as age and socioeconomic status. When we then turn to what parents say about mediation, we do so knowing what patterns of children's access are common, but also where there is variation, since this in itself might have a bearing upon mediation practices. The other background information sought concerns children's perceptions of whether they are more skilled users of smartphones compared to parents. While these are only perceptions, to an extent they may act as a proxy for being more skilled, and that can become relevant to what parental mediation options are open to parents. These data are derived from two questions reported by children (aged 9–16) in the Net Children Go Mobile survey, which covered Belgium, Denmark, Ireland, Italy, Portugal and the UK (Mascheroni and Ólafsson, 2014). The main focus of parental motivations, concerns and mediation then draws upon qualitative research involving interviews with parents in Belgium, Denmark, Germany, Ireland, Italy, Portugal, Romania and the UK (Haddon and Vincent, 2014).

Children's reports on ownership, access and skills

Smartphone ownership and getting the first device

As background, Net Children Go Mobile results show that European children reported they got their first mobile phone at least one year later than their first use of the internet (9.5 compared to 8.5 years on average), while the first smartphone was only obtained two and half years later (Mascheroni and Ólafsson, 2014). In Table 4.1,

Table 4.1 Smartphone ownership, age of first smartphone and self-confidence in smartphone use as compared with parents

		% of children who own or have a smartphone for private use	Average age when children got their first smartphone	'I know more about using smartphones than my parents' (%)		
				Not true	A bit true	Very true
Belgium	9–12 yrs	19	11.2	10	38	52
	13–16 yrs	48	13.5	14	9	77
	High SES	45	12.9	25	18	57
	Medium SES	41	13.1	2	18	81
	Low SES	22	13	5	8	87
	Total	36	13	13	16	71
Denmark	9–12 yrs	75	9.5	37	19	43
	13–16 yrs	92	12.3	5	19	76
	High SES	79	11	28	25	48
	Medium SES	82	11.6	12	18	70
	Low SES	95	10.5	17	14	69
	Total	84	11.1	19	19	62
Ireland	9–12 yrs	22	9.2	64	14	22
	13–16 yrs	62	13	14	21	65
	High SES	39**	11.2	52	24	24
	Medium SES	55***	12.3	19	19	62
	Low SES	35***	11.9	41	10	50
	Total	40	11.7	41	17	42
Italy	9–12	25	10.3	14	64	22
	13–16 yrs	65	13	2	38	60
	High SES	50*	12	16**	40**	45**
	Medium SES	41*	12.7	7**	40***	53***
	Low SES	46*	12	2**	51**	48**
	Total	45	12.2	5	46	49

Portugal	9–12 yrs	20	10.8	13**	26**	61**
	13–16 yrs	45	12.8	4**	23**	73**
	High SES	41*	12.5	7	23	70
	Medium SES	39*	11.7	26	37	37
	Low SES	32*	12.3	3	21	76
	Total	34	12.3	6	24	71
Romania	9–12 yrs	20	9.8	9*	32*	60*
	13–16 yrs	32	13.5	8*	24*	69*
	High SES	41**	11.4	9*	24*	68*
	Medium SES	26**	12.6	2*	32*	66*
	Low SES	23**	12.8	14*	22*	63*
	Total	27	12.4	8	27	65
United Kingdom	9–12 yrs	34	10.4	32	15	53
	13–16 yrs	76	12.9	8	15	77
	High SES	70	12	10*	18*	73*
	Medium SES	62	12.3	17*	13*	70*
	Low SES	35	13	23*	10*	67*
	Total	58	12.3	14	15	71
Total	9–12 yrs	31	9.9	40	23	37
	13–16 yrs	60	12.9	8	21	71
	High SES	55	1.7	28	23	50
	Medium SES	50	12.2	12	22	66
	Low SES	38	12	18	21	61
	Total	46	12	20	22	58

Source: Net Children Go Mobile survey 2014. Base: all children who use the internet.

Notes

All differences are statistically significant ($p < 0.001$), except otherwise noticed.

* Non-significant.

** $p < 0.01$.

Gender differences were limited and are not reported.

above, on average, 46 per cent of children in the countries covered owned a smartphone or had one for private use in 2014. However, this varies from 84 per cent in Denmark to 27 per cent in Romania, so there was substantial national variation, meaning questions of parental mediation of these devices were faced by parents in some countries more than others at that time. Smartphones are eminently a part of specifically teenage culture: on average, around 60 per cent of 13–16 year olds said they own or have one for private use, almost twice the proportion of 9–12 year olds. Except for Denmark and the UK, all countries range from 19 to 25 per cent in this younger age group. This gap between young children and teenagers illustrates differences in relation to the centrality that smartphones have in teenagers' lives and how they are connected with different practices and daily activities. This means that although mediation itself may be different for different aged children, the whole issue arises more in relation to teenagers because more of them have these devices.

In most countries children from higher socioeconomic status (SES) were more likely to own or have a smartphone for private use than their lower SES counterparts.

Although smartphones are eminently related to teenage culture, there are variations across countries regarding the age of first ownership. Danish children have the lowest average age (11.1), confirming their position of being at the forefront of smartphone culture, while Belgium children were the oldest when they first acquired smartphone (13). The age when children start using smartphones is dropping, following the tendency detected in relation to internet access: teenagers were on average given a smartphone at the age of 12.9, whereas for children who are aged 9–12 the age was 9.9. The issue of parental mediation may currently arise more with teenagers, but the trend is that more parents of younger children will in the future face these decisions.

Self-confidence in relation to smartphones skills

Teenagers are more likely to perceive their smartphone skills to be higher than those of their parents: 71 per cent of 13–16 year olds claim that is 'very true' they know more about smartphones than their parents, compared to 37 per cent for the 9–12 year olds. That said, another way of looking at the figures is that even quite a few younger children believe that they know more about smartphones than their parents – which may reflect the trend noted above whereby children are getting familiar with digital cultures at ever earlier ages.

By SES, the general pattern indicates that children from middle and low socioeconomic backgrounds are more likely to say that it is 'very true' they know more about smartphones than their parents, compared to half of the children from higher SES backgrounds. However, socioeconomic differences are small and tend to be less clear within the countries. In sum, in addition to how the patterns of smartphones penetration may affect where parental mediation is taking place, these different perceptions in relation to parental skills may well have implications for the challenges parents face when it comes to mediating the use of devices they are less familiar with.

Parents' perspectives on children and smartphones

Concerns

The opinions of parents about the smartphone's positive or negative challenges are quite diverse. Some even doubt that smartphone use requires special parental mediation, as they consider the smartphones to be just another device that allows children to connect to the internet. The main types of parental concerns are related to child's future and to family and social connectedness (Clark, 2011b).

Parents expressed a wide range of concerns about their child's future. Some are based on older fears linked to the TV or the desktop-internet era. Other fears have been adapted to the new affordances of smartphones. Finally, yet others are specifically linked with smartphone use. A number of topics are seen as problematic by parents. These include the online content that the child is exposed to via public sites or private messages, including content produced by other children, addiction and internet excessive use risks and (unwanted) costs incurred by smartphone use (i.e. the internet plan) and by the consumerist attitude of children who desire the most expensive devices (two risks that are seen as more specific for girls). Other concerns relate to the redesigned new privacy issues that smartphone apps can trigger, which potentially has consequences for children's present and future reputation, as one Danish father reported to have explained to his pre-adolescent sons:

> Because you can just take a screenshot of a Snapchat, and then everyone can have the picture. And then suddenly they send it out to their friends, and then it's on Facebook.

Some parents worry about certain cognitive and developmental problems, such as laziness, impatience or difficulty in focusing on a task due to the continuous distraction of the smartphone. There is the risk of delays in the child's social and emotional development, when children keep texting rather than making phone calls that require more social skills. There are concerns about the deterioration of written language abilities due to the intensive and careless use of texting. Physical safety is a worry, as there is always the risk of being robbed as is the risk of road accidents, when children are distracted and engaged in their always-with-them online world. There are concerns about health problems, from the negative impact of smartphone radiation to eyes damage and lack of physical activity. There is the worry that children are moving too rapidly from childhood to adolescence for which they are not yet matured. Last, there are time-space issues, framed as children's need for exclusive offline time (for homework and school, sleep or social activities) and smartphone-free spaces (e.g. bedrooms, the 'upstairs' zone, or the lunch/dinner zone).

Parents can be ambivalent about children's lack of social connectedness that parents attributed to their use of smartphones. Most parents fear that because of intensive smartphone use, children can no longer engage in face-to-face inter-actions with peers. However, some actually appreciate the way smartphones can also facilitate children's communication processes, not only technically, but socially, when children are at an age when their behaviour is under the strict control of their peer group (Pasquier, 2008):

> It's true that they communicate less face to face, but their shyness, their insecurity ... thanks to these devices they are able to overcome these difficulties.
>
> (Italian mother, of an 11-year-old child)

Parents seem to worry less about any lack of face-to-face interaction within the family. Some might assume that the child's social misuse of the smartphone within the family can be corrected easily and immediately by parents, as one Danish father noted:

> If you are having a conversation and then someone takes their phone and uses it, then we comment on it. 'Wow, that is nice ... you sit with your phone while we are talking!'

Interestingly, not all parents regret the decrease in family communication result-ing from the use of smartphones. One German parent observed that it also reduces family conflicts, suggesting the self-preservation concern identified by Clark (2011b).

Positive motivations

One positive motivation for actively supporting the child's smartphone use is the idea that it also enhances family emotional and communicative bonds, as it allows parents to coordinate with their children, to keep a remote eye on them whenever they are hanging out and, equally important, to have the feeling of being in control. Most parents keep to classical phone calls and text messages (e.g. SMS, WhatsApp), and have not used the new applications for monitoring or control (only one Danish father mentioned that he uses geo-location tools to track his 11-year-old son). Those strategies may either lead to a gain in the child's agency – especially for younger children who could increase their per-sonal space as a result of this permanent phone contact with parents – or lead to a decrease in children's responsibility, if they always rely on their smartphones in any situation, thus not developing 'real life' social skills:

> We should provide them with opportunities to develop their autonomy and responsibility ... otherwise they always stick with the phone.... 'If I get lost I have my phone'. No, I don't like it this way, you get lost and try to do something.
>
> (Italian mother, ten-year-old boy)

While parental concerns about the child's future were many and diverse, only two positive aspects were mentioned. One was the easier access to information – although even this was sometimes also framed as a risk, one that could lead to laziness and shallowness. The other related to reading practices – counterbalancing the concern regarding the impairment of writing skills. As one British mother of a teenage girl put it: 'even if she is reading rubbish, she is still reading!'

Mediation strategies

Parents often have concerns and actively take steps to address them, some of which do not fall neatly inside the typologies of parental mediation reviewed earlier. What seems to be non-action can itself be a form of mediation. For example, one Italian mother decided not to activate a mobile internet plan for her son but instead only allows him to go online using Wi-Fi networks for which she herself gives him the password each time. In fact, mediation comes in various guises as in the case of another Italian mother who imitated her daughter's style of writing messages in order to make her aware of how poorly she texts.

In line with previous studies (Mascheroni, 2014), the Net Children Go Mobile data show that the choice of parental mediation strategies is greatly influenced by parents' perception of digital technology. When parents see digital technology as being ubiquitous, they tend to teach children to use the smartphone responsibly, as a tool. When parents see children's use of devices as just being 'cool', they tend to be more relaxed in mediation. If the parent is him- or herself a smartphone user (as most younger parents are), he/she mediates more, with more understanding of the child's usage as they share the same smartphone ethos with their child. Furthermore, parents' own technical skills also enhance or limit the mediation strategies, as suggested in the statistical analysis above: quite a few parents complained that they were not able to practice proper mediation as they were not familiar with the settings and applications on the smartphone and the technical options available for mediation (e.g. to check child's history on the browser).

The other important factor that impacts on the mediation strategies that parents adopt is their wish to appear to be 'good parents' (Aarsand, 2011). Looking back at her own childhood and taking it as the model, one Belgian mother of an adolescent boy said that parents should trust children and allow them a safe autonomous space, a process facilitated by smartphones because it enables one to keep in touch without being too intrusive. In contrast, an Italian father of a ten-year-old girl set strict rules for the child's smartphone, in line with the model of an American mother, who was intensely publicized in the Italian media at the time of the interview.

This idea of good parenting often pops up when parents contrast their own parenting style with that of others'. For example, when Portuguese and Romanian parents (from countries where the fewest children had smartphones) were critical of parents who allow their children to have these devices they sometimes argued along the lines that 'good parents' do not need to provide a smartphone as a substitute for the parent's physical, mental or emotional presence or – as one Portuguese mother put it – a 'way of compensating for their lack of support'. Likewise, one German mother talked about other parents' disengagement from parenting: 'they do not really want to deal with their children'.

By contrast, other parents welcome this technology in their children's life, adapting the mediation process to perceptions of their child's current demands (i.e. to be in contact with their peers or just to entertain themselves in spare time). Thus, one Danish father of two pre-adolescent girls opposed the strict mediation strategy employed by some of his friends in comparison to his own practices, which took into account his girls' timetables, rather than stressing abstract and general rules. Less common, some parents explicitly characterized themselves as not being 'good parents' or good smartphone role models, as they could not stay away from their own smartphone.

Often parents preferred to take small steps on this parental mediation route, initially allowing only Wi-Fi connection, which enabled them to monitor the child's early online activities on the smartphone, only later allowing the children to have a 3G connection as a 'sign of trust'. Usually there is also an evolution of parental mediation practices in relation to younger siblings, as parents adjust their strategies compared to how they dealt with their older children, if they decide that another approach might be more effective. For instance, one Romanian mother mentioned that she was quite keen on buying such devices for her younger children, because she had seen in the case of her older daughter the interest in the device decreased once a child had it.

Another factor leading to a change in mediation is sometimes the child's opposition to the parent's attempt to check his or her smartphone. This seems to be an important challenge for parents as the child grows older, as British mothers of adolescent girls acknowledged: 'we are not even allowed to touch the smartphone', otherwise 'they would go completely ballistic'. These cases reveal an inversion of roles, where the adolescent determines the mediation process. It is worth adding that sometimes parents disagree with each other about the suitability of a specific mediation strategy, for example, as regards monitoring strategies, due to the mother's and father's different opinions about their children's rights to privacy.

Transforming mediation concepts into practice

Rules are a manifestation of parental concerns and important instruments for parental mediation. Some parents did not want to set up strict rules or did not see the necessity, because the media use of the child had never caused problems. Others emphasized the obligation of parents to mediate the use of smartphones by setting rules.

Finally, the parents' answers suggest different parenting styles as regards finding the balance between setting rules and giving advice. Some pointed out the importance of setting rules and sanctioning misbehaviour; others tended to give advice, especially with regard to social practices on the internet, like 'delete people you don't know' or 'stay off certain websites'.

Types of rules

Rules about the smartphone use can be divided into those covering aspects such as time of use, location and situation where the smartphone is used, and regarding the level of differentiation (e.g. rules about the internet in general, rules about platforms like Social Networking Sites, or rules about activities like posting pictures). While some parents try to regulate the internet use totally on the smartphones, others make distinctions with regard to different online programs. Meanwhile, some children are not allowed to play violent videogames or download apps that cost money – if they want to download something they have to ask their parents for permission. Others are not allowed to have a Facebook account or to post any pictures (or post pictures of others without permission).

Rules regarding content were mentioned quite rarely and mostly in relation to violent videogames or 'inappropriate content' (e.g. sex, violence and bad language), which includes both downloading and uploading inappropriate content like intimate revealing pictures. Rules regarding the amount of time spent on smartphones were seen as being important tools to regulate media consumption, but due to the diversification of devices and programs and with regard to different age groups it was quite complicated for parents to find the right balance. Some parents set a general limit for all screen media, while others tried to limit the time for each single device. The limit seems to be set rather intuitively and individually without necessarily considering the characteristics and affordances of the particular medium. Parents mentioned that children have to switch off the smartphone at 8 or 9 p.m. and/or during the night, and/or to leave it outside the bedroom. In fact, parents from Belgium and from Romania often noted that their children are not allowed to take the mobile or smartphone into their bedrooms at all.

Although many parents said at first that they did not have rules for mobile devices, in practice they quite often went on to say that they did in fact check the smartphones and have a look what kind of pictures the child uploaded on Instagram or WhatsApp. This control procedure sometimes seemed quite arbitrary as parents sometimes jumped to conclusions. Parents sometimes referred to the importance of the consistency in applying rules, while admitting that it is sometimes not easy to ensure due to the two parents' different ideas about mediation and their own different media habits. Apart from consistency, parents also acknowledged that rules are not ubiquitous or set in stone forever, but have to be adapted with regard to the context and also to the development of the child. Most parents seem to agree that the older the children become, the less the parents are able to regulate the media use and the more trust they need to have in their children. Some parents had set up rules but with the increasing age of the child, they realized that they could not control everything. Some examples of 'bypassed' rules showed that rules are not seen as mandatory. One Italian mother admitted that she felt guilty, because in general she did not allow the use of the smartphone during dinner, but nevertheless she allowed its use to keep the child quiet at a restaurant. In Italy, Belgium and Romania, interviewees complained that the parents themselves do not respect the rules in school when calling their children during the school time. This parental behaviour might give children the impression that compliance with rules is not really necessary.

Conclusion

This panorama of parental mediation of smartphones first set the scene by identifying similarities and differences in smartphone access by children across Europe. Apart from country variation in adoption, differences are mainly visible in the age of first ownership of these devices. Socioeconomic status also makes some difference. This is also relevant because, as parents say, the very first act of mediation is whether to provide children with devices at all. Finally, the growing familiarity of children with smartphones at younger ages, also observable in their perception of their own smartphone skills when compared with those of their parents, suggests particular challenges to parental mediation and opportunities for 'participatory learning' (Clark, 2011a).

The next step in the analysis was to chart the broad range of concerns about smartphones, including ones where there was occasionally ambiguity, such as the fear about the devices making children anti-social. The range of such concerns that motivate parental mediation contrasts with the far smaller range of positive reasons for children to have smartphones. While many concerns about smartphones echo sentiments about previous technologies – e.g. internet addiction, the cost of using mobile phones – some related to specific new affordances of the technology or the great intensity with which the device was used. We saw how parental mediation strategies, some of which do not fit neatly into the typologies identified in the literature review, were greater influenced by parental perceptions of the technology, whether they had smartphones themselves and their desire to appear to be 'good parents'. The process of mediation can be incremental and can change both as children grow up and resist some forms of mediation, and because parents learn from mediating the smartphones of older siblings.

The last section specifically explored variations in parental rules in relation to smartphones, including finding a balance between setting rules and giving advice. In fact, studying the mediation of the smartphone reveals the huge range of different types of rules and levels at which rules are nowadays applied (some being very general, about the internet, and some being very specific about particular applications). Rules about time use are very common, but again, there is considerable variation – e.g. total screen time vs. time for a specific online activity. There is sometimes a difficulty in being consistent about applying rules, especially when the parents do not share the same views on this issue, but the application of rules can also change, often decline, over time as it is less easy to enforce them.

In general, our analysis confirms that and shows how mediation strategies are complex, combine different approaches and are affected by public representations on media and good parenting. They reflect parental attention to sociocultural challenges their children are experiencing and old and new concerns about media impacts.

References

Aarsand, P. (2011) Parenting and digital games: on children's game play in US families, *Journal of Children and Media*, *5*(3), 318–333. http://doi.org/10.1080/17482798.2011. 584382.

Austin, E. W. (1993) Exploring the effects of active parental mediation of television content, *Journal of Broadcasting & Electronic Media*, *37*(2), 147–158. http://doi. org/10.1080/08838159309364212.

Baumrind, D. (1971) Current patterns of parental authority, *Developmental Psychology*, *4*(1, Pt.2), 1–103. http://doi.org/10.1037/h0030372.

Clark, L. S. (2011a) Parental mediation theory for the digital age, *Communication Theory*, *21*(4), 323–343.

Clark, L. S. (2011b) A multi-grounded theory of parental mediation: exploring the complementarity of qualitative and quantitative communication research. In Jensen, K. B. (ed.) *Handbook of qualitative and quantitative methodologies for communication* (chapter 17). New York, Routledge.

Darling, N. and Steinberg, L. (1993) Parenting style as context: an integrative model. *Psychological Bulletin*, *113*(3), 487–496. http://doi.org/10.1037/0033-2909.113.3.487.

Gebel, C. (2013) Medienerziehung aus elternsicht. ergebnisse der repräsentativen elternbefragung [Parental mediation from a parent's perspective]. In Wagner, U., Gebel, C. and Lampert, C. (eds) *Zwischen anspruch und alltagsbewältigung: medienerziehung in der familie* [Between aspiration and coping with every-day life: media education in the family] (pp. 65–140). Berlin, Vistas.

Green, N. and Haddon, L. (2009) *Mobile communications: an introduction to new media*. Oxford, Berg.

Haddon, L. and Vincent, J. (2014) *European children and their carers' understanding of use, risks and safety issues relating to convergent mobile media*. Milano, Educatt. Retrieved from: http://netchildrengomobile.eu/reports/.

Johnson, R. (1986) What is cultural Studies anyway? *Social Text*, *16*, 38–80. http://doi. org/10.2307/466285.

Knop, K., Hefner, D., Schmitt, S. and Vorderer, P. (2015) *Mediatisierung mobil. Handyund mobile internetnutzung von kindern und jugendlichen* [Mediatization mobile. mobile internet use of children and adolescents]. Leipzig, Vistas.

Lee, N. (2001) *Childhood and society: growing up in an age of uncertainty*. Maidenhead, Open University Press.

Lim, S. S. (2016) Through the tablet glass: transcendent parenting in an era of mobile media and cloud computing, *Journal of Children and Media*, *10*(1), 21–29. http://doi. org/10.1080/17482798.2015.1121896.

Ling, R. and Bertel, T. (2013) Mobile communication culture among children and adolescents. In Lemish, D. (ed.) *The Routledge international handbook of children, adolescents and media* (pp. 127–133). London, New York, Routledge, Taylor & Francis Group.

Livingstone, S., Haddon, L., Görzig, A. and Ólafsson, K. (2011) *Risks and safety on the internet: the perspective of European children. Full findings*. LSE, London, EU Kids Online.

Mascheroni, G. (2014) Parenting the mobile internet in Italian households: parents' and children's discourses. *Journal of Children and Media*, *8*(4), 440–456.

Mascheroni, G. and Ólafson, K. (2014) *Net Children Go Mobile: risks and opportunities*. Second edition. Milano, Educatt.

Pasquier, D. (2008) From parental control to peer pressure: cultural transmission and conformism. In Drotner, K. and Livingstone, S. (eds) *The international handbook of children, media and culture* (pp. 448–459). London, SAGE.

Ribak, R. (2013) Media and spaces: the mobile phone in the geographies of young people. In Lemish, D. (ed.) *The Routledge international handbook of children, adolescents and media* (pp. 307–314). London, New York, Routledge, Taylor & Francis Group.

Thomson, R. and Holland, J. (2004). *Youth values and transitions to adulthood: an empirical investigation*, London, Families & Social Capital ESRC Research Group.

Wagner, U., Gebel, C. and Lampert, C. (eds) (2013) *Zwischen anspruch und alltagsbewältigung: medienerziehung in der familie* [Between aspiration and coping with every-day life: media education in the family]. Berlin, Vistas.

Wyness, M. (2006) *Childhood and society: an introduction to the sociology of childhood*. Basingstoke, Palgrave Macmillan.

5 Older people, smartphones and WhatsApp

Mireia Fernández-Ardèvol and Andrea Rosales

Introduction

Els meus WhatsApps amb la mama
> ([My WhatsApp messages with mom] (Orsini, 2014a))

'CijkiopplypMpo' is the first WhatsApp message a mother sends her son with her new Smartphone. Having just started to use new technologies and excited about the ease of barging into the daily life of her offspring, she learns to handle the new phone at the expense of the young man's patience.

Modern, fresh and fun, this story shows that, nowadays, stories are also written through WhatsApp.

A ... hilarious novel, speaks of the ties between parents and children and the generational gaps.[1]

News, short films, songs and TV parodies reflect WhatsApp's omnipresence (Ballesteros, 2016). In the context of Barcelona, it seems that anyone having a smartphone is supposed to have WhatsApp – not Telegram or Line, though. The book *Els meus WhatsApps amb la mama* [My WhatsApp messages with mom] (Orsini, 2014a), published simultaneously in Catalan and Spanish, illustrates the importance of WhatsApp in this cultural context. Interestingly, the original edition, in French, refers to SMS instead of WhatsApp (Orsini, 2014b).

WhatsApp is the most popular mobile messaging app, worldwide (Sun, 2015). Mobile messaging apps allow mass self-communication (Castells, 2009): from one-to-one communication – in the same way as SMS, to many-to-many communication – thanks to the groups. As communicants are (mostly) known to each other within a WhatsApp environment, interactions bring a sense of togetherness and intimacy (O'Hara *et al.*, 2014) different to social network sites (SNS) – such as Facebook – where the audience is not that easily controlled. Messages include text, voice, pictures and videos that can be combined in flexible ways. In this sense, WhatsApp is often described as a traditional SMS with augmented capabilities. Two main characteristics help to create the analogy. On the one hand, it is linked to a specific phone number that recognizes other WhatsApp users whose numbers are stored in the mobile device; on the other, it is a multiplatform app available for the most common devices and mobile operation systems. It is also a convenience and a nuisance (Ahad and Lim, 2014), like the mobile phone, because it allows permanent contact (Katz and Aakus, 2002). These metaphors that help us to understand the app (Lakoff and Johnson, 2008), themselves contribute the representation process – in terms of the circuit of culture (du Gay *et al.*, 2013).

Launched in 2009 (Rowan, 2014), WhatsApp has almost one billion users (Sun, 2015). It is part of the everyday life communication practices in an increasing number of contexts, from the UK (O'Hara *et al.*, 2014) and Germany (Montag *et al.*, 2015) to Brazil (Wojahn *et al.*, 2015); or from Israel (Aharony and Gazit, 2016) to Brunei (Ahad and Lim, 2014). Yet, its popularity is uneven, as WhatsApp stands out in most countries in South America, Europe, Africa, Asia and Oceania, but not in North America (Schwartz, 2016). To understand the context of Barcelona we must look at the Spanish telecommunication market and its price structure. Mobile data are mostly commercialized through flat rates that exclude traditional SMS (CNMC, 2016),[2] which significantly fostered the replacement of SMS worldwide (*The Economist*, 2015), a process the industry regulator explains:

> The surge in the use of mobile broadband on voice terminals is giving rise to a process where traditional SMS messaging is being replaced by new online instant messaging services such as WhatsApp, Telegram and others. As well as not representing costs to users in addition to those of the mobile broadband connection, these … services have similar or even superior features to those of SMS, since they allow not only the delivery and receipt of messages, but also communication between the members of a group of individuals and free transfer of all manner of files, such as photos or videos.
>
> (CNMC, 2015: 97)

Young people, as early as 2011, identified WhatsApp as a meaningful app (Rubio-Romero and Perlado Lamo de Espinosa, 2015), and the trend expanded to society in general. A recent survey shows that almost all internet users in Spain (90 per cent) find mobile messaging, mobile phone calls and face-to-face communication to be of similar importance for communicating with friends and relatives. Two out of three (66 per cent) consider that mobile messaging impacts the way they communicate with a majority (58 per cent) reporting an increase in the frequency of contacts with relatives and friends (Fundación Telefónica, 2016). Tracking studies point out that WhatsApp tends to be the most used app on smartphones (Montag *et al.*, 2015). Regarding multi-screening practices, mobile messaging is also the most common activity carried out while watching TV (57 per cent of the cases; Clarke *et al.*, 2015). Mobile messaging plays a role in the so-called war of screens (Tubella *et al.*, 2008), and particularly WhatsApp became a social TV app to share broadcasted contents (Krämer *et al.*, 2015).

The smartphone is the most popular digital communication device in Spain – used by 61 per cent of the population aged 15 and over (ONTSI, 2016); and the most pervasive channel to go online – as reported by 88 per cent of internet users (Fundación Telefónica, 2016). Seven out of ten adults use instant messaging apps in Spain, a proportion which lowers to 20 per cent among those aged 65 and over (CIS, 2016). While these figures can bring the idea that WhatsApp has no importance (at all) for older segments of the population, previous research shows that older individuals who have a smartphone do consider WhatsApp as one of its most important apps (i.e. Rosales and Fernández-Ardèvol, 2016b). Some moved directly from SMS to WhatsApp, while others had experience in participating in SNS, such as Facebook, on their mobile devices. In any case, it is worth analysing the transformation in everyday digital practices of older individuals that multimedia (MM) apps are bringing about.

Networked individualism (Wellman, 2001) defines our societies. Sociability increasingly depends on (and is enabled by) mobile digital technologies, a trend no generation can ignore. We consider of utmost importance the inclusion of older people in the analysis of digital transformations, the least studied age group in this area (Richardson *et al.*, 2011). First, because it is a mistake to ignore part of the population when it comes to understanding social phenomena. Second, and more importantly, because the digital environment is in permanent change and we, as individuals who grow older, will keep facing a number of decisions on acquisition, adoption, appropriation, and eventually stop using (new) artefacts.

WhatsApp is a cultural artefact intrinsically linked to another cultural artefact, the smartphone. Both can be analysed, from the perspective of older people, in terms of specific forms of consumption, representation and regulation within the framework of the circuit of culture (du Gay *et al.*, 2013). Therefore, the chapter focuses on the tensions between values, identities and the changes in interpersonal communication that have come with smartphones and WhatsApp, and how they have been integrated into the everyday life of older individuals while dealing with social regulations.

Empirical evidence

Dating from late 2010, more than five years of research on the mobile phone use of older people in Barcelona (Catalonia, Spain) are drawn upon in this chapter. During this period, smartphones and WhatsApp became pervasive, making them a relevant entering point to analyse the changes, if any, in communication practices.

Research activities included, first, semi-structured interviews around mobile communication with 52 participants aged 60 to 96 years (i.e. Fernández-Ardèvol and Arroyo, 2012, Fernández-Ardèvol, 2013). Conducted between 2010 and 2011, these conversations explored everyday life uses of communication media, with a specific focus on mobile phones – if they were used. We discussed both the drawbacks and advantages of mobile telephony, as well as motivations, opinions and personal experiences regarding the decision to have, or not have, this device. Second, in 2014 we tracked the smartphone activities of 238 Spanish individuals, aged 16 to 80, through a commercial panel (Rosales and Fernández-Ardèvol, 2016a). Third, we immersed ourselves in the weekly meetings of a smartphone learning club of older people that belongs to Àgora – a participative, lifelong-learning community committed to strengthening social inclusion (Sanchez Aroca, 1999). The activity, which started in 2014 and continues as we write these lines, explores participants' experiences with mobile devices, mainly smartphones and smartwatches, from an ethnographic approach (Rosales and Fernández-Ardèvol, 2016b). Thirty-four participants, aged 55 to 86 – mostly over 65 (66 per cent) – were involved in the learning club. Weekly sessions attract between seven and 30 participants, as attendance is not compulsory. All participants had a smartphone and different levels of experience – from brand new users to those with more than two years of use. In addition, we involved eight participants from the club in a project that provided them smartwatches to study how they appropriated them. Within this context, the relevant studies for this book chapter are: three focus groups with 25 participants in which we discussed their uses of smartphones (2014); interviews with eight participants around their use of smartwatches (2016); and participation in two WhatsApp groups – one about smartphones (since 2014) and the other about smartwatches (since 2015) – aimed to share doubts and help among peers, and to coordinate specific activities of the project.

Activities in the projects were held in Catalan, Spanish, or both. The authors took care of the translations into English. To guarantee anonymity, we identify participants by referring to their sex and age. A correlative letter will be used in case of individuals with coincident characteristics.

The empirical evidence comes from a specific urban setting, Barcelona, and so does not claim to be generalizable. However, the experiences participants shared with us are relevant for understanding the forms of appropriation of smartphones and WhatsApp among older individuals. In terms of the circuit of culture (du Gay *et al.*, 2013), they allow us to discuss how representations and regulations are negotiated when these two digital artefacts are consumed.

Results and discussion

The smartphone gets home…

When it comes to buying a smartphone, responding to offers by telecommunication providers is common – as two participants explain (Man 63, Woman 61). However, similarly to what we found in 2010–2011 regarding featured phones, the purchase can also be expressed as a response to external pressures:

> I bought it because I've a group of friends, and all of them had smartphones, they're pushing me, and finally I gave up and bought one of those phones.
>
> (Woman, 77)

It was a gift from my daughter, I used to send [her e-mails and] pictures [on the computer], because my daughter lives in Japan, and she sends me pictures.

(Man, 72)

Sometimes, the older individual who aims at having a brand new smartphone might face the opposite pressure which, based on stereotypes, could even put limits to adoption (Ling, 2008):

I went to the store to buy a new smartphone, I wanted to have a better one, and they stared at me like, 'Why would this old woman like such a smartphone?' Everyone's free to have a desire, and this was my desire.

(Woman, 76)

Mobile devices are surrounded by stereotypical assumptions that depict older people as limited users or laggards (Rogers, 1995), leading to situations in which older individuals are far from being seen as autonomous users of sophisticated devices. We found another attitude that challenges stereotypes is the willingness, the desire to learn, which becomes relevant for inter-generational relationships and fosters participation in the learning club:

You know why I want to learn new things (about the smartphone)? Then I can go back to my children, show it to them, and ask them, did you know this?

(Man, 76)

With the smartphone, social interaction is combined with other forms of digital entertainment, which might involve creation, edition, publication and circulation of media content, activities that are not strange at all for older users:

I take a picture of my grandchildren, then I put a frame on it, and I send it. It's so entertaining.

(Man, 78)

Even though smartphones are designed for individual use, appropriation processes often challenge industry expectation (Bar *et al.*, 2016). This is the case with shared devices. When individuals decide not to have their own mobile phone, they could regularly borrow one from somebody else, often a close relative – as we already observed among older individuals (Fernández-Ardèvol and Arroyo, 2012). We distinguish between hands-on sharing and minimal sharing (Weilenmann and Larsson, 2002). In hands-on sharing, borrowers use the device by themselves – making calls, messaging or taking pictures. In minimal sharing, only the contents are shared and the device owner will perform the tasks on behalf of the other person.

For the same reason, one participant reports that she does not need her own smartphone because she has permanent access to her husband's one (Woman,

60). In a similar vein, another participant explained that his wife would use his smartphone regularly because she does not have her own mobile phone. In fact, he usually dials their daughter's number for her (Man, 72). The sharing of the device, and the collaborative use attached to these practices, both play a role in the maintenance and reinforcement of existing links (as already described in relation to youth – Castells *et al.*, 2006: 155–156). Primary and secondary users – the lender and the borrower of the device respectively – continuously negotiate the interactions around the mobile device to decide who, how, when and where the smartphone is used. This is the case with regard to a couple (Woman 65, Man 70), who refer to the smartphone as a shared device and explain that they use it indistinctly. Consequently, everybody in their personal network would know that their WhatsApp is shared – even though on certain occasions there are misunderstandings, the couple do not perceive as troublesome.

... and it comes with WhatsApp

Back in 2010–2011, SMS were significantly popular and MM apps were just taking off. Our participants mirrored this situation, with almost all mobile users relying on SMS but only one mentioning an MM app. She could only use WhatsApp with her daughter 'because she is the only one who has it' and friends and relatives 'don't want to know anything about it' (Woman, 62). This generational discourse, slightly suggested by the comparison between her daughter (young) and her peers and relatives (older adults), also appeared in relation to SMS, as argued by a participant who did not use texting for communicating because people in his network 'they are not like the youth, … always with texts here and there' (Man, 70).

The massive movement from SMS to WhatsApp became evident in the focus groups we conducted in 2015. Participants expressed its meaningfulness in different ways:

> I use [the smartphone] for pictures, WhatsApp and calls.
>
> (Woman, 81)

> I only use the smartphone when needed, and to check all the rubbish people send through WhatsApp.
>
> (Man, 69)

Described as important as voice calls – and pictures – WhatsApp is a relevant socializing channel attached to the smartphone. It favours expressive interactions aimed at conveying social relationships, what the participant identifies as 'rubbish', which usually help to maintain both strong and weak personal ties. In addition, even external actors will expect any smartphone owner to use this app:

> WhatsApp's the most important thing in this [smart]phone. I bought it and, without asking or anything, they installed it in the store.
>
> (Woman, 77)

The pervasiveness of WhatsApp redefined phone calls, and at the end of the day, interactions increase in frequency while voice calls still take place:

> For something long, I prefer a phone call. But it's a cost issue. If we said on the phone all that we say on WhatsApp, it wouldn't be possible [to afford] it.
>
> (Woman, 70)

A young senior woman complained about the incremental change in communication that now intensifies non-oral communication based on text and images. She also faces social pressure to use WhatsApp:

> I make more calls than I receive. People don't like calling anymore. Me, I don't like WhatsApp, I use it because I have no choice, but I don't like it at all. Because I like talking to people and meeting them. We've gone already from not meeting each other to talking on the phone. And now, with WhatsApp, you no longer talk. I find it awful.
>
> (Woman, 60)

In addition, she complained about the lack of interest of people on calls, despite the introduction, in 2015, of WhatsApp calls.

Voice calls seem to be more suitable for communicating with closer friends and closer relatives (strong links), while weak links would be maintained mostly through WhatsApp – but also through SNS. In this sense, a participant refers to the multimodal communication she maintains with her daughters during the day on an ordinary basis: 'Also, for other things you talk on the phone with your daughters' (Woman, 70). Pictures and text messages would go through WhatsApp, she explains, which substitutes and augments the role e-mails used to play. But voice calls have no substitution. In our Mediterranean setting, daily voice conversations with (adult) children tend to be essential, because, as another mother explained in 2011, 'hearing [their] voice' gives a 'real sense of how are they doing' – something a text message could hide (Woman, 62).

It seems to be generally accepted that some conversations are more suitable for voice calls – for instance, when nuances are difficult to translate in a text message. Conversely, others are more suitable through MM – for instance, when an image would save extended explanations. With no discussion, voice calls are also necessary when fast reaction is needed – for micro-coordination (Ling and Yttri, 2002) and urgent things:

> You have to distinguish between what is imminent, and what's not, because [interactions on WhatsApp] can take long.
>
> (Man, 68)

WhatsApp groups, a huge innovation

Groups are the most striking feature of MM apps. Groups are not new in the digital environment, but their specific materiality has brought innovations in communication practices. Both the app, WhatsApp, and the device, the smartphone, have specific affordances and limitations that shape the way groups are used. We highlight some of them. First, the keyboard is not as user friendly as that of a computer, which might decrease the willingness to write while increasing spelling typos. Second, mobile images already became pervasive; they are used to report personal activities and as substitutes of texts, opening the door to new creative uses. Groups have an image, which any participant can change. Third, voice messages, videos and other MM contents are easily shared in these groups. Fourth, group administrators are in charge of incorporating new users to the group. And fifth, groups can be muted during different periods of time. These characteristics, which shape the use of WhatsApp groups, are negotiated and regulated by their users, a process that never ends due to permanent updates of the app.

Groups with relatives are common and meaningful for participants (Aharony and Gazit, 2016):

> I have WhatsApp split in three, my wife's family, my family and mysons.
>
> (Man, 64)

> I have a family group, so my son in Australia can be updated with all that we say here in the group.
>
> (Woman, 70)

By allowing permanent connection with children abroad, groups seem to increase the emotional attachment to (and through) the mobile device (Aharony and Gazit, 2016; Vincent, 2010) thanks to the intimate communication they allow. That can include sharing both everyday life moments – such as the growth of the plants in the backyard of the son's home in Australia – and important life moments – as the first steps of the grandchild. This turns WhatsApp into a powerful life-logging tool (Karapanos et al., 2016).

Groups can be easily compared with Facebook. WhatsApp is perceived as being safer, in terms of controlling the final audience for messages, which was problematic with Facebook (Righi et al., 2012). Being always aware of who the receivers of the messages are, the audience, was a relevant factor in the adoption of WhatsApp. Participants in the 2015 focus groups explained they widely used Facebook and WhatsApp. However, the conversations did include much discussion about WhatsApp and almost no comments about Facebook. Not so long before, Facebook was the topic of controversy (Gibson et al., 2010) but the attention has moved to the MM app. In fact, most club participants were passive users of Facebook:

I'm not concerned with this, this thing with knowing about somebody else's life. If I want to know about somebody I'd contact them.

(Woman, 76)

They had Facebook accounts that they checked often, but most of them never published:

I'm on Facebook, but I'm a reluctant user. [In my profile] there's not my name, nor my last name or my photo, I don't like seeing somebody else's photos.

(Man, 78)

One participant does not use Facebook nor Twitter, because 'they don't fit' her. She explains how WhatsApp became the perfect channel for sharing contents and socializing:

I think it's a tool to bring joy to people ... to break the monotony. Whenever I receive a nice WhatsApp, I forward it immediately; I want others to enjoy it. I don't want to be the only one who can enjoy it.

(Woman, 81)

WhatsApp groups are often created for a goal (preparing a party or following a course, for instance). Yet, on occasion, they might evolve and mix together greeting cards, general interest topics and issues regarding the original topic of the group. Thus for most users, these spaces for cultivating social relationships also bring tensions:

Groups are interesting, if I'm planning to go out with seven people, I don't have to call each one. Then they start sending those funny things.

(Woman, 61)

These groups are both the most useful and most useless tool you can find.

(Man, 68)

Participants made it clear that the evolution of groups comes together with regulations. Topics outside the central thematic of the group can be explicitly banned, as well as political opinion, sensitive news, non-socially acceptable contents, etc. Limits are put in place to maintain the interests of all the group members.

The negotiation is usually conducted first in face-to-face conversations, where the regulation tends to be agreed among group members. Negotiations lead to different norms of use in different settings, in response to specific social learning processes, shaped by existing social norms – as we have already learnt for mobile phones worldwide (Castells *et al.*, 2006: 94–97). Therefore, what is suitable for one WhatsApp group is not necessary suitable for another, in terms of norms of use and contents. In the learning club, we discovered a controversy around the appropriate time of day for sending WhatsApp messages. A rule was stated, but the norm was often broken:

> We have a rule in the group, you can't send WhatsApp messages later than 10:30 p.m.
>
> (Woman, 79)

> Usually they scold me, because sending messages during the night is not the right time to send messages.
>
> (Man, 76)

For other users, the technical features provided by the smartphone would be enough to control when to receive messages. However, those conflicts can remain active despite knowing how they could be controlled from the smartphone:

> One day, I was, in the car in the middle of the street, waiting for an urgent message from my son, and I received a message from the group, some nonsense. I get bothered in these cases.
>
> (Man, 68)

WhatsApp is meant for non-synchronic communication, however through its use, people can build expectations about synchronic communication, at least with some of their contacts. This sense of immediacy (Wojahn *et al.*, 2015) leads to more social norms:

> You're used to quick responses, if someday they don't answer you get worried.
>
> (Man, 64)

> You have immediate answers, this is good.
>
> (Woman, 81)

> It depends on who, some can take longer to answer.
>
> (Man, 55)

Yet, other users do as they have always been doing with mobile phones, in some instances they just ignore the device:

> They can keep calling, they don't bother me – I have it shelved. I'll catch up whenever I decide to pick up my phone.
>
> (Man, 75)

Conclusions

The main conclusions point to the importance of WhatsApp for older individuals as a socializing channel, both within the family and with peers. For former SMS users, WhatsApp became an easy app to get used to. Its augmented features allow sharing MM content that can be either personal or not, personally created or forwarded. Of particular interest are the negotiations of social norms around the chat groups that – as a relatively new phenomenon – bring with them controversies and new regulations that might shape specific forms of consumption. These regulations, in some cases, seem to reflect social norms that come from the landline – as when participants complained about receiving messages too late at night. Therefore, as part of the smartphone experience, mobile messaging etiquette, as a form of regulation, is negotiated and builds upon the personal experiences of the social group that appropriates the app.

Participants in the 2015 focus groups explained how they use Facebook and WhatsApp. Conversations did raise a lot of discussion about WhatsApp and almost no comments about Facebook. The lack of attention seems to point either to a *naturalization* of Facebook or to the beginning of a process of migration to other digital environments. Conversely, participants still have much to say about WhatsApp – especially, but not only, new users. We argue that, within the circuit of culture framework, these conversations constitute evidence of the on-going process of the construction of the representation of WhatsApp.

The path of constant innovation that characterizes digital communication is most striking in the case of mobile apps. Changes immediately reach final users through regular updates. Text, images, voice messages and video were the basic features of WhatsApp during most part of our study, while voice calls were incorporated at the end of the period in 2015. In this sense, new processes of regulation of appropriate uses and new forms of consumption might arise if voice calls on WhatsApp become popular. At some point, WhatsApp might be displaced by a new service of asynchronous, intimate communication leading to a new iteration of the circuit of culture.

All in all, even though data paint a picture in which mobile messaging apps are comparatively less important among older individuals in Spain, which might suggest that this is not a relevant phenomenon for the senior population, our research shows that WhatsApp is essential in the everyday life practices of some older individuals. We identify specific forms of appropriation among older participants, such as shared smartphones between couples; and specific approaches to new digital devices, with some participants willing to get the breaking novelties and others reacting to pressures to have an smartphone – essential to support WhatsApp.

Results suggests the need for further research in this area on older populations from a non-patronizing perspective, particularly in search of more evidence on the specific ways of appropriation with same age peers.

Acknowledgements

We are indebted to all participants who took part in the studies. We acknowledge the support from the Ageing+Communication+Technology project http://actproject.ca/ (ref. 895–2013–1018, Social Sciences and Humanities Research Council of Canada). Adrien Semail helped on language revision.

Notes

1 Book review in a Spanish bookstore (www.casadellibro.com/libro-els-meus-whatsapp-amb-la-mama/9788415961277/2296433, accessed 10 October 2016).
2 Since 2006, when short messages (SMS and MMS) reached a maximum of 13.4 million in Spain, they are constantly decreasing, reaching 1.9 million in 2015 (CNMC, 2016).

References

Ahad, A. D. and Lim, S. M. A. (2014) Convenience of nuisance? The 'WhatsApp' dilemma. *Procedia – Social and Behavioural Sciences*, 155: 186–196.

Aharony, N. and Gazit, T. (2016) The importance of WhatsApp family group: An exploratory analysis. *Aslib Journal of Information Management*, 68 (2): 174–192.

Ballesteros Doncel, E. (2016) Circulación de memes en WhatsApp: ambivalencias del humor desde la perspectiva de género [WhatsApp memes: Humor's ambivalences from a gender perspective]. *Empiria. Revista de metodología de ciencias sociales*, (35): 21–45.

Bar, F., Weber, M. S. and Pisani, F. (2016) Mobile technology appropriation in a distant mirror: Baroquization, creolization, and cannibalism. *New Media & Society*, 18(4): 617–636. DOI 10.1177/1461444816629474.

Castells, M. (2009) *Communication power*. Oxford, Oxford University Press.

Castells, M., Fernández-Ardèvol, M., Linchuan Qiu, J. and Sey, A. (2006) *Mobile communication and society: A global perspective*. Cambridge, MA, MIT Press.

CIS. (2016) *Barómetro de Febrero 2016. Avance de resultados. Tabulación por variables sociodemográficas. Estudio no 3128. Centro de Investigaciones Sociológicas (CIS)*.

Clarke, J., Montesinos, M., Montanera, R. and Bermúdez, A. (2015) Estudio mobile. Retrieved 8 December 2015, from www.iabspain.net/wp-content/uploads/downloads/2015/09/Estudio-Mobile-2015.pdf.

CNMC. (2015) *Telecommunications and Audiovisual Sector Economic Report 2015. CNMC (Spanish National Markets and Competition Commission)*. Madrid, Spain.

CNMC. (2016) Informe económico cectorial de las telecomunicaciones y el audiovisual. España, informe anual 2016: CNMCDATA – Statistical data. CNMC (Spanish National Markets and Competition Commission). Retrieved 3 October 2016, from http://data.cnmc.es/datagraph/files/informe_anual_2016_14-10-2016.zip.

Du Gay, P., Hall, S., Janes, L., Madsen, A. K., Mackay, H. and Negus, K. (2013) *Doing cultural studies: The story of the Sony Walkman* (2nd edn). London, Sage.

Fernández-Ardèvol, M. (2013) Deliberate missed calls: A meaningful communication practice for seniors? *Mobile Media & Communication*, 1(3): 285–298. DOI 10.1177/2050157913493624.

Fernández-Ardèvol, M. and Arroyo, L. (2012) Mobile telephony and older people: Exploring use and rejection. *Interactions: Studies in Communication & Culture*, 3(1): 9–24. DOI 10.1386/iscc.3.1.9_1.

Fundación Telefónica. (2016). *La Sociedad de la Información en España 2015.* Barcelona, Ariel; Fundación Telefónica.

Gibson, L., Moncur, W., Forbes, P., Arnott, J. and Martin, C. (2010) Designing social networking sites for older adults. *Focus*, 44(0): 181–189.

Karapanos, E., Teixeira, P. and Gouveia, R. (2016) Need fulfillment and experiences on social media: A case on Facebook and WhatsApp. *Computers in Human Behavior*, 55(part b): 888–897. DOI 10.1016/j.chb.2015.10.015.

Katz, E. and Aakhus, M. (eds) (2002) *Perpetual contact: Mobile communication, private talk, public performance.* Cambridge, Cambridge University Press.

Krämer, N. C., Winter, S., Benninghoff, B. and Gallus, C. (2015) How 'social' is social TV? The influence of social motives and expected outcomes on the usage of social TV applications. *Computers in Human Behavior*, 51(part A): 255–262. DOI 10.1016/j.chb.2015.05.005.

Lakoff, G. and Johnson, M. (2008) *Metaphors we live by.* Chicago, IL, University of Chicago Press.

Ling, R. (2008) Should we be concerned that the elderly don't text? *The Information Society*, 24(5): 334–341.

Ling, R. and Yttri, B. (2002) Hyper-coordination via mobile phones in Noruega. In *Perpetual contact. Mobile communications, private talk, public performance* (pp. 139–169). Cambridge, MA, Cambridge University Press.

Montag, C., Blaszkiewicz, K., Sariyska, R., Lachmann, B., Andone, I., Trendafilov, B., Eibes, M. and Markowetz, A. (2015) Smartphone usage in the 21st century: Who is active on WhatsApp? *BMC Research Notes* 8: 331 https://doi.org/10.1186/s13104-015-1280-z.

O'Hara, K. P., Massimi, M., Harper, R., Rubens, S. and Morris, J. (2014, February) Everyday dwelling with WhatsApp. In *Proceedings of the 17th ACM Conference on Computer Supported Cooperative Work & Social Computing* (pp. 1131–1143). ACM. DOI 10.1145/2531602.2531679.

ONTSI. (2016) *Las TIC en los hogares españoles. Estudio de demanda y uso de Servicios de Telecomunicaciones y Sociedad de la Información. XLIX Oleada. Julio-Septiembre 2015. ONTSI (Observatorio Nacional de la telecomunicaciones y de la SI).* ONTSI.

Orsini, A. (2014a) *Els meus WhastApps amb la mama.* Barcelona, Rosa dels Vents.

Orsini, A. (2014b) *Avec maman* [With mum]. Paris, Chiflet.

Richardson, M., Zorn, T. E. and Weaver, C. K. (2011) Older people and new communication technologies: Narratives from the literature. In Salmon, C. T. (ed.) *Communication yearbook 35* (pp. 121–154). London, Taylor & Francis.

Righi, V., Sayago, S. and Blat, J. (2012) Older people's use of social network sites while participating in local online communities from an ethnographical perspective. In *Proceedings CIRN 2012 Community Informatics Conference: Ideals Meet Reality* (pp. 7–9).

Rogers, E. M. (1995) *Diffusion of innovations.* New York, Free Press.

Rosales, A. and Fernández-Ardèvol, M. (2016a) Generational comparison of simultaneous internet activities using smartphones and computers. In *International Conference on Human Aspects of IT for the Aged Population* (pp. 478–489). Cham, Switzerland, Springer.

Rosales, A. and Fernández-Ardèvol, M. (2016b) Smartphones, apps and older people's interests: From a generational perspective. In *Proceedings of the 18th International Conference on Human-Computer Interaction with Mobile Devices and Services (Mobile HCI'16)* (pp. 491–503). Florence, Italy, ACM.

Rowan, D. (2014) WhatsApp the inside story, *Wired*, 19 February. Retrieved 7 March 2017, from www.wired.co.uk/article/whatsapp-exclusive.

Rubio-Romero, J. and Perlado Lamo de Espinosa, M. (2015) El fenómeno WhatsApp en el contexto de la comunicación personal: una aproximación a través de los jóvenes universitarios [WhatsApp in the personal communication context: An approach through undergraduate young ones]. *Icono*, 14, (13): 73–94. DOI 10.7195/ri14.v13i2.818.

Sanchez Aroca, M. (1999) Voices inside schools – La Verneda-Sant Martí: A school where people dare to dream. *The Harvard Educational Review*, 69(3): 320–336. DOI 10.17763/haer.69.3.gx588q10614q3831.

Schwartz, J. (2016) The most popular messaging app in every country – 2016, 24 May. Retrieved 10 October 2016, from www.similarweb.com/blog/worldwide-messaging-apps.

Sun, L. (2015) Facebook Inc.'s WhatsApp hits 900 million users: What now? 11 September. Retrieved 10 October 2016, from www.fool.com/investing/general/2015/09/11/facebook-incs-whatsapp-hits-900-million-users-what.aspx.

The Economist. (2015) Messaging apps. What's up?, 25 March. Retrieved 3 May 2016, from www.economist.com/blogs/graphicdetail/2015/03/messaging-apps.

Tubella, I., Tabernero, C. and Dwyer, V. (2008) *Internet i televisió : la guerra de les pantalles*. Barcelona, Ariel.

Vincent, J. (2010). Emotions and the mobile phone. In Greif, H., Hjorth, L., Lasén, A. and Lobet-Maris, C. (eds) *Cultures of participation: Media practices, politics and literacy* (pp. 95–110). Berlin, Peter Lang.

Weilenmann, A. and Larsson, C. (2002) Local use and sharing of mobile phones. In Brown, B., Green, N. and Harper, R. (eds) *Wireless world: Social and interactional aspects of the mobile age* (pp. 99–115). London, Springer.

Wellman, B. (2001). Physical place and cyber-place: Changing portals and the rise of networked individualism. *International Journal of Urban and Regional Studies*, 25(2): 227–252.

Wojanh, R. M., de Oliveira, A. L. and de Souza Domingues, M. C. J. (2015) Intensity of use of social networks in Southern Brazil. Complex, intelligent and software intensive systems (CISIS) 2015 ninth international conference 8–10 July.

Part III

Developing domestication through empirical studies

6 Domestication and social constraints on ICT use

Children's engagement with smartphones

Leslie Haddon

Introduction

Domestication analysis helps to make sense of people's engagement with technologies through understanding the broader context of their lives (Silverstone *et al.*, 1992; Berker *et al.*, 2006; Haddon, 2006, 2011). This framework enables us to appreciate how they acquired (or acquired access to) information and communication technologies (ICTs), the nature of that access, their uses of the technologies, the location and timing of that use and how and why they talk about or otherwise display their devices and services. That entails understanding people's circumstances, their biographies, the meanings that ICTs have for them and, as part of this, their relations and negotiations with others.

Sometimes that background can lead people to reject technologies altogether, be that through an antipathy towards what an ICT might threaten (e.g. as when interviewees in the past have said things like 'That will lead us to watch even more television!') or its perceived irrelevance (e.g. 'Why do I need that? I can already do what I want to do with this new technology!'). Sometimes a technology is adopted, it has some value for people, but it simply has a narrowly defined, limited, place in their lives.

What is of interest in this chapter is how, even when technologies are accepted, the contextual factors noted above can also be viewed as social constraints, restricting what people do with their devices. In other words, these factors not only steer use but also they can also be considered to circumscribe how people deal with their technologies. The reason why it is sometimes useful to explore this emphasis is because we are often confronted with celebratory accounts of our relations with technologies, as captured in marketing slogans about our ability to use them 'anytime, anywhere' and accounts of the 'endless' possibilities they promise. Like the cases of technology rejection and limited use noted above (and elaborated in Haddon, 2004), the focus on social constraints certainly provides something of an antidote to these enthusiastic claims, enabling us to understand some of the reasons why people do not always embrace the technological affordances on offer. But more generally in an academic literature that often addresses social consequences of ICTs, including what people can achieve through them, it is important to question any assumptions about people's unrestricted ability to use these technologies in the first place.

In fact, in the light of the some particularly positive images of how children often embrace new technologies, as in the claims about them being 'digital natives' (Prensky, 2001, or for one of many critiques of this claim see Selwyn, 2009) the empirical data reported in this chapter will focus on the particular constraints that children experience in their use of smartphones. More specifically, this allows us to explore the financial limitations faced by a group that is still economically dependent on parents as well as the social concerns that both adults and children have about children's use of ICTs. These lie behind restrictions on when and where children use or do not use these technologies – in other words, time and space constraints. Before moving on to the specificities of children and smartphones, a few more general points will be made about financial constraints, time and space considerations and the social evaluations of technologies that inform those adult interventions.

Social constraints on ICT use

Although not stressed in the original classic text on domestication (Silverstone *et al.*, 1992), the financial circumstances of individuals and households are an important part of the social context influencing ICT adoption and use. One early quantitative analysis using the domestication framework showed the extent of this in a survey of five European countries, France, Germany, Italy, Spain and the UK (Haddon, 1998). Of the Europeans surveyed, 24 per cent received complaints from other household members about the cost of outgoing telephone calls, 64 per cent rationed their own use of the phone and 42 per cent tried to persuade others in the home to limit their calls. Unsurprisingly, such financial constraints were most visible in domestication studies of poorer households, as exemplified in UK and US qualitative studies of single parent families (Haddon and Silverstone, 1995; Russo-Lemor, 2006).

Financial constraint can be exemplified even more strongly and in more detail through a Kenyan domestication study of mobile phone use by people living in slum next to Nairobi (Mwithia, 2016). Keeping in contact with extended family in rural areas of Kenya, including sending money to them and arranging to visit, was very important in this African context (also noted in Brinkman *et al.*, 2009, pp. 77–78). The study showed how existing ways of doing this – such as passing on messages via others travelling to the country areas, using rare public telephones or sending money – were all problematic. In desperation, people sometimes borrowed the mobiles of others to achieve those goals, but that could also be socially difficult for both the lender and the borrower. As a result, many participants acquired mobile phones. But even the cheapest models and minimal running costs constituted a high proportion of the income of these slum dwellers. Hence this study is useful for highlighting a whole range of financial constraints at work.

Cost was the key factor influencing what models were bought, so fashion played less of a role in the choice of mobiles than occurs in some of the European and Asian studies. It often led these users to limit the number of calls made, not just because of the telephone tariffs but also because of the cost of electricity for charging the mobile phone. Financial constraint was also the reason for the practice of 'beeping' (ceasing to ring before the person can answers), which did not incur charges, but nonetheless signalled to someone else that the mobile phone owner was free to be called (a practice also noted in some other Global South countries, Donner, 2007). Financial considerations limited other uses of the mobile – the participants in the Kenyan study would download music rather than stream it onto the phone so that they did not incur repeated costs when listening to music. Finally, because of the context in which they lived, mobile phones were generally concealed on the body, and not used at all in certain parts of the slum because the interviewees feared that their devices would be stolen. So apart from constraints on use, there was little of the display of mobile phones to others that has been noted in the European and Asian literature on mobile phones.

Turning to time and space issues, from its earliest formulation, domestication analysis highlighted the importance of these in its discussion of 'incorporation' and 'objectification', covering how ICTs are fitted into people's temporal routines and those of social networks and how ICTs are located and used (or not) in certain spaces (Silverstone *et al.*, 1992). Those particular social constraints have received considerable attention subsequently (reviewed in Haddon, 2004; Green and Haddon, 2009), but while the reason why they exist can reflect social contexts such as working times or housing types, they can also arise from people's values. In its discussion of the 'moral economy' of the home, the classic domestication text drew attention to the importance of values that motivate technology choices (as well as resistance to some technologies) and also shape rules governing how ICTs may or should be used (Silverstone *et al.*, 1992). Perhaps the clearest example of how these act as constraints on use within the ICT literature more generally is the body of work on the parental mediation of children's experience of ICTs. This covers parental rules, other interventions such as the guidance that parents give to children and actions such as monitoring children's use of technologies like the internet (for a review, see Mascheroni, 2014). The focus in these studies is often on which strategies parents use and on which are most effective. However, some studies have also noted the history of moral panics that often underlie adult (and by implication parent) concerns about children's experience of technologies (e.g. Critcher, 2008), evaluations that in turn lead to those various parental interventions. To refer to the circuit of culture model that frames this book, using terms from the Du Gay *et al.* (1997) version this chapter mainly focuses on the 'regulation'; of smartphones, specifically the regulation of children's use, although this history noted above means that we also need to appreciate the 'representations' of technology that motivate that regulation by parents and other adults. One last caveat about those social evaluations of technologies is that while some children may themselves acknowledge and reflect the worries of their parents, they also have their own agency, including their own values and perceptions of technology that influence their use or non-use of ICTs such as the smartphone. In other words, we need to remember that regulation includes self-regulation.

Children and smartphones

The Net Children Go Mobile *project*

Net Children Go Mobile was a multi-country European project lasting from 2012–2014 that was funded by the European Commission's Safer Internet Programme (for further details of this project, see the chapter by Mascheroni in this book). Its aim was to look at possible online risks faced by children as smartphones and tablets provided a new channel for accessing the internet. Mascheroni and Ólafsson (2014) reported the quantitative findings from Net Children Go Mobile while Haddon and Vincent (2014) discussed the European qualitative research covering Belgium, Denmark, Germany, Ireland, Italy, Portugal, Romania, Spain and the UK. In addition, there was a specifically UK qualitative report, which is why there are slightly more UK quotations in this section (Haddon and Vincent, 2015). Since there was limited research on smartphone use by children, the qualitative research reported here had to cover more general questions about adoption, use and consequences before dealing with the risk agenda and it is some of this material that forms the basis for the analysis below.

The main fieldwork was carried out from January to September 2014, and was conducted in two phases: interviews and focus groups with children were generally completed by the end of April 2014. The focus groups with adults (parents, teachers and youth workers) continued in certain countries until September 2014. There were 55 focus groups with children ($N=219$) and 107 interviews ($N=108$) across the nine countries.[1]

Financial constraints

The amount of money involved in buying and subsequently using smartphones was especially important for both children and their parents at various stages. When initially acquiring the devices, many parents clearly took these costs into account, in part referring to smartphones as expensive items that might potentially be lost or stolen or that the children might simply break. The cost of smartphones also influenced which model of phone parents bought. Marco: 'my mother says it doesn't have to be beautiful for me to show off. It has to be useful' (boy, 12, Italy).

While some children may be more fashion-conscious than others and lobby for brands like the iPhone, many of the young people interviewed were themselves cost conscious, often complaining about the price of (some) smartphones, especially when they appeared to be fragile. And some of those interviewed mentioned their everyday anxieties about losing or damaging such a dear possession.

> DANIEL: I need to be careful how I'm going to use it, where I'm going to use it, where to put it. Because people put their phone in their pockets and then they just drop out and they lose it. So I'd usually put mine in

my top left blazer pocket so I know it's there at all times. (... you can have) panic attacks when you're: 'Oh, where's my phone, where's my phone! And to feel it's there; or have these check-ups, to check it's still there.'

(Boy, 15, UK)

After acquisition financial considerations could have a bearing on which apps children downloaded. Across countries, and not just in less economically prosperous families, parents had often advised their children to stick to free downloads (free apps, free games and free music downloads), occasionally adding that if the child really wanted to download something expensive, they would have to pay for it themselves. Where the parents had agreed to pay for downloads, younger children in particular had to ask their parents' permission first. In practice, many of the young people interviewed only downloaded free apps, especially games, at times arguing that they are good enough and the games they had had to buy were too expensive.

Running costs also influenced usage. Some, often older, children were very knowledgeable about the Service Provider tariff plans for their smartphones, and even when they did not know all the details with a few exceptions they had a good deal of awareness of the package they were on. This could influence their evaluation of various smartphone apps, several appreciating Snapchat and WhatsApp because these apps were free and hence could replace texting. Some recalled how they had first become aware of some costs:

> WILSON: I remember, I went on holiday ages ago and I wanted to watch 'The Simpsons' on YouTube. And I was on this journey, in the car, and I was using 3G. Then my dad said: 'How are you watching this?' And I said: '3G'. And he said: 'No, get off it, it costs'. I didn't even know that so I'd been using 3G for ages.

(Boy, 12, UK)

In the most extreme cases, the internet facility of the smartphone was either not used or abandoned. Ricardo (boy, 13, Portugal) had a smartphone but simply did not use it to access the internet – he did not want to spend money 'on this stuff'. Marco (boy, 15, Portugal) had recently deactivated his 3G access because his internet tariff had become too expensive to go online 'wherever he wants'. He was planning to return to an older tariff. Last, Vasco's (boy, 11, Portugal) parents had said that his smartphone was mainly to be used for phone calls, that he should not use it much to go online or to exchange online messages. In fact, one day he had forgotten that the internet was switched on and when the higher than normal bill came in part of his pocket money was deducted to pay it. As a result, Vasco decided to avoid going online from his smartphone and used the laptop and free WiFi instead. Even without the experience of a large bill many sought out WiFi in public places. Children like Trine, (girl, 12, Denmark), would check to see if access to WiFi was available before she turned on 3G, or else, like Griet (girl, 12, Belgium), they rationed their time online: 'I try to turn (3G) off most of the time, otherwise it would cost a lot of money. If I want to go on Facebook or Snapchat, I turn it on. But immediately afterwards, I turn it off again'.

This was also true for those not on a pay-per-use tariff but who had a tariff with internet access (however measured) up to a certain point. Sometimes their parents had imposed these limits, just as in the past other parents had imposed limits on how much money their children could spend on traditional mobile phones. Or else the parents had negotiated a deal whereby their child would pay the extra if they crossed that threshold. While some children admitted to going over their limit, more monitored their usage and tried to stay below their limit. For example, whenever Alana (girl, 12, Romania) received a notification that she was about to surpass her internet limit she stopped going online from her phone. Meanwhile:

> ANUJ: I check how much data I have left normally. And then if there is WiFi I'll use it. But if there isn't I won't mind using my internet, but only if it's somewhere when I really need it. If I don't need to go on my phone for something important then I'll wait till I get home or later on.
>
> (Boy, 12, UK)

One common tactic to save money was to switch from texting via the phone to online app alternatives using free WiFi. Several interviewees also mentioned using some form of online textual messaging option when abroad because it was cheaper than speaking on the phone. An alternative strategy to reduce costs lay in the choice of what service to access. For example, Emile (boy, 15, Denmark) would not use YouTube on his smartphone when out because it 'eats up data' while Gaia (girl, 15, Italy) said the same but specifically about viewing longer videos on the smartphone. Another example of finding cheap alternatives is when Massimo (boy, 14, Italy) noted that the mobile version of the newspaper *Repubblica* required a subscription, so he went to the newspaper's homepage instead because it was free. Paulo (boy, 12, Portugal) provided an illustration of a 'workaround' (Ito *et al.*, 2010) whenever he was in a shopping centre: if he wanted to send a message to a friend, he would first check whether there is free WiFi and if there was he would send the message through Facebook, avoiding costs. If there was no WiFi, he would send the message by short message service (SMS) because it was cheaper than activating 3G, going to Facebook, going to Facebook Chat and sending the message via that route.

As we saw earlier, some of the motivation to be careful about costs came from bad personal experiences. For example, Cătălin (boy, 14, Romania) only used the internet for about ten minutes per day but at first had not known how to shut down apps and his bill had mounted by €10 per day. He had been too scared at first to tell his mother but eventually he did and Vodafone let the family pay just half the bill (€65). When Marius (boy, 11, Romania) had been at his grandmother's he had sent messages and watched films unaware of how much it would cost – and had cried when he received a bill of €80 (although his parents subsequently had not told him off).

This section has demonstrated how costs remain an issue and in fact shape the acquisition and use of smartphones in a variety of ways. Arguably, money concerns are more acute for children than adults because of their financial dependence, meaning limited personal funds, as well as parental pressures on them to be frugal (also suggested by analysis of earlier data from the 2010 EU Kids Online survey: Haddon and Ólafsson, 2014). This may be exacerbated in some countries, given the many examples from Portugal and Romania.

The social nature of time and space constraints

Time constraints were often imposed by parents. This frequently reflected concerns about the general amount of 'screen time' that their children experienced either because this was perceived as making children less sociable, less physically active, taking time away from homework or more 'worthy' pursuits, causing eyestrain or leading their children to have insufficient sleep (a theme explored more in the EU Kids Online research – Smahel and Wright, 2014; see also the chapter by Ponte *et al.* in this book). In other words, many of these concerns carried over from earlier fears about the effects of TV and subsequently about the internet in general.

Although they sometimes objected and tried to get around these constraints, many children agreed with their parents' assessments. These concerns often led parents to impose limits on the total amount of time children could spend using these devices, or else the parents intervened when they perceived that the children had been using them too much (in one session). But sometimes it was the timing of use that was controlled, as when children were allowed to use devices only after finishing homework, or not during 'family times' such as communal dinners or holidays together.

Even without parental pressure, some children exercised their agency by, for example, preferring to do their homework first before using devices, including portable ones, for recreational purposes – even turning these devices off so that they could not be disturbed by incoming messages. For certain young people their after-school activities, their hobbies, their sporting interests, etc. took precedence, meaning that in effect they were not using devices, including smartphones, at these times. Or to be more exact, they were not undertaking tasks that took up blocks of time on these devices. Communication could be another matter, as some children checked incoming communications regularly, fitting this in between other activities, while others did not. How many personal commitments children had depended on the individual, but in general older children were more likely to mention these as reasons for not using the phone at certain times.

How young people evaluated the time spent on devices could also lead them to limit their use. While many were quite positive about their usage, some also recognised how the devices, smartphones especially, could be time-consuming. Occasional comments from children in a variety of countries suggested using smartphones could be seen as 'wasting time' that children could use for doing other things, including schoolwork.

NORA: Another disadvantage is that it distracts a lot of attention from home-work. Instead of doing homework and studying for a test, you prefer spending time on the phone because the phone is always on and you don't notice how much time goes by. You just wanted to look something up quickly but in the end you spend half an hour or more, because you lost yourself somewhere.

(Girl, 14, Germany)

Hence, to return to the discussion of constraints on use, some children actually restricted their own use of portable devices to go online, not just because they had got better things to do (as in the earlier examples of turning off smartphones when doing homework) but also because they were themselves wary of using devices too much, as when Lilya (girl, 11–13, Romania) felt that some of her peers were 'addicted' to using smartphones and she was afraid that she could become like that too. Others, like Stefania below, noted how they had overcome this temptation.

STEFANIA: Initially, when I first had my smartphone, I used to be connected for long periods and as a consequence I did my homework later and it took me longer, until the evening. Then of course I learned how to self-regulate and this does no longer happen, but it did at first.

(Girl, 13, Italy)

Turning to space issues, regulation of mobile phone use on school premises varied across countries[2] as well as to some extent between individual schools (for a fuller discussion of school regulation see the chapter by Vandoninck *et al.* in this book). Even in less strict schools there was an understanding that devices could not be used in lessons when paying attention to teachers, but many other schools banned their use for longer periods, as in some UK schools, especially junior schools up to age 11, where phones were not even allowed on the school premises (even if children often broke this rule in practice). One key reason for banning smartphones in lessons was that their use could be disruptive. But it became clear from some interviews with teachers that they had similar concerns to parents about children's excessive use of (this) technology as well worries as about the smartphone's potential negative consequences for children's face-to-face sociability.

Smartphones were often not used in those public spaces where they might be stolen.

ANTONY: I go to Peckham Bus Station to go to cadets and I never get my phone out there. You'd literally get dragged behind ... someone would take it!

(Boy, 15, UK)

In fact, children across countries, especially younger ones, often said themselves they would be wary of using smartphones in (certain) public spaces, walking home or on buses. And if children did use the smartphone in such spaces they would often do so carefully. In part this reflected parental advice, based on fears that the device would be stolen – including very specific advice about certain locations, for example, that children should not take smartphones to football practice.

In the UK, the interviews with teachers showed how these staff went out of their way to warn their students to be careful not to show their smartphones when walking home while listening to music with headphones, for example. This was a concern based on the fact that a number of these phones had been stolen in the local area. Indeed, the police who gave talks at the school advised such caution, partly because of a concern that children would be less attentive to traffic if listening to music or being otherwise pre-occupied with their phones. Perhaps it is not surprising, then, that this awareness about use in public spaces was expressed most by the UK children, for example Daniel (boy, 15, UK):

> If I'm on the bus without my friends and there's a group of people behind me, then I'm wary of how I use it. You won't go through just poking the screen – because that's asking to get your phone stolen.

Previous research on mobile phones had shown that these devices are used less in certain spaces because of social norms (e.g. in theatres during shows; reviewed in Haddon, 2004 and Green and Haddon, 2009). The same was clearly true for smartphones, as some young people told embarrassing anecdotes about their phones ringing in places like churches during a service. Thus, in some places smartphones were not used or even switched off.

Finally, young people also limited their use in public spaces (and at certain times) out of a sense of what was socially appropriate behaviour. Pilar (girl, 16, Spain) was one of the children interviewed who did not check her smartphone when out with friends out of respect for those co-present – that was as a form of etiquette. Fabio, below, had reduced his use when in company as he reflected on this

> FABIO: I used to be very attached to Facebook, but after a while I understood that … I mean, I see all my friends that are always on Facebook. They hang out with friends and they are stuck on their phones. That is not real life. It is not good. On Saturday night you go out to have fun and (they are) with their phones in their hands all the time. It is good to use it when you can, not using 24/7.
>
> (Boy, 16, Italy)

While there are some practical reasons for time and space constraint on smartphone use, such as mobile signal coverage, this section has underlined some of the social reasons for restrictions on the use of technology, both reflecting parental concerns about technology but also children's own perspectives on the social implications of technology use.

Conclusions

In his book *What is history?* (1961), the historian Carr likened his discipline to fishing. What fish you catch will depend on, among other things, where you go fishing and the type of fish you are trying to catch (that will also influence the type of fishing equipment that you use). In other words, what historical accounts researchers generate will depend on where they look and what they are looking for (influencing what methods of analysis they use). Carr's analogy could certainly be applied in other domains, including the study of ICTs. Although domestication analysis has become a very diverse corpus of work, and different contributions to that literature can have different goals, the classic work and some of those who subsequently used this framework were to varying degrees contextualising people's experience of ICTs. That does not mean that domestication analyses automatically dwell upon the issue of social constraints, but it is easy to see why these might sometimes be striking when conducting this form of research. The question has been raised about whether domestication analysis could ask a range of further questions, to use the fishing metaphor, whether there are other things researchers could fish for. For example, should domestication analysis pay more attention to the social consequences of ICT use, and whether this could be empowering (Bakardjieva, 2006). These are indeed worthy questions. But to turn this the other way around, when looking at social consequences in terms of at what people – in this case children – achieve with their technologies, how they can be creative, what problems they face, what risks they run, how it could change the organisation of their lives, etc. it is important to first pay attention to the social constraints that restrict, or 'regulate', what they do in practice. And these can reflect the values and perceptions of others (here, parents, teachers and adults more generally) as well as of children themselves, when they self-regulate their own use.

Notes

1 In some of the focus groups we only had the age range that had guided the choice of the sample (e.g. 11–13 years old). When this happens in the quotes an average figure is given (e.g. 12).
2 In the UK, 63 per cent of children are not allowed to use smartphones in school. The fact that for Denmark the figure is only 18 per cent shows the national variation in how smartphone use is regulated, implying different degrees of constraint on use in different countries.

References

Bakardjieva, M. (2006) 'Domestication running wild. From the moral economy of the household to the mores of culture', in Berker, T., Hartmann, M., Punie, Y. and Ward, K. (eds) *Domestication of media and technologies*, Maidenhead, Open University Press, 62–79.

Berker, T., Hartmann, M., Punie, Y. and Ward, K. (eds) (2006) *Domestication of media and technologies*, Maidenhead, Open University Press.

Brinkman, I., De Bruijn, M. and Bilal, H. (2009) The mobile phone, 'modernity' and change in Khartoum, in De Bruijn, M., Nyamnjoh, F. and Brinkman, I. (eds) *Mobile phones: the new talking drums of everyday Africa*, Bamenda, Cameroon and Leiden, the Netherlands, Langaa and African Studies Centre.

Carr, E. (1961) *What is history?* London, Macmillan.

Critcher, C. (2008) Historical aspects of public debates about children and media, in Drotner, K. and Livingstone, S. (eds) *The international handbook of children, media and culture*, London, Sage, 91–104.

Donner, J. (2007) The rules of beeping: exchanging messages via international missed call, *Journal of Computer Mediated Communication*, 13 (1), 1–22.

Du Gay, P., Hall, S., Janes, L., Mackay, H. and Negus, K. (1997) *Doing cultural studies. The story of the Sony Walkman*, London, Sage.

Green, N. and Haddon, L. (2009) *Mobile communications. An introduction to new media*, Oxford, Berg.

Haddon, L. (1998) Il controllo della comunicazione. Imposizione di limiti all'uso del telefono, in Fortunati, L (ed.) *Telecomunicando in Europa*, Milano, Franco Angeli, 195–247

Haddon, L. (2004) *Information and communication technologies in everyday life*, Oxford: Berg.

Haddon, L. (2006) The contribution of domestication research to in-home computing and media consumption, *The Information Society*, 22 (4), 195–203.

Haddon, L. (2011) Domestication analysis, objects of study, and the centrality of technologies in everyday life, *Canadian Journal of Communication*, 36 (2), 311–323.

Haddon L. and Ólafsson, K. (2014) Children and the mobile internet, in Goggin, G. and Hjorth, L. (eds) *The Routledge companion to mobile media*, Abingdon, Routledge, 300–311.

Haddon, L. and Silverstone, R. (1995) *Lone parents and their information and communication technologies*, SPRU/CICT Report Series, No. 12, University of Sussex, Falmer. http://eprints.lse.ac.uk/62461/.

Haddon, L. and Vincent, J. (2009) Children's broadening use of mobile phones, in Goggin, G. and Hjorth, L. (eds) *Mobile technologies: from telecommunications to media*, Abingdon, Routledge, 37–49.

Haddon, L. and Vincent, J. (eds) (2014) *European children's and their carers' understanding of use, risks and safety issues relating to convergent mobile media*, Report D4.1. Milano, Unicatt. http://eprints.lse.ac.uk/60147/.

Haddon, L. and Vincent, J. (2015) *UK Children's experience of smartphones and tablets: perspectives from children, parents and teachers*, London, LSE, Net Children Go Mobile, http://eprints.lse.ac.uk/62126/.

Ito, M., Baumer, S., Bittanti, M., Boyd, D., Cody, R., Herr Stephenson B., Horst, H. A., Lange, P. G., Mahendran, D., Martinez, K. Z., Pascoe, C. J., Perkel, D., Robinson, L., Sims, C., Tripp, L., with Antin, J., Finn, M., Law, A., Manion, A., Mitnick, S., Scholssberg, D., Yardi, S. (2010) *Hanging out, messing around and geeking out: kids living and learning with new media*, Cambridge, MA, MIT Press, https://mitpress.mit.edu/books/hanging-out-messing-around-and-geeking-out.

Mascheroni, G. (2014) Parenting the mobile internet in Italian households: parents' and children's discourses, *Journal of Children and Media*, 8 (4), 440–456.

Mascheroni, G. and Ólafsson, K. (2014) *Net children go mobile: risks and opportunities* (2nd edn), Educatt, Milan, Italy.

Mwithia, J. (2016) *Domesticating the mobile phone in Kibera: how Nairobi's poor are integrating the mobile phone into their everyday lives*, Doctoral Thesis, University of Technology, Sydney, Australia.

Prensky, M. (2001) Digital natives, digital immigrants', *On the Horizon*, 9 (5), 1–6.

Russo Lemor, A-M. (2006) Making a 'home'. The domestication of information and communication technologies in single parents' households, in Berker, T, Hartmann, M., Punie, Y and Ward, K. (eds) *Domestication of media and technologies*, Maidenhead, Open University Press, 165–184.

Selwyn, N. (2009) The digital native – myth and reality, *Aslib Proceedings: New Information Perspective*, 61 (4), 364–378.

Silverstone, R., Hirsch, E. and Morley, D. (1992) Information and communication technologies and the moral economy of the household, in Silverstone, R. and Hirsch, E. (eds) *Consuming technologies*, London, Routledge, 15–31.

Smahel, D. and Wright, M. (2014) *The meaning of online problematic situations for children: results of cross-cultural qualitative investigation in nine European countries*. London, LSE, EU Kids Online.

7 Domesticating smartphones

Troels Fibæk Bertel

Introduction

Recent developments in the media landscape have pointed towards complex processes of convergence and diversification exemplified not least by smartphones.
The smartphone is an example of media convergence par excellence (Cumiskey
and Hjorth, 2013); it is a meta-technology (Jensen, 2010), capable of representing all previous media forms on a single, mobile material platform. At the same
time, it is used in connection with a multitude of services and content forms
across media. This chapter discusses the smartphone as an object of domestication by examining a number of general themes related to the domestication of
this type of media technology. Some of these themes are well known from
research on other media technologies (see Haddon, 2016), but have become re-
actualized in the context of smartphones and an increasingly complex and interconnected media landscape. Furthermore, in the course of this discussion the
chapter asks how to approach the complexities associated with smartphones in
the domestication framework.

The domestication perspective

The domestication perspective is a theoretical framework for studying how users
appropriate media technologies (Silverstone *et al.*, 1992). It emphasizes the
active role of individuals and groups in shaping technologies as they are integrated into the contexts and practices of everyday life. The metaphor 'domestication' connotes the taming of wild animals and suggests that media and
technology, too, in a sense are tamed when users make them their own. The
domestication of media technologies is, however, never complete since their
meanings and uses are continuously renegotiated as technologies, content and
contexts change (Haddon, 2011). Employing the domestication perspective
implies a focus on the meanings that technologies have for individuals and
groups and the capacity these actors have for exercising agency in the use of
technology. The perspective is mainly preoccupied with the meaning-making
and use of media in small social worlds (e.g. groups of friends, households and
computer clubs), although it has also been used for macro-level analysis of the

appropriation of technology – e.g. the domestication of the car in Norway (Sørensen, 2006) and the mobile phone in Estonia (Bolin, 2010). Domestication theory was first developed in the UK in the 1980s in studies of the use of media (particularly TV) in the context of households, but has since been applied in a range of other contexts as well (Haddon, 2011, 2016).

When relating domestication theory to cultural studies and the circuit of culture framework used in this anthology (Du Gay *et al.*, 2013), it is clear that the process of domestication has a fundamental rooting in the moment of *consumption*. As such, domestication theory offers a perspective with which to examine, in detail, one aspect of the circuit of culture. Having made this point, it is, however, also clear that the entire circuit – *representation, identity, production, consumption, regulation* – is relevant to the domestication perspective in different ways. How technologies are represented and regulated in the culture at large clearly influences the role that technologies come to play in the lived experience of individuals and groups. Meanwhile, the meanings that are inscribed into technologies in design and production become starting points for domestication in the everyday lives of users. Thus, the entire circuit to varying extents is reflected in domestication's microcosmic view on how users make technology their own.

Smartphones and the domestication perspective

Smartphones have greatly expanded the functionality available on mobile platforms. The mobile phone was predominantly a device for text and voice communication between (two) individuals, whereas smartphones are general platforms for networked communication, information and the production and consumption of content. This chapter will not go into a detailed discussion of the differences between the mobile phone and smartphones or the different practices they support, but rather use an example from recent empirical research to illustrate a number of themes pertaining to the domestication of smartphones. Following this example, the rest of the chapter will discuss these themes.

'Peter', a man in his 50s, suffers from incapacitating long term illness.[1] Online, he actively participates in a number of Facebook groups about illness, political issues and music among other things and this engagement is important to him. Having limited eyesight and lacking the financial means to buy new eyeglasses, Peter prefers using his old second-hand computer over his smartphone for accessing the internet because of the bigger screen. However, when the power to his house was cut off for a period of time and he subsequently had to stay at a relative's house, he depended on his phone for going online. Since reading on the smartphone is a challenge to Peter, and he still wanted to keep updated on the topics he is interested in, he needed a way to save links and information to read later. He came up with the solution of creating closed and secret Facebook groups with himself as the only member where he would store the information to read on the computer once the power came back:

I actually made some groups myself which I'm the only one who uses. I made them but you need one other user apart from yourself in order to make a group. Then I invited my daughter and as soon as I'd done making the group I deleted her again. I have one called 'the memory group' [laughs] and one called 'politics for later use', 'music for later use' and so on and so on. (Peter, male, 50s)

(Bertel, 2016a)

This small example illustrates the complexity of how smartphones are integrated into everyday life. In so doing, it also highlights a number of themes that merit discussion in relation to the domestication perspective.

A first theme is how domestication applies in the context of mobile use. Smartphones travel with users across the situations of everyday life and are not tied to specific and bounded contexts such as households, which have traditionally been a central focus in domestication research. As Peter leaves his home to stay at a relative's house as a guest, he adapts his media use practices to his changing surroundings, domesticating the various media he uses across contexts.

A second theme is the individual dimension of media use. A tenet of the domestication approach has been its focus on the negotiation of meaning in social contexts. The use of smartphones is, however, to a high degree individualized: Peter uses his computer and smartphone for communicating with others, but to a significant degree also uses it for consuming content (e.g. keeping up with the topics he is interested in) without the direct involvement of other individuals.

A third theme is the 'malleability' of smartphones. Smartphones can be configured in countless ways and so what they mean to users is arguably more variable than many other technologies and may change as configurations and services change. Peter's use of the smartphone is quite specific: he uses it as a terminal for saving links in private groups on Facebook, something few other users would likely do. Thus the meanings a smartphone has for Peter likely differ from those of other users, which to some extent challenges the analytical precision in analysing the domestication of 'the smartphone' as the unit of analysis, as if it were a unidimensional and static object.

Finally, a fourth theme is how domestication theory deals with cross-media communication and services. The smartphone is embedded in an interconnected network of other technologies and its use is to a large extent cross-media. Peter uses his phone and his computer to access Facebook and participate in groups, and the meanings of all these technologies are connected and interdependent. The rest of this chapter will discuss these four themes in turn.

Domestication in households and beyond

The first theme pertains to the applicability of domestication research in and outside of households. Domestication theory was first developed and applied in the context of studies of how TV and other media were consumed by families and households. Thus, it was in this context that the basic vocabulary of the perspective was introduced: domestication was theorized to take place in an interplay between the public world and the private 'moral economy' of the household, in which media were 'consumed' and domestication occurred through four phases: *appropriation, objectification, incorporation* and *conversion* (Silverstone *et al.*, 1992). Since this early formulation of the approach, a number of studies have applied the perspective outside of its original context, not least in mobile communication. The application of the perspective in such varying contexts has become part of its body of knowledge, highlighting 'what can be done with this framework, how it can be used, and also how it can be developed' (Haddon, 2016, p. 21). When the perspective has been used outside of households, some of the original concepts and the model of the domestication process have sometimes not been included. Instead, such studies have most commonly used the concept of domestication in a general sense, referring to 'the social character of media technologies that do not develop to an inner logic, but are related to negotiations, social interactions and changing discourse' (Peil and Röser, 2014, p. 236). That is, they point to what is arguably the tenets of the perspective: user agency and social negotiations of meaning in context.

In a previous article (Bertel, 2013), I used an example from an empirical study of the domestication of smartphones among young Danes, conducted in 2011–2012, which might illustrate the relevance of such an approach. In the example, the respondent, a teenage girl, described a situation where she was going to a party by bike and got lost. This was not the first time; she often has difficulty finding her way around. Prior to owning a smartphone, she would get lost and call her friends and ask for directions. Then they would help her but might also tease her because she was not able to find her way. Using a map application on her smartphone, she was happy that she no longer had to call her friends to ask for directions and disclose the fact that she could not find her way. In this example, the smartphone is being domesticated as a go-to medium for wayfinding, partly because it is easy to look up such information on modern smartphones, but importantly also because of more or less explicit negotiations with her network of friends whose expectations and behaviour she takes into account when making communication choices. Clearly, this can be described as domestication despite not occurring in the context of the household. The girl actively makes choices about which media to use for what purposes but this agency is constrained and shaped by the social and other contexts.

Having this broad focus on agency and social negotiation, one might reasonably ask how, at a concrete level, to delimit the unit of analysis is such studies. The concept of 'communicative figurations' developed in mediatization theory (Couldry and Hepp, 2017; Hepp, 2013) might be helpful in this context. In the above example, the group of girls can be said to manifest a particular communicative figuration consisting of a constellation of human actors (the girls), who are guided by some relevance frame or purpose (doing teenage friendship), are engaged in a set of communicative practices (talking, calling, texting and using a map application) and are using a specific ensemble of media (phones, Facebook and applications). Using this vocabulary as a guide, the task for domestication theory would be to examine how technologies are appropriated into such varying (and sometimes overlapping) communicative figurations in everyday life. This has the advantage of being conceptually more flexible than geographically bound and narrowly defined units such as households. Furthermore, the household can itself be described in terms of its communicative figuration(s). This is significant because, as Bakardjieva has pointed out, the idea of the household being a delimited private space that is separate from a wider public world, which lies behind the early formulation of domestication theory, may be difficult to uphold in the face of the internet and mobile media perforating its boundaries (2006). In this way, the concept of communicative figurations may provide a common and flexible framework for analysing domestication across contexts.

Smartphones as individualized media

The second theme pertains to individualized use of media. In its original focus on families and households, domestication theory emphasized the negotiations between individuals of the role technology comes to play in everyday life. Individual use of technology, however, has been less explicitly discussed. In the context of mobile communication, a focus on social negotiation has been particularly understandable; mobile communication in the context of mobile phones was to a large extent social as many of the central concepts from the literature suggest. 'Perpetual contact' (Katz and Aakhus, 2002), 'micro-coordination' (Ling and Yttri, 1999) and 'connected presence' (Licoppe, 2004) all described practices that directly involved two or more individuals and thus a focus on social negotiation, not least about norms and appropriate phone behaviour, was obviously relevant. Although individual use practices (e.g. playing games, listening to music or using a calendar application) were long present in the context of mobile phones, they have been dramatically expanded in the context of smartphones. This has also been reflected in newer concepts from the literature. The concept of 'flexible alignment' (Bertel, 2013), for instance, captures the fact that users routinely consult online information systems just-in-time (e.g. maps, weather apps and bus schedules), which provides them an increased flexibility in their individual management of everyday life. The concept of 'listening in' (Crawford, 2012) on the ongoing conversation in one's network (e.g. in social media) without communicating actively with these contacts similarly points to the individualized use of mobile media.

The above is not to say that the individual perspective has been absent from domestication theory. The fact that agency is central to the domestication perspective points to the level of individuals even if, as Haddon argues, the focus has been on 'agency that acted within social constraints' (2016, p. 20). Also, some empirical studies have focused explicitly on the individual use of media (Aune, 1996; Berg, 1996; de Reuver *et al.*, 2016). In general, however, this aspect has been less pronounced.

This does, however, not necessarily imply that smartphones demand new ways to approach domestication in this regard. The point of the following discussion, rather, is to underscore the perhaps somewhat obvious point that the individual and social use contexts are connected and that both are relevant in domestication. As a first observation to that effect, it seems obvious that direct social negotiations entail the presence of individuals with differing perspectives, wants and needs. Here the connection between individual and the collective is immediately clear. As a second observation, individual use of technology that enters indirectly into social relationships can arguably be considered to be negotiated to some extent. The example above, where a teenage girl uses a map application to avoid calling her friends, illustrates this point well. Although her media use in this situation does not involve her friends directly, it is nonetheless influenced indirectly by them because it occurs with reference to them. Finally, use that does not enter into social relations (or happens with reference to them) can also be said to have a social component in so far as it builds on the meanings that media technologies have for users. One way to clarify the connection between the individual and collective levels in such cases would be to point to a meta-theory of meaning, for instance symbolic interactionism. While the space of a brief chapter such as this one does not allow for a detailed discussion of this perspective, it should suffice to refer to Blumer's three tenets of symbolic interactionism to illustrate the point. These, briefly put, are: (1) that people act towards objects (e.g. things, situations and other people) based on the meanings the objects have to them; (2) that these meanings are constructed and negotiated in an interplay with other individuals; and (3) they are interpreted and applied by the individual, who 'selects, checks, suspends, regroups, and transforms the meanings in the light of the situation in which he is placed and the direction of his action' (Blumer, 1969, p. 5). Meaning, then, is both socially negotiated and individually interpreted.

Returning to Peter's example, a symbolic interactionist perspective would stress that although Peter uses Facebook groups to save and store information in an individualized manner, such use is always connected to the collective through the meanings with which it is associated. And these meanings are socially shaped – e.g. through design, marketing, regulation, practices, experience and social context (Du Gay *et al.*, 2013; Silverstone and Haddon, 1996). Furthermore, when Peter uses his smartphone as a terminal to store information for reading later on the PC, this is not an isolated act pertaining only to the meanings associated with those platforms but is connected to the social value and wider set of meanings the information has for Peter – e.g. when he participates in collectives online discussing the information.

In focusing on negotiation and the meanings technologies have for users both the individual and the collective perspectives are in that sense arguably inherent to domestication theory – even if the research interests of concrete studies have tended to place more emphasis on the collective aspects than on the individual.

Smartphones as malleable media

The third theme centres on the variable configurations of smartphones. The mobile phone was, in most regards, a tool for voice and text communication and this functionality was a fixed part of the device. This meant that when Scandinavian teenagers were using a Nokia mobile phone in the late 1990s, there was a good chance they were texting with other teens. On smartphones there is not an equally strong connection between the material device and its symbolic contents. Smartphones are malleable devices in so far that the content and services to which they provide access may to a high degree be selected and configured by the individual user. That material platforms may be used for the consumption of variable content is, of course, not a new phenomenon with smartphones; it was also the case for the personal computer, and to a lesser extent for TV, radio and so on. However, since such malleability is a defining characteristic of smartphones, they provide a good opportunity for revisiting what such malleability means for the domestication perspective.

Arguably, one consequence is that smartphones may be too broad a unit of analysis in many cases. In my empirical research on the domestication of smartphones among Danish high school students, it was clear that the participants, at an abstract level, domesticated smartphones in similar ways; it was used, in particular, to provide a more flexible access to the internet across the contexts of everyday life (Bertel, 2013). However, looking deeper into the use of different services and functionalities on the phone, practices, experiences and meanings varied. It was also clear that symbolic content on smartphones was being domesticated relatively independently from the material platform. A case in point was the 'check-in' functionality on Facebook that many of my respondents did not use but about which they often had quite strong (predominantly negative) feelings (Bertel, 2016b). In this example, the smartphone was not the logical unit of analysis despite the fact that check-ins were done using this platform. Instead, what was being domesticated was a very specific type of communicative text on Facebook, a service that, from the user's perspective, resides in the cloud rather than on any material platform. This highlighted the need for an increased level of specificity in the analysis.

One way of approaching this issue is suggested by Hartmann's (2006) discussion of the different levels of media articulation. In her discussion, Hartmann returns to the notion of the 'double articulation' of media technologies, a concept that has long been part of the vocabulary of domestication theory. The concept highlights the way that media are special technologies in that they are both material objects and conduits of symbolic content and that both these articulations should ideally be studied in domestication research. Hartmann's argument, then, is that this understanding of media has led to a certain neglect of the analysis of individual texts, and Hartmann proposes that media should instead be considered triply articulated as material platforms, symbolic environments and texts. In the present context, this specification is relevant because it allows us a higher degree of precision in the analysis of what is being domesticated. Are we, at any given point of analysis, looking at the smartphone as a material object? Or is it rather a specific symbolic environment such as the Facebook app (or class of symbolic environment such as social network sites) or the reception of a specific text (or class of texts)?

Smartphones as cross-media

Finally, the fourth theme is how domestication theory might deal with cross-media use. Smartphones are to a significant degree used for cross-media communication as services increasingly reside in the cloud and can be accessed from many different material platforms. This means that smartphones cannot be considered in isolation but must be placed in the context of the wider media ecology of which they are part. This, of course, points back to the above discussion of the levels of material platforms, symbolic environments and texts; the symbolic environment of Facebook is a good example of such a cross-media service. Drawing attention to the symbolic environment or category of texts being domesticated is helpful for narrowing the analysis, but, on its own, is less helpful for addressing cross-media communication, where more explicit contextualization is needed.

Two concepts that might aid with such an analysis are intertextuality and intermediality, which would point, respectively, to the levels of texts and the combination of material platform and symbolic environment in Hartmann's distinction above. Intertextuality refers to the fact that texts get their meaning from their position within a context of other texts (Jensen, 2008). Referring again to the reluctant use of the check-in functionality on Facebook among young Danes, it was clear that this rejection was influenced by how the content of these messages was received and interpreted in the context of other messages. Specifically, the communicative purpose and relevance of the check-in messages was unclear due in part to the 'thinness' of this form of communication (a person was at a place at a specific time) relative to, say, a motivated textual description of where a person is and what he is doing (Bertel, 2016b). Explicitly situating a check-in message on Facebook within all other kinds of texts available to users across platforms and symbolic environments (SMS, instant message, email, snap, photo and so on) would thus help with establishing the meaning of the text in a domestication context.

The concept of intermediality shows that while each medium has affordances of its own that influence how it is chosen and used, 'actual communicative processes often involve the combination of several media, requiring that the affordances of all the media involved are taken into account in order to describe the choices that have resulted in a given process' (Helles, 2013, p. 16). The concept thus highlights how use of any one medium always happens with reference to other available media and their affordances e.g. the modalities, levels of synchronicity, types of flows, types of interactivity and practices they support. Referring to the similarities, differences and interconnectedness of the affordances of various media available in a given situation, the concept of intermediality may be a useful starting point for contextualizing media choices as well as how individual media are integrated into and influence cross-media practices. Not only the affordances of media need to be taken into account in such analysis, however; the sociological significance of media and their meanings need also be addressed. A perspective that may be helpful in supplementing intermediality on this account is the concept of polymedia (Madianou and Miller,

2013). This perspective, similar to intermediality, argues that users approach media not in terms of their individual affordances, but as an integrated web of affordances. Users chose among possible media based on what they logistically want to achieve as well as, importantly, the wider set of meanings these technologies have for them. The perspective stresses a sociological 'emphasis upon the social and emotional consequences of choosing between those different media' (Madianou and Miller, 2013, p. 170). An intermediality approach that takes into account both logistical and sociological consequences would seem to be very well aligned with the domestication perspective. Returning again to the check-in example, the fact that these messages occurred in the semi-public many-to-many communication flows characteristic of 'mass self-communication' (Castells, 2009) arguably made their communication content less immediately relevant than had the same content been sent via the one-to-one communication of a SMS text message, where the intended recipient would be immediately specified and the meanings of the exchange could be inferred to a higher degree. The fact that it is an SMS text would signal that this information was somehow important and relevant to the receiver because SMS tended to be used for direct communication to aid such activities as coordination (Bertel, 2016b).

Conclusion

This chapter has discussed smartphones as objects of domestication; four general themes were discussed with reference to four characteristics of such devices. A first theme was the consequences of the mobility of smartphones for domestication analysis. Smartphones travel with users across situations in everyday life and domestication occurs continuously. Originally, the focus of the domestication perspective was on media use in families and households, but such a focus is challenged when media move across contexts. When the domestication perspective has been used outside of households, they have often done so by pointing to the tenets of the perspective (e.g. that the user has agency and that meanings of technologies are negotiated socially in everyday life). This application of the perspective has proven fruitful, but raises the question of what the unit of analysis might be in such studies. The chapter suggested that the concept of communicative figurations developed in mediatization theory might be useful as a common approach to framing units of analysis in domestication studies across a range of contexts, including households.

A second theme was individualized use of smartphones. One of the tenets of the domestication approach is social negotiations of the meaning of technology, but the role of the individual has often been implied rather than made explicit. The chapter has argued that the individual perspective has, however, been part of the domestication approach even if concrete studies have focused less explicitly on this aspect. Social negotiations entail the presence of individuals and when individuals use technology with reference to (but not directly with) other individuals this arguably may be considered negotiation, too, albeit indirect. Furthermore, domestication is a perspective that is interested in the meanings that technologies have for humans, and meanings highlighted by symbolic interactionism are socially negotiated and individually interpreted and applied. Both dimensions are present and relevant in domestication.

A third theme addressed the fact that smartphones are malleable media in the sense that their configurations and meanings may differ among users. This arguably calls for a higher level of specificity than merely referring to 'smartphones' as if they were a uniform and stable object. The chapter has suggested that Hartmann's argument that media are triply articulated as material platforms, symbolic environments and texts could be a useful way of specifying the level at which domestication is taking place, allowing for more detailed and precise discussions.

Finally, the fact that smartphones are often used with cross-media applications and services was discussed. The chapter has argued for the necessity of situating smartphones (as texts, symbolic environments and material platforms) in the context of the wider mediascape of which they are part; the concepts of intertextuality and intermediality were discussed in this context.

Note

1 This example comes from empirical research conducted by the author in 2013–2014 in Denmark on the use of cross-media communication for civic participation among individuals suffering from long term illness who experience being 'caught up' in the municipal system.

References

Aune, M. (1996) The computer in everyday life – patterns of domestication of a new technology, in Lie, M. and Sørensen, K. H. (eds), *Making technology our own?: Domesticating technology into everyday life* (pp. 91–120). Oslo; Boston, Scandinavian University Press.

Bakardjieva, M. (2006) Domestication running wild. From the moral economy of the household to the mores of a culture, in Berker, T., Hartmann M., Punie, Y. and Ward, K. (eds), *Domestication of media and technology* (pp. 62–79). Maidenhead, McGraw Hill/Open University Press.

Berg, A.-J. (1996) Karoline and the cyborgs: The naturalisation of a technical object, in Frissen, V. (ed.), *Gender, ICTs and everyday life – proceedings from COST A4, Granite workshop, in Amsterdam, the Netherlands, 8 to 11 February, 1996* Vol. 6, pp. 7–36. Amsterdam, European Commission.

Bertel, T. F. (2013) 'It's like I trust it so much I don't really check where it is I'm going before I leave': Informational uses of smartphones among Danish youth. *Mobile Media & Communication, 1*(3), 299–313.

Bertel, T. F. (2016a) 'There's just nowhere else to turn': Illness and mundane citizenship on Facebook, in Sandvik, K., Thorhauge, A. M. and Valthysson, B. (eds), *The media and the mundane* (pp. 91–104). Gothenbur, Nordicom.

Bertel, T. F. (2016b) Why would you want to know?: The reluctant use of location sharing via check-ins on Facebook among Danish youth. *Convergence: The International Journal of Research into New Media Technologies, 22*(2), 162–176.

Blumer, H. (1969) *Symbolic interactionism; perspective and method.* Englewood Cliffs, NJ, Prentice-Hall.

Bolin, G. (2010) Domesticating the mobile in Estonia. *New Media & Society, 12*(1), 55–73.

Castells, M. (2009) *Communication power.* Oxford; New York, Oxford University Press.

Couldry, N. and Hepp, A. (2017) *The mediated construction of reality.* Cambridge, Polity Press.

Crawford, K. (2012) Four ways of listening with an iPhone: From sound and network listening to biometric data and geolocative tracking, in Hjorth, L., Burgess, J. and Richardson, I. (eds), *Studying mobile media: Cultural technologies, mobile communication, and the iPhone* (pp. 213–228). New York, Routledge.

Cumiskey, K. and Hjorth, L. (2013) Between the seams – mobile media practice, presence and politics, in Cumiskey, K. and Hjorth, L. (eds), *Mobile media practices, presence and politics: The challenge of being seamlessly mobile* (pp. 1–11). New York, Routledge.

de Reuver, M., Nikou, S. and Bouwman, H. (2016) Domestication of smartphones and mobile applications: A quantitative mixed-method study, *Mobile Media & Communication, 4*(3), 347–370.

Du Gay, P., Hall, S., Janes, L., Madsen, A. K., Mackay, H. and Negus, K. (2013) *Doing cultural studies: The story of the Sony Walkman.* Milton Keynes; Los Angeles, CA, Open University Press; Sage.

Haddon, L. (2011) Domestication analysis, objects of study, and the centrality of technologies in everyday life. *Canadian Journal of Communication, 36*(2), 311–323.

Haddon, L. (2016) The domestication of complex media repertoires, in Sandvik, K., Thorhauge, A. M. and Valthysson, B. (eds), *The media and the mundane* (pp. 17–30). Gothenburg, Nordicom.

Hartmann, M. (2006) The triple articulation of ICTs. Media as technological objects, symbolic environments and individual texts, in Berker, T., Punie, Y., Hartmann, M. and Ward, K (eds), *Domestication of media and technology* (pp. 80–102). Maidenhead, Open University Press.

Helles, R. (2013) Mobile communication and intermediality. *Mobile Media & Communication, 1*(1), 14–19.

Hepp, A. (2013) The communicative figurations of mediatized worlds: Mediatization research in times of the 'mediation of everything'. *European Journal of Communication, 28*(6), 615–629.

Jensen, K. B. (2008) Text and intertextuality, in Donsbach W. (ed.), *The international encyclopedia of communication.* Oxford, Blackwell Publishing.

Jensen, K. B. (2010) *Media convergence: The three degrees of network, mass, and interpersonal communication.* London; New York, Routledge.

Katz, J. E. and Aakhus, M. (eds) (2002) *Perpetual contact: mobile communication, private talk, public performance.* Cambridge, University Press Cambridge.

Licoppe, C. (2004) Connected presence: The emergence of a new repertoire for managing social relationships in a changing communications technoscape: *Environment and Planning: Society and Space, 22*(1), 135–156.

Ling, R. and Yttri, B. (1999) *'Nobody sits at home and waits for the telephone to ring': Micro and hypercoordination through the use of the mobile telephone.* Kjeller, Telenor forskning og utvikling.

Madianou, M. and Miller, D. (2013) Polymedia: Towards a new theory of digital media in interpersonal communication: *International Journal of Cultural Studies, 16*(2), 169–187.

Peil, C. and Röser, J. (2014) The meaning of the home in the context of digitization, mobilization and mediatization, in Hepp, A. and Krotz, F. (eds), *Mediatized worlds: Culture and society in a media age* (pp. 233–249). Basingstoke, Palgrave Macmillan.

Silverstone, R. and Haddon, L. (1996) Design and the domestication of information and communication technologies: Technical change and everyday life, in Mansell, R. and Silverstone, R. (eds), *Communication by design: Politics of information and communication technologies* (pp. 44–74). Oxford, Oxford University Press.

Silverstone, R., Hirsch, E. and Morley, D. (1992). Information and communication technologies and the moral economy of the household, in Silverstone, R. and Hirsch, E. (eds), *Consuming technologies* (pp. 15–31). London, Routledge.

Sørensen, K. H. (2006) Domestication: The enactment of technology, in Berker, T., Hartmann, M., Punie, Y. and Ward, K. (eds), *Domestication of media and technology*. Maidenhead, Open University Press.

Part IV
Managing sociability

8 Collective uses of mobile phones in the global South

Cultural diversity among low-income groups in Brazil and in South Africa

Carla Barros

Introduction

The purpose of this chapter is to discuss certain consumption practices relating to communication technologies among low-income groups in which collective uses emerge as a central aspect of the cultural dynamics in question. To do so, the results of an ongoing ethnography conducted in the city of Rio de Janeiro will be analyzed and then placed in perspective by making comparisons with studies conducted in South Africa. The search for a comparative dimension between the Brazilian and South African contexts first arose as an attempt to think about the discontinuity between how cultural forms, in this case artifacts, are anticipated in production and how they are experienced in consumption outside of the cultural experience of most economically developed countries. It is known that this discontinuity has a long tradition related to reception studies, be they of British or Latin American origin. Parallel to these studies, another type of research can be conducted that focuses on understanding different experiences with these technologies, which also emphasize the ways in which individuals create meaning in their interactions with communication goods. As some scholars (Sahlins 1976; Miller 1987) have emphasized, production "is completed" through consumption, since it is in the latter dimension that objects produced in series gain singularity through the appropriations made by them of individuals inserted in a given culture. Therefore, the ways by which goods were planned in the production sphere can be significantly changed in their everyday uses, through a wide variety of consumption practices.

The anthropological approach adopted here approximates, in certain aspects, the "circuit of culture" concept adopted by Du Gay et al. (2013). In this concept, the meanings of a cultural product are determined by the articulation of certain processes that, although distinct, are interrelated and overlapping. The perspective of Du Gay et al. allows the integration, among other factors, of the domains of production and consumption, which are perceived as mutually constitutive of each other. Thus, there is no fixed meaning for a cultural product that can be transported in a stable manner to different moments of the global process. This process has affinity with the anthropological perspective adopted in this chapter, which emphasizes that a series of contingent meanings will be attributed to a product in various situations. Another point of approximation of the concept of "circuit of culture" and the anthropological perspective is the central importance given to culture as an instance in which things "make sense" and where the "work of construction of meanings" takes place in the way that we represent them and how we construct our practices.

It is also possible to make a connection between Du Gay et al.'s concept and the vision of the cultural process of constitution of goods defended by Kopytoff (1986), which proposes the idea of a "cultural biography of things," where the meanings and values of goods are resignified in circulation, varying according to the context. In Kopytoff's vision, it is up to the researcher to accompany the daily circulation of objects in different contexts of value and meaning—from an object of greater value to its decline, for example, passing through various owners and uses. In both approaches, therefore, the meanings of cultural products are provisory, and must be understood in their specific contexts.

The focus of this chapter is to investigate certain uses of technology among low-income groups in Brazil—adding comments from studies conducted in South Africa—to analyze how individuals in their daily lives relate to consumer goods that are created based on models predominant in the European and North American contexts. The majority of the analysis focuses on research conducted about the habit of watching TV on smartphones. The counterpoint made with South Africa indicates the importance of comparative studies that consider the cultural diversity among South Atlantic countries and differences with those that are more economically developed.

In the specific field of television studies, Silveira (2004) has emphasized that both ethnographic studies of media consumption in the British tradition of cultural studies, as well as those produced in the Latin American context of reception studies, almost always identify the domestic space and the family group as "basic structural units of the standardized situationality of the television audience" (Silveira 2004: 65). These studies examine the rhythms of domestic dynamics related to television programs, as seen in the exemplary ethnography by Silverstone (1996), in which in addition to an analysis of the family nucleus, a description is made of furniture and other household objects to portray the situation where experiences with television take place. The author questions the existence of "a natural and universal way" of watching television, associated with domesticity and the family group. It is common for studies to emphasize television in its domestic locus, giving little importance, or even ignoring, other spaces and contexts outside the home where the medium is present. What is the reason for this tendency for research to consider TV in connection with domestic environments? Is there a certain "Eurocentrism," due to the influence of the family experience of most of the scholars who write about this topic in which the television's context is the home?

To escape this perspective, the "naturalization" of TV in the domestic environment has begun to be relativized by a relatively small number of empirical studies that present other media experiences found in public and urban settings. The audience in this research has always been in spaces outside the home, which has intensified with the arrival of new technologies—technological convergence in particular—and the advancement of mobility, which took the television and its audiovisual appeal outside the boundaries of the home. In several Brazilian cities in the interior, one can witness scenes where a TV set is taken onto sidewalks on the streets, mobilizing the neighborhood around it, or even the people who are walking by, to watch a program together. Tufte (1997) did a reception study in Rio Grande do Sul—a Brazilian state—regarding the telenovela *Rainha da Sucata* (*Queen of Scrap*), which shows that the boundaries of public and private dissolve when "windows and doors open," allowing you to watch TV from the street.

To investigate contexts of audience found in urban environments, the reflection presented in this chapter focuses on a different type of situation than mentioned previously. It specifically involves the adoption of smartphones as television reception platforms, which provokes a reflection on the traditional public/private dichotomy. The point here is to consider devices created for individual use, such as smartphones, which in certain situations in public spaces are appropriated for collective uses. In addition to the uses related to forms of watching TV on smartphones, the chapter will extend the discussion to other situations in which there may be a distancing from the individualistic form of dealing with information technology that is predominant in European and North American contexts. To begin the analysis of the Brazilian case, here is a brief presentation of the device most commonly found in this ongoing study, the so-called XingLing phones.

The emergence of XingLings

The situation chosen for observation in this study involves the use of so-called "MPX" or XingLing smartphones. The name "MPX" refers to phones that are widely consumed in low-price markets in large cities across Brazil. It is important to remember that consumers present at these locations belong not only to the lower and working classes, but also to the urban middle class, although the former are the large majority. These devices are generally smuggled and counterfeits of famous brands such as Sony, Nokia, Motorola, and Apple—and for the most part of Chinese origin, hence the nickname XingLing. Their main features are analog broadcast TV reception and that they can be used with more than one chip, which allows users to avoid the high cost of telephone services in Brazil by adhering to promotions from various carriers. The MPX devices are sold in Rio de Janeiro and in other urban centers in informal street markets and technology shopping malls aimed at a low-income public. They are offered at reduced prices because they enter the country without paying taxes. In general, MPXs have touch screens, front and rear cameras, wireless Internet, room for two or more chips, and broadcast TV reception. In the formal smartphone market there are models with "mp3" and "mp4" audio and video compression, while in the "pirate" market there are a range of devices that claim to have from "mp5" to "mp 20." In the fieldwork done in these low-income markets, one could find the extension of this classification to an "MPX 20" device—the salespeople do not always have the same understanding regarding the technical specification of each device, but the differences are related to the presence of features such as GPS, the number of chips (two, three or four chips on the same machine), Wi-Fi, analog and digital broadcast TV, and others.

Despite the issue of piracy, an interesting phenomenon in the context of low-income markets occurred—the wide diffusion of MPX-type gadgets helped accelerate the habit of watching TV on smartphones. Another dynamic was found that is not very common—a technological "novelty," in this case, the ability to watch TV on a smartphone, was pioneered and broadly disseminated among a low-income public. The acceptance of products with analog TV in the informal market, especially among low-income groups, sparked corporations to market this type of phone in Brazil legally. The first to venture into the market was EUTV, which in 2009 obtained the approval of the Brazilian regulatory agency to market a model produced by the Chinese company *E-Techco*. The CEO of EUTV made it clear when the device was released that the company's commercial strategy was to tackle the "gray market" of smuggled smartphones by offering a model with two SIM cards and access to broadcast television, two of the most attractive MPX features.

Thus, the practice of watching TV on smartphones was not only pioneered by low-income groups but inspired companies such as Samsung and Motorola to produce and sell devices to compete with the MPXs that were widely consumed in informal markets. The important thing to note is that the wide diffusion of MPX-type phones helped to accelerate the habit of watching TV on smartphones in the context of low-income groups, and not in the middle and upper classes, as would be expected. Therefore, the "novelty" of TV on smartphones did not spread through a "trickle-down" (Simmel 1957) effect—in which the subordinate classes imitate fashions that arise among the upper classes—but from increased consumption among low-income groups. As Miller and Horst (2006) noted in their ethnography of cell phone use in the lower classes of Jamaica, consumer practices often follow very different paths than those planned by technology developers.

Watching TV on a smartphone: conversations in movement

Unlike situations where television is inserted in a context of public and collective reception—such as a television in a bar turned on for the enjoyment of customers—the focus here is on situations that "by definition" are intended for individual use, but are transformed into collective audiences. The research results that will be presented below refer to an ethnographic study in progress, whose first phase was conducted from February to May 2013, in the city of Rio de Janeiro, Brazil. The work was interrupted in July 2013, for academic reasons, and resumed in the first semester of 2016.

The ethnographic methodology was chosen due to the primordial attention it gives to social practices. Ethnography allows a deep plunge into the perspective of the agents in specific situations, revealing how the meanings created in the productive sphere are appropriated and resignified. This methodology uses the techniques of participant observation and individual in-depth interviews to attain the so-called "native perspective" (Geertz 1976), that is, the internal logic that guides people in their daily actions. The researcher thus conducts a prolonged immersion with the group studied to understand how the various social spheres articulate among each other.

In the first phase of the study, predominated by observation, the interest focused on public spaces of circulation of people who had smartphones of the XingLing type that provides access to TV programming. Within the scope of the chapter, the analysis will focus on the use of these smartphones on urban train trips.

There is a certain methodological difficulty in capturing less obvious moments of television watching, outside domestic routines, ones that multiply in numerous situations with varying audiences, such as passengers riding in taxis with TVs. In the specific situation of the smartphone TV audience, the challenge of observing is intensified by the erratic character of an audience who are in a state of mobility and without a predetermined moment at which the experience with the media takes place.

The city of Rio de Janeiro receives a high number of workers who live in neighboring cities, and who spend about four hours a day commuting from home to work and back. Some of these people have low-skill jobs, and use various forms of urban mass transportation including trains, subways, and buses. Thus far the fieldwork has been concentrated in the context of the rail network known as the *SuperVia* that transports passengers from neighboring municipalities to the city of Rio de Janeiro. The *SuperVia* trains circulating in the city are strongly criticized by the population — the poor maintenance of the cars and the delays are constant complaints. The travel environment is very noisy, aggravated by the shouting of the many vendors who circulate among the cars, offering various types of goods. Food is the most common, but other products are present such as DVDs, fingernail painting kits, and various electronic goods. Since the trips are long, one way commuters pass the time is by sharing what they are doing on their phone with someone else. In one scene observed, a mother showed her friend a photo of her child on her phone that she will post on Facebook. In another situation, three young men talk while one of them asks another if he can plug his headphones into his friend's phone while he is listening to a local radio on the device. The music is loud enough for all those around to hear. In several other scenes observed, phones serve a collective purpose, linked to entertainment, exercising an intense sociability among peers, and their use is not restricted to the sole enjoyment of the device's owner.

The telenovela *Avenida Brasil*, broadcast by TV Globo in 2012 with high ratings and a strong presence in social networks, deserves more detailed comments regarding the reception context addressed here. Those who returned later from work in public transportation watched the telenovela which begins just after 9 p.m. on their mobile devices, often sharing the broadcast content with those around them, thus initiating a broad conversation about the program. Accordingly, the material regarding the reception of the *Avenida Brasil* was not collected on the trains, but in other conversations with the house cleaners and in this regard I would like to highlight the reception of the program by women who work as full time maids or house cleaners. The plot of the novel revolves around Rita, who was abused in childhood by her former stepmother Carminha. To get revenge, Rita adopts the name Nina to take a job as a cook in Carminha's house. She winds up feeling the pain of the maids working at the house, who were constantly being humiliated by their employer. When watching the soap opera on their smartphone, along with other house cleaners heading home, a certain "class sensibility" arose among this social group, and the women would criticize the authoritarian and arrogant attitude of Carminha's character. It became a time that they could also criticize their employers and their excessive arrogance toward the house cleaners, as the conversation revolved around their real situations. The house cleaners did not participate in the intense activity on social networks caused by the soap opera because they were not Twitter users, but they amplified the program's reception in daily conversations on the way to and from work, both while watching on their phones, or when commenting on the previous day's episode. At times, this collective conversation about the soap opera continued at the employer's house. Conversations about television programs may prove to be a privileged type of dialog, opportunities to exchange information, moral judgments, and knowledge of new lifestyles between the worlds of the house cleaners and their employers (Barros 2007).

This "shared repertoire" (Hamburger 1998), created by the fact that the telenovela is viewed throughout the country by all social classes, is structured and strengthened each day as maids and their employers comment and discuss the content of various programs, especially the telenovelas. Regarding *Avenida Brasil*, the house cleaner-employer relationship became the subject of many conversations in workplaces, in which on the one hand, the house cleaner did not achieve the "catharsis" in relation to her domestic employment that occurred on the trains, but, on the other, she would discuss with her employer the absurdities of the authoritarian behavior and ill-treatment the character Carminha imposed on her employees. In a country with strong oral tradition and intense sociability (DaMatta 1981) such as Brazil, the opportunity to talk about the telenovela is just as important as watching it, especially when the televised product interests people in many walks of life, as was the case with *Avenida Brasil*. The act of watching TV on a smartphone allows conversations that were previously restricted to homes and the workplace to be expanded to public space. It has long been a custom in the country to talk about the previous day's episode; to be able to watch it on a smartphone when the program is being aired increases the engagement of all who are in the environment, creating a large collective conversation.

Orality and collective uses surrounding media

Based on this point, we can now think about the importance of orality in Brazilian society and how communication phenomena in the country were strongly marked by sociability and interaction, even before the advent of new media. In fact, these more recent technologies came to accentuate certain cultural aspects that already existed. The anthropologist Gilberto Freyre (1987), in his classic *Casa Grande & Senzala* [*The Masters and the Slaves*], emphasized the strong oral tradition of Brazilian society since the colonization period, expressed in animated conversations in the streets and in oral narratives with which slaves, great storytellers, entertained the children of plantation owners. This was a social context in which conversation predominated over writing, which had always had airs of excessive formality in comparison with the "relaxed" speech found in the streets, the result of cultural exchanges between the groups that formed the country—slaves, Portuguese colonists, and Indians. Examining everyday moments in Brazilian society where media consumption takes place in a shared manner, it is worth highlighting a typical scene in the city of Rio de Janeiro, which is the collective reading of news in the newspapers on display at newsstands in the city streets. Newsstand owners hang the daily newspapers outside their stalls in the morning, and passersby gather in front of the headlines, occasionally commenting on the various issues printed on the front pages.

In the ongoing research discussed in this chapter, it was also possible to observe a variation of this collective conversation around a media source. In addition to monitoring individuals in urban trains, the ethnography extends to a low-income community in the city of Rio de Janeiro. In the location being studied, a cable car takes residents to the highest points of the community. The driver of the car always left a popular newspaper inside the car, which was read and commented on by the driver or by passengers, drawing comments from other people. In one scene observed on the cable car, after reading his own newspaper, someone loudly made an ironic comment about the behavior of a controversial football player, receiving opinions of support and disapproval from other passengers. On the same trip, other people read a newspaper headline. The newspaper was not read introspectively; on the contrary, it was common for the person reading the paper to externalize their feeling to others, expecting some kind of comment. This "socialized" reading relates to counter position discussed by Chartier (1993) in relation to possible forms of relationships between readers and the object being read. Chartier affirms that there was a kind of intensive reading that marked a historical period in which reading was scarce and was connected to various practices, such as reciting what was read to others. This is opposed to extensive reading, which would be imposed as of the eighteenth century, when texts came to be read individually, in intimacy and silence. Chartier suggests that the first mode was not exactly replaced by the second, but that they coexist in reading experiences in different social groups. Reports of socialized reading observed during the fieldwork could, to a certain extent, be associated with this idea of extensive reading, in which the collective context is emphasized through sharing of the content read with the group. Some authors are especially concerned about emphasizing the socio-cultural environment where communication technologies are inserted, inviting a closer look at the interactions, networks, and sociability that precede experiences with the media and which are reconfigured by them.

In previous work by this author (Barros 2009) about videogame enthusiasts in popular Internet cafes in Rio de Janeiro, a reception context was observed where learning the game took place through strong collective sharing. The group in question consisted of World of Warcraft gamers, classified within the Massive Multiplayer Online Role-Playing Game category (MMORPG). The use of computers at the Internet cafe was interesting due to a specific aspect—not only were the users connected and interacting with other players online; there was also intense interaction with other people in the physical environment of the Internet cafe. Young people, whether they were in front of the computer or not, communicated constantly, swapping tips on the best strategies and actions to be used during the game. The "teaching" was passed on by someone who had greater expertise in the game than the others, a role that was taken alternately by multiple actors—the Internet cafe staff, and more experienced players. At various times, navigation was truly shared when someone would take the mouse from the person who was in front of the computer, playing for a while, and then return the game control.

There could be two, three, or four people around a single computer, with one "officially" starring in the adventure, another with more expertise taking the mouse at times to advance through steps, and others commenting on the game or just "kibitzing." In a way, here is a counterpoint to the original idea of the personal computer—in the Internet cafe environment I found machines that were used collectively to some extent, functioning collaboratively, as a kind of "shared personal computer."

This is a scenario where the relationship with the computer must be seen beyond the individual level—or as a strict man-machine relationship—seeking to understand the communication phenomenon from the perspective of interactions that show the importance of conversation and sociability in the constitution of the experience with the media.

Comparative dimensions between Brazil and South Africa

Shifting the reflection from Brazil to South Africa, some studies in this country found consumer practices related to technology similar to those found in the Brazilian context being studied. The survey by Walton et al. (2012), for example, investigates sociability among young residents of Khayelitsha, a poor community on the urban outskirts of Cape Town, through certain uses of cell phones in a context where the devices are often shared. As other studies with low-income groups show (Silva 2010; Smyth et al. 2010), the use of Bluetooth in the community appears to be an important recourse for dealing with high Internet costs. The study shows how the way the industry thinks about the uses of the objects can become very distant from the social practices of some groups. Thus, certain device features related to "protection" and "privacy" wind up creating problems in contexts such as those found in the South African study, where the emphasis is on sharing. While smartphone manufacturers assume that "personal privacy" is universally desirable, in the daily lives of the young people studied, use of a device's privacy features can lead to conflict, either by expressing an anti-social behavior that hinders sharing, or by suggesting that the person has "something to hide."

An important point to note is that cell phone sharing should not be seen in a deterministic way or as a simple consequence of "economic scarcity," because even in poor locations where people have their individual phones, collective uses can be observed. These group practices should also not be seen as a kind of "communal culture," since the maintenance of mechanisms of distinction and hierarchy are seen. This is presented in Burrell's (2010) study in Uganda, where women were excluded from cellphone-sharing practices. Schoon (2013), Schoon and Strelitz, (2014), in turn, conducted an ethnographic study with low-income youth in the city of Grahamstown in South Africa, which had high unemployment. The author shows that the observed use of mobile phones is very different from the prevailing habits in developed countries, where ownership of the devices usually facilitates mobility, providing a broadening of geographic barriers and freedom from ties to one's original community. In the South African case study, a middle class notion of "privacy" did not exist, since a busy social life takes place in the street for everyone to see. In Grahamstown, the uses of mobile phones, with widely used features such as chat applications, intensify local experiences, strengthening community ties, thanks to the incorporation of technology in situations like the "gossip and dating rituals." The result, according to Schoon, is a condition of "immobility," since the young people remain attached to social facts defined by race, class, and gender.

The author (Barros 2009) of this chapter, in a study conducted in a poor community in the city of Rio de Janeiro, found results similar to those of Schoon (2013) and Strelitz (2014), with respect to an emphasis on local sociability in the use of social networks through computers. In this study, posts on the Orkut social network were primarily about comments on and photos of events with friends from school or the neighborhood, whom they had just seen or spoken to, reinforcing existing ties. Users even denied the possibility of a "true friendship" emerging from the virtual world, as one young informant stated:

> A friend from my daily life is with me, knows what I do, what I don't do, and knows what I like and don't like. But an Internet friend has no idea what I like or what I don't like.

Thus, the South African and Brazilian studies discussed here show, as a whole, forms of technological appropriations that find a special stage for the dynamics of local sociability through the collective and shared dimensions of these technologies.

Concluding remarks

This chapter sought to discuss certain technology consumption practices among low-income groups, where collective uses appear as a central aspect of the observed cultural dynamics. The uses of smartphones with TV occur in a specific cultural context, marked by strong orality and sociability; a person's smartphone provides content for conversation and fun for others, besides the owner, extending the moment of reception to a permanent process of interpersonal relations. As seen in the example of the house cleaners and the telenovela *Avenida Brasil*, watching TV on a smartphone during the commute to and from work allows expanding the discussion about the relations between maids and employers.

After incorporating the investigation of certain situations in the South African cultural context, the need for the relativization of individual consumption methods of communication goods is suggested as part of the effort to better understand collective uses of television, mobile phones, and computers. This involves thinking in a broader way about the person-machine interface and emphasizing interaction dynamics that occur in these practices and in the cultural systems that are the backdrop for technological experiences. The Brazilian and South African studies mentioned found that technology is used in ways that relativize the dominant model in developed countries, where mobile phones are usually synonymous with individualization and geographic and social mobility.

As seen, this chapter approximates Du Gay et al.'s proposal of the circuit of culture and the work of anthropologists such as Kopytoff (1986), by analyzing the trajectory of a product in its various moments, from the logic of production to the consumption practices of the social agents, which create new meanings in their daily life. Thus, the cell phone, and now smartphone, conceived in the sphere of production as an object for individual use, appears in the consumption of some groups of Brazil and South Africa as a good that can also be collectively appropriated.

The meanings of cultural products are the provisory results of a combination of processes. The parts of the circuit of culture—consumption, production, regulation, identity, and representation—are therefore interlinked in a complex and contingent manner. The discontinuity between the spheres of production and consumption points to technology consumption practices that are based on a public, collective and shared approach.

References

Barros, C. (2007) *Trocas, hierarquia e mediação: as dimensões culturais do consumo em um grupo de empregadas domésticas.* Tese (doutorado em Administração) – COPPEAD/UFRJ, Rio de Janeiro.

Barros, C. (2009) "Usos juvenis de computadores na lan da periferia: um estudo sobre cultura, sociabilidade e alteridade," *Anais do Congresso Brasileiro de Ciências da Comunicação, 32º.* Curitiba, Intercom. Disponível em: www.intercom.org.br/papers/nacionais/2009/lista_area_DT6-CU.htm (accessed July 21, 2016).

Burrell, J. (2010) "Evaluating shared access: social equality and the circulation of mobile phones in rural Uganda," *Journal of Computer-Mediated Communication*, V15, 2, 230–250.

Chartier, R. (1993) "Du livre au lire," in Chartier, R. (ed.), *Pratiques de la lecture*, Paris: Editions Payot & Rivages.

DaMatta, R. (1981) *Carnavais, malandros e heróis: por uma sociologia do dilema brasileiro*, 3. ed., Rio de Janeiro: Zahar.

Du Gay, P., Hall, S., Janes, L., Koed Madsen, A. Mackay, H., and Negus, K. (2013) *Doing cultural studies: the story of the Sony Walkman*, 2 ed., London, Thousand Oaks, CA: Sage.

Freyre, G. (1987) *Casa Grande & Senzala*, 25 ed., Rio de Janeiro: José Olympio.

Gastaldo, E. (2005) " 'O complô da torcida': futebol e performance masculina em bares," *Horizontes Antropológicos*, V11, 24, 107–123.

Geertz, C. (1976) "From the native's point of view," in Basso, K. H. and Selby, H. A. (eds.) *Meaning in anthropology*, Albuquerque: University of New Mexico Press.

Goffman, E. (1963) *Behavior in public places*, New York: The Free Press.

Hamburger, E. (1998) "Diluindo fronteiras: a televisão e as novelas no cotidiano," in Schwarcz, L. (ed.) *História da vida privada no Brasil: contrastes da intimidade contemporânea*. V4, São Paulo: Companhia das Letras.

Kopytoff, I. (1986) "The cultural biography of things: commoditization as process," in Appadurai, A. (ed.) *The social life of things: commodities in a cultural perspective*. Cambridge, MA, Cambridge University Press.

Miller, D. (1987) *Material culture and mass consumption*, Oxford: Blackwell.

Miller, D. and Horst, H. (2006) *The cell phone: an anthropology of communication*, Oxford, Berg.

Rocha, E. (1985) *Magia e capitalismo*, São Paulo, Brasiliense.

Sahlins, M. (1976) *Culture and practical reason*, Chicago, IL: The University of Chicago Press.

Schoon, A. (2013) "Exploring participatory video journalism in the classroom and community," *Communitas*, 18(1), 57–75.

Schoon, A. and Strelitz, L. (2014) "(Im)mobile phones: 'stuckness' and mobile phones in a neighbourhood in South Africa," *Communicare*, Dec, V33: 2, 25–39.

Silva, S. R. (2010) *Estar no tempo, estar no mundo: a vida social dos telefones celulares em um grupo popular*. Tese (doutorado em Antropologia), UFSC, Florianópolis.

Silveira, F. (2004) "Sobre a 'naturalização' da domesticidade televisiva: uma problematização e um protocolo para a observação empírica," *Alceu*, V4, 8, 65–77.

Silverstone, R. (1996) *Televisión y vida cotidiana*, Buenos Aires: Amorrortu.

Simmel, G. (1957) "Fashion," *The American Journal of Sociology*, V62, 6, 541–558.

Smyth, T. N., Kumar, S., Medhi, I., and Toyama, K. (2010) "Where there's a will there's a way: mobile media sharing in urban India," in *Proceedings of the 28th International Conference on Human Factors in Computing Systems*. CHI'10. New York: ACM Press, pp. 753–762.

Tufte, T. (1997) "Questões a serem estudadas em estudos etnográficos de mídia: mediações e hibridização cultural na vida cotidiana," in Lopes, M. I. V. (ed.) *Temas contemporâneos em comunicação*, São Paulo, Edicon/Intercom.

Walton, M., Haßreiter, S., Marsden, G., and Allen, S. (2012) "Degrees of sharing: proximate media sharing and messaging by young people in Khayelitsha," in *Proceedings of the 14th International Conference on Human-Computer Interaction with Mobile Devices and Services* – Mobile HCI '12. New York, ACM Press, pp. 403–412.

9 Adolescents and smartphones

Coping with overload

Maialen Garmendia, Miguel Casado del Río and Estefanía Jimenez

Introduction

Public concern related to the risk that young people might overuse electronic devices is not a new issue. For example, the amount of time children spend either watching TV or playing videogames has been for a long while, and still is, a preoccupation of populist writers (Winn, 1977), academics (Griffiths and Meredith, 2009; McIlwraith et al., 1991; Skoric et al., 2009; Vandewater, 2006), and policy makers (as in advice about the amount of screen time children should watch). Such has been the case with mobile phones and, more recently, smartphones. We have to consider that both of these are portable devices which children and young people can always bring with them wherever they go and, hence, they provide them with the potential for *anytime, anywhere, always on* connectivity (but for the constraints on this, see Haddon in this volume). In particular, smartphone apps have increased the number of potential communication channels and the scope for broadcasting information, as well as providing mobile access to social networking sites. Thus, it may be worth asking whether there are overload issues in relation to this technology and how do children cope with the potential deluge of messages?

In research and policy-making young people have very often been regarded as passive subjects who are not fully aware of the implications of their own use of technology and devices and as lacking the required skills for coping with problematic situations. As Staksrud and Livingstone state "when it comes to risks they are instead portrayed as potential victims in an Aristotelian state of *tabula rasa*, vulnerable to the wide array of harmful contents and contacts afforded by the internet" (Staksrud and Livingstone, 2009: 364). But especially within the new sociology of childhood, children are not simply regarded as passive users anymore, as their agency when growing up with information communication technologies (ICTs) has been increasingly recognized (Haddon, 2004). In this respect, children can play an active role in the changing conditions of childhood through their very own new media practices (Livingstone and Bober, 2003).

In fact, the problem of managing excessive information is not a new concern. Toffler referred to it as information overload in 1980. But today, the smartphone has become the central focus for studying what has been termed *infoxication*. Most of the research on this issue is related to information management in a work context, emphasizing the stress this information overload produces on employees (Bucher et al., 2013; Derks and Bakker, 2014; Jackson and Farzaneh, 2012). Outside the work context, Hargittai et al. explored whether the typical new media consumer actually feels overwhelmed by information (Hargittai et al., 2012). According to their research—12 focus groups in the US—most of the participants did not feel that "overload" but sometimes they show "annoyance at the distracting trivialities associated with social networking sites such as Twitter and Facebook" (2012: 165). In a similar vein, in communication studies some researchers have referred specifically to the "social media fatigue" of those who are leaving social networking sites not just because of information overload but also because of the lack of relevance of some of the material that circulates in social media (Bright et al., 2015).

There are two further points to add when we shift the focus specifically to young people. The first is that there is a literature on "overuse" issues separate from "overload" ones. Researchers looking at overuse have paid plenty of attention to "internet addiction" among young people generating addiction measuring scales (Grecu, 2013; Km et al., 2011; Kwon et al., 2013). In contrast, the overload issue, that is the way adolescents manage vast volumes of information or messages, has received scarce attention.

Second, when looking at adolescents and young people's use of the smartphones, it is worth adding that they mainly engage in communication and entertainment practices (Mascheroni and Cuman, 2014). Therefore, even though "information overload" is a far more common term than "communication overload," when analyzing children's management of overload in this chapter the issue will be basically related to coping with messages or communication rather than with information.

Before moving on to those findings, a few final words need to be added about the broader framework informing the analysis. Mobile communication studies have focused on the way communicative affordances of the mobile phone became socially embedded. For example, Ling (2012) has traced the domestication of the mobile phone and its transition to an integral taken-for-granted part of our social ecology. In the course of this, mobile communication affordances (Hutchby, 2001; Schrock, 2015) contribute to shaping—either enabling or constraining—the modes of social interaction that emerge. On the other hand, children also exert agency. In that process they can use different technologies for different activities and can attribute different meanings to their communicative practices or habits.

To summarize, the main aim of this chapter is to explore adolescents' agency when using smartphones in their everyday life, in order to see how young users cope with the volume of data, in the form of information and communication happening in their mobile devices. Our analysis of the emerging practices and communication patterns among European adolescents draws upon the qualitative and quantitative research data from the countries that took part in the Net Children Go Mobile project (Mascheroni and Cuman, 2014; Mascheroni and Ólafsson,

2014—for methodological details see Mascheroni's chapter in this book). First, we will focus on whether these young people have any perception of overload (i.e., their awareness) and, later, we will try to see how they deal with the issues they have to confront—such as time and space constraints—when managing all the messages coming into their mobile devices (i.e., their coping strategies).

"Always on" availability

Mobile devices provide their users with permanent access to their social and communicative affordances. For example, one of the advantages of smartphones consists in enabling users to experience "perpetual contact" (Mascheroni and Vincent, 2016) to its owner/user. Previous research has shown how mobile communication can facilitate contact with family and friends, make it easier to manage everyday life activities and mobility, enable better employment of "dead" time, and so on. Research specifically on what children do with mobile phones shows that they mainly use them for the "intensive exchange of short messages among intimate and homogeneous peers" (Kobayashi and Boase, 2014). This intensive exchange can be, at the same time, a source for stress and pressure to be "always on," as children are expected to reciprocate in real time. So, some of the previous research questions concerned with the threat of too much screen time for children and young people need to be complemented by or reformulated into questions about the implications of adolescents now being "always on" (Mascheroni and Vincent, 2016).

On the positive side, and as a general rule, respondents in the Net Children Go Mobile study are pleased about the possibility of having permanent connection through their smartphones:

> It's smaller so you have it always with you. So you can always use it…. if the possibility is there, you'll just use it more.
>
> (Boy, 15–16, Belgium)

For some of them this is a clear advantage, as they feel more connected to their friends. For instance, in the Net Children Go Mobile survey most children stated this is "a bit" (39 percent) or "very" (42 percent) true of them. Therefore, smartphones are vital for communicating and socializing with their peers for most of them:

> I feel more connected with people, as I have freedom to talk to them whenever I can.
>
> (Girl, 11–13, Ireland)

> You can communicate much better, and to the question if I communicate more with friends with the smartphone, yes. I started befriending them more because of WhatsApp, going into groups and finding more things about them.
>
> (Girl, 10, Romania)

Adolescents emphasize the opportunity to develop and strengthen friendship ties, even if, permanent availability through mobile devices can be particularly complex for them to manage.

> I don't know, I don't know how to explain ... but you have, when you're connected you can ... I mean, if someone needs you they can look for you immediately. Not saying to talk non-stop but to be there connected.
>
> (Girl, 15, Italy)

In this respect, Turkle observes some of the social pressures on young people to make themselves available:

> the adolescent wants both to be part of the group and to assert individual identity, experiencing peers as both sustaining and constraining. The mores of *tethering* support group demands: among urban teens, it is common for friends to expect that their peers will stay available by cell or instant message.
>
> (Turkle, 2008: 126)

However, for some children—particularly for older ones—peer pressure to be "always on" may be regarded as a disadvantage. In the Net Children Go Mobile survey nearly three out of four children (72 percent) agree that they feel they have to be always available to family and friends, which for some children implies "losing their freedom" (Girl, 15–16, Belgium).

The way availability becomes normative due to peer group pressure has been noted in other research (Hall and Baym, 2012) especially regarding how sometimes young people find it difficult to manage these expectations. This is shown in the following excerpts, which highlight the need for perpetual contact and for reciprocating messages in real time.

> KRISTINE: Well.... You spend a lot of time on it because.... When you have done your homework, you just have to go to Instagram and write a little message, and then you have to do some more homework, and then suddenly someone replies your text, and then you have to write back!
> SARAH: And there are three new pictures that have been posted.
> KRISTIEN: Yes, and then you have to like them! Like all the time....
>
> (Girls, 11–13, Denmark)

Communication overload

Nowadays nearly all young people have their own profile in some social networking site. In the Net Children Go Mobile survey, on average around 70 percent of young people (aged between nine and 16) have a profile on a social networking service (SNS), most of them in Facebook, however among 15–16 year olds 93 percent have a profile. Moreover, some affordances of smartphones and new messaging services—such as WhatsApp and Snapchat—are widely used by young people and the fact that they are free of charge or very cheap, encourages a continuous flow of communication. Taking into account that most young people say they have more than 50 contacts in their SNS it is easy to imagine the volume of messages they can get every day. In relation to the use of these social networks on smartphones, Salehan and Negahban found that

> mobile social networking applications are significant predictor of mobile addiction. The use of these applications can be influenced by the network size and SNS intensity of the user. SNS intensity is also affected by network size which may be a sign of extensive use of SNS for connecting to weak ties.
>
> (Salehan and Negahban, 2013: 2637)

> having a smartphone always at hand, you immediately receive notifications of all incoming messages, of everything. Then you are inclined to check it continuously, being it is so at your fingertips. On the computer, I used to do many things during the day, check at night, but that was it. Now instead, as these notifications continue to arrive, it turns into something....
>
> (Boys 14–15, Italy)

> like 5 years ago, people would have to go to their computer to check their Facebook or Twitter. But now if you have iPhone/smartphone, you wouldn't have to log in, you are just few clicks away, it's like you are constantly online nowadays, with your phone if you are not having a Wi-Fi you have 3G or 4G. So you are constantly connected to the internet, Facebook, Twitter, and stuff like that.
>
> (Boy, 16, Ireland)

So, even if young people sometimes complain about all these incoming messages, many try to keep up with them, in order to avoid exclusion from the peer group. Sometimes, when time or space constraints prevent them from using the smartphone—at school or family meals—or if their use is restricted by the lack of availability of networks or even by batteries, they may discover a backlog of hundreds of messages on their devices.

> Once I went away for a week, I left my mobile at home, and when we got back I had 500 messages.
>
> (Boys, 11–13, Spain)

> Sometimes if the phone turns off, if you forget to recharge the batteries, I mean, if you recharge it over night, when you turn it on, WhatsApp doesn't work because you find over 300 messages.
>
> (Boys, 12–13, Italy)

This vast volume of data coming in can cause adolescents some anxiety related to the sheer difficulty of being able to look through all the messages. That is another reason why some adolescents feel compelled to be always available in order to be able to read the messages as they come in.

> Mostly I check it most of the time because when I'm on my phone I just … everyone's talking on that and posting things.… So, I just check it most of the time.
>
> (Girl, 11–13, UK)

The Net Children Go Mobile survey also gave evidence that as on average 45 percent of the children surveyed in the UK stated that "I felt bothered when I cannot check my smartphone" "very" or "fairly" often, above the average for the seven countries surveyed (36 percent). Below, we can see an example of this feeling in Bea's description of her reaction to being without the mobile internet.

> INTERVIEWER: Do you think, Bea, that now, when you're sitting here without your phone because you're talking to me, when you go back and pick it up again are you going to feel you've missed out on something because you haven't been able to follow it?
> BEA: I don't think like an hour would make that much difference to me.…
> ELSA: What about a week?
> BEA: A week! Oh gosh, I'd die, I couldn't live with that.
>
> (Girls, 14–16, UK)

As other chapters in this volume have noted (Haddon and Vandoninck et al.) mobile phones and smartphones are banned from use in some social settings, such as schools. There are huge variations related to smartphone use regulations across the European countries studied. On average, 54 percent of the children surveyed claimed that they were not allowed to use their smartphones at school, the usual reason for restrictions being that the devices may cause distractions among students and, therefore, negatively affect their school performance, as was noted by some of the young people themselves:

> A lot of students check Facebook, watch videos, etc., in class so it has become the biggest problem.
>
> (Boy, 14, Denmark)

Even so, some students feel the "need" to look at the messages coming in on their smartphones in school time. Although in most schools smartphone use can be sanctioned by confiscating the device, some children say they cannot help checking and even replying to the messages.

> It is stronger than me … I cannot avoid replying to messages, because not replying.…
>
> (Girl 15, UK)

> At school? I use it anyway. I have been caught using my phone and it has been confiscated, but [laughing] it is stronger than me: I can't help replying to messages.
>
> (Girl, 15, Italy)

As they say, their need to keep their connection with their friends is stronger than their will power and they keep replying even in school time, no matter what sanction they may get for doing it. Therefore, "the normative character of "availability" emerges especially when this affordance is constrained by technical or social limitations" (Mascheroni and Vincent, 2016: 10), such as school regulations.

Even outside of school time, some children say that smartphones interfere with their attention when doing their homework:

> Also, less studying maybe [laughs]. Because it distracts me, and my smartphone is always with me when I'm doing my homework.
>
> (Girl, 12–13, Belgium)

Apart from the "interference" with time devoted to homework, some children also lamented how the smartphone had changed some of their past habits with "Facebook" substituting "board games," as one 15-year-old Belgian boy observed.

In sum, adolescents feel compelled to be "always on" their smartphones and reciprocate in real time to their peers' messages. Therefore, availability can become normative, even when there are institutional rules try to prevent their use at schools and keeping on top of messages takes time away from activities outside of school.

Coping with communication overload

In the previous section we have seen how children are able to identify settings where or when smartphone use can be regarded as inappropriate or even negative for them. Now we will look at the strategies children develop to cope with such situations. After analyzing the children's discourses on smartphone use and communication overload the young people's coping strategies can be classified into the two main types of strategy outlined below.

Keeping notifications out of sight

This first strategy seems to be very obvious; children very often mention it when referring to the need to concentrate for studying or doing homework. Sometimes they turn the smartphones off voluntarily, while sometimes they are asked to do so by their parents. But children are usually willing to comply with this request as they consider it helpful in order to be able to concentrate on their schoolwork. In such cases, since the child is not able to hear the notifications this avoids having any contact with the new messages:

The negative side of smartphones is that they distract you, I know that many study with their smartphones turned on and ... well, it is not a very efficient method because, it's true, you got distracted. It is for this reason that I leave my smartphone in the dining room.

(Girl, 13, Italy)

The first time we had a lot of tests to write I simply could not concentrate because the phone always vibrated. And then I looked up how I could switch this off, so that it doesn't give a signal. And then I switched it off and now, when I have switched it off, the messages on WhatsApp no longer appear on the display, even if it is locked.... Since doing that, I can concentrate much better, because I had partly ... I used to sit there for 3 hours and some-how learned for just one hour ... and the rest, I spent on the phone in the groups, where they said: you should do it this way. And sometimes they explained it wrong.

(Girl, 14, Germany)

Some children also note that they do not bring their smartphone to some activities such as sports training because they regard it as inappropriate. Such cases could also fit into this strategy as far as it implies avoiding any contact with the smartphone for some period of time.

The other main way to avoid using the device is based on the technical facilities that the smartphone offers. The device can often be set to mute or even to "do not disturb" mode in order to avoid the notifications being shown on the screen. As Andrea says:

I think I would be more affected if I just put it on silent and put it in my pocket. Because if I do not switch on the "do not disturb," then I can still feel that something is coming, since it vibrates. And so, in fact I think you are more ... "okay, now I've got something" ... and then you want to check what it is and things like that....

(Girl, 14–16, Denmark)

Some children try combining both types of strategies using the technical features of the devices as well as placing the device in another room. They can do this either voluntarily or at their parents' request. Such is the case of the 13-year-old boy who says "I keep it muted and in another room."

Prioritizing messages

As an alternative to putting the smartphone completely aside, some adolescents say they are able to keep the device on and next to them in order to read those messages regarded as relevant, while not paying attention to the rest. Children claim that some of the information coming through WhatsApp groups or SNS is very often trivial and unnecessary. Therefore, the child will decide whether a message is worthy of attention or else he/she may consider more important the task being done:

> You get things like people instagramming their food which I don't see the point in to be honest because it's just food. It's nice but there's no need to share it with the world!
>
> (Boy, 14, UK)

Sometimes, for instance, adolescents say that they do not pay attention to Whats-App messages coming through groups and they only read private messages. It is necessary to keep in mind that very often the information sent through instant messaging groups is just for pure entertainment:

> And when you go on WhatsApp you find a lot of messages, they might be interesting but you don't bother to read them all and then the next day in class they talk and you don't know what they are talking about.
>
> (Girl, 11–13, Italy)

> [when the smartphone beeps] I check to see if it's WhatsApp. If it is from the basketball team I may reply later, if it comes from a private chat I will reply then. I don't look at any other messages, I only reply immediately if the message comes from a private chat.
>
> (Boy, 14–16, Italy)

This strategy implies a more developed skill for managing the communication, as instead of temporarily ignoring the incoming messages, the young person takes decisions depending on the relevance of the content or the sender's identity. Based on this, they will consider whether to take the opportunity to reply or not.

Inappropriate use

Some of the adolescents seem to be aware of the need to set some rules about smartphone use. In their view, rules should preserve some time for some other activities such as school, sports training, or sharing meals with the family. They are aware that smartphone use interferes with the attention required by such activities:

> So, there should be some rules on how much we have to use it, I think. But it must be like … we also just like to check it sometimes. I understand you probably should not use it when you are training, in school and when you sit and eat and stuff. I think there you should probably not use it. It's like … that way you don't get a lot out of teaching.
>
> (Girl, 14–16, Denmark)

The demand for rules does not merely reflect a desire for some external pressure to reduce their own use. It can also be based on their critical evaluation of the actions of their peers. For example, some note that their friends tend to be stuck on these devices even when they go out, instead of enjoying and having fun:

> I used to be very attached to Facebook, but after a while I understood that … I mean, I see all my friends that are always on Facebook. They hang out with friends and they are stuck on their phones. That is not real life. It is not good. On Saturday night you go out to have fun and he is with his phone in his hand all the time. It is good to use it when you can, not using it 24/7.
>
> (Boy, 16, Italy)

Some of them openly demand some sort of rules to be applied while meeting face to face with friends or people, arguing that it is not appropriate to be on the smartphone all the time while they are with someone else. Or else that checking the smartphone can be OK, but not all the time. Some of them even claim that smartphone use can make people more introverted:

> I am always with people. When I am with them and they are listening to music, I say to them: "Stop that, you are with people."
>
> (Boy, 14–16, Spain)

> And if someone has a 3G connection, maybe he is always with his phone in his hands. It is not a good thing. He will shut himself away. So maybe you ask for a ride, or rather he asks you for a ride and you are there with your smartphone in your hand. And I say "no." You became more introverted, I don't know how to explain it.
>
> (Boy, 16, Italy)

More rarely, some children even say they have given up internet connection, even if only temporarily, as in the case of 15-year-old Spanish boy who for a while swapped his smartphone for an "old phone in order to avoid permanent availability."

In short, even though adolescents appreciate the chance for perpetual contact with their peers through mobile devices, some of them are able to identify some everyday life contexts when smartphone use can regarded as inappropriate. Accordingly, they demand some rules be established for the "always on" availability and the demand for reciprocating.

Conclusion

By exploring the smartphone's communicative practices that are experienced among some European children and young people, this chapter has provided evidence on the way users cope with the data overload coming onto their devices. We have seen how adolescents can be active when managing the communicative affordances of mobile communication as well as its constraints. So, the evidence shows that what sometimes seems to be obligatory availability can actually be negotiated or even resisted. "Perpetual availability" (Mascheroni and Vincent 2016) as an affordance of mobile communication has increased exponentially the volume of communication reaching smartphone users. Managing all this communication has become a challenge for adults as well as for young people.

As some previous research referring to adults suggested (Lee, 2012), the more they use smartphones the more they develop the ability to distinguish its content's relevance. As far as children and young people are concerned, the same pattern emerges from the Net Children Go Mobile qualitative fieldwork: the older and hence generally more experienced the children are with smartphones the less compelled they are to feel permanently available and obliged to reciprocate to their peer group, and they can control that availability either through technical affordances of the device or where they locate it in physical space. In addition, the more familiar they are with the smartphone the more capable some of them have become at identifying trivial communication, such as the flood of messages coming from groups or simply irrelevant information (e.g., pictures of food). As Hargittai et al. (2012) suggested referring to adults, some redundant or superfluous comments can be annoying and the *social media fatigue* they cause can lead people to avoid permanent availability.

It is worth emphasizing the fact that it was older children who tended to want to avoid permanent availability and resist its normative character. This may in part be because, as Mascheroni and Vincent argued: "as teenagers gain independence and autonomy, the feeling of missing out and being isolated becomes less compelling" (2016: 322). This can in turn support their desire for rules or a set of *ethics*, which should identify appropriate/inappropriate use of smartphones in some social settings.

Finally, this study captures a moment in time when children and young people appear to be working out how to manage their availability and when to reciprocate. In other words, they are still in the process of learning how to domesticate these devices. On the other hand, as the technology itself is still fairly new, different practices and norms, including different strategies for managing communication overload, may yet emerge as communicative affordances are shaped and reshaped by future adolescents.

References

Bright, L. F., Bardi, S., and Landreth, S. (2015) Computers in human behavior too much Facebook? An exploratory examination of social media fatigue. *Computers in Human Behavior*, 44, 148–155. http://doi.org/10.1016/j.chb.2014.11.048.

Bucher, E., Fieseler, C., and Suphan, A. (2013) The stress potential of social media in the workplace. *Information, Communication & Society*, 16(10), 1639–1667. http://doi.org/10.1080/1369118X.2012.710245.

Derks, D. and Bakker, A. B. (2014) Smartphone use, work-home interference, and burnout: A diary study on the role of recovery. *Applied Psychology-an International*

Review-Psychologie Appliquee-Revue Internationale, 63(3), 411–440. http://doi.org/10.1111/j.1464-0597.2012.00530.x.

Grecu, C. (2013) The new generations and the addictions to technology. *European Journal of Science and Theology*, 9(1), 99–110.

Griffiths, M. D. and Meredith, A. (2009) Videogame addiction and its treatment. *Journal of Contemporary Psychotherapy*, 39(4), 247–253. http://doi.org/10.1007/s10879-009-9118-4.

Haddon, L. (2004) Cultural differences in communication: Examining patterns of daily life. In Mobile Communication and Social Change. *Paper for the Conference "Mobile Communication and Social Change"* Seoul, October 17–18, 2004.

Hall, S. and Baym, N. (2012). Calling and texting (too much): Mobile maintenance expectations, (over)dependence, entrapment, and friendship satisfaction. *New Media & Society*, 14(2), 316–331.

Hargittai, E., Neuman, W. R. and Curry, O. (2012) Taming the information tide: Perceptions of information overload in the American home. *The Information Society*, 28(3), 161–173. http://doi.org/10.1080/01972243.2012.669450.

Hutchby, I. (2001). Technologies texts and affordances. *Sociology* 35(2), 441–456.

Jackson, T. W. and Farzaneh, P. (2012) Theory-based model of factors affecting information overload. *International Journal of Information Management*, 32(6), 523–532.

Km, W., Park, B.-W. and Lee, K. C. (2011) Measuring smartphone dependence: A first step with emphasis on factor analytic evidence. *Information-an International Interdisciplinary Journal*, 14(9, SI), 3031–3047.

Kobayashi, T. and Boase, J. (2014) Tele-cocooning: Mobile texting and social scope. *Journal of Computer-Mediated Communication*, 19(3), 681–694. http://doi.org/10.1111/jcc4.12064.

Kwon, M., Lee, J.-Y., Won, W.-Y., Park, J.-W., Min, J.-A., Hahn, C., Gu, X., Choi, J.-H. and Kim, D.-J. (2013). Development and validation of a smartphone addiction scale (SAS). *PLOS ONE*, 8(2). http://doi.org/10.1371/journal.pone.0056936.

Lee, D.-H. (2012) "In bed with iPhone": The iPhone and hipersociality in Korea, in Hjorth, L., Burgeuss, J. and Richardson, I. (eds), *Studying mobile media. Cultural technologies, mobile communication and the iPhone* pp. 63–81, New York, Routledge.

Ling, R. (2012) *Taken for grantedness: The embedding of mobile communication in society*, Cambridge MA, MIT Press.

Livingstone, S., and Bober, M. (2003) *Report UK children go online: listening to young people's experiences*. London. Retrieved from http://eprints.lse.ac.uk/388/1/UK ChildrenGoOnlineReport1.pdf (accessed February 11, 2016).

Mascheroni, G. and Cuman, A. (2014) *Net Children Go Mobile final report* (with country fact sheets). Retrieved from file:///C:/Users/Casa/Downloads/NCGM_FinalReport_Country_DEF (3).pdf (accessed February 11, 2016).

Mascheroni, G. and Ólafsson, K. (2014) *Risks and opportunities*. Second edition. Net Children Go Mobile (May).

Mascheroni, G. and Vincent, J. (2016) Perpetual contact as a communicative affordance: Opportunities, constraints, and emotions. *Mobile Media & Communication*, 4(3), 310–326. Retrieved from http://eprints.lse.ac.uk/66938/1/Vincent_Perpetual%20 contact.pdf (accessed February 11, 2016).

McIlwraith, R., Jacobvitz, R. S., Kubey, R. and Alexander, A. (1991). Television addiction: Theories and data behind the ubiquitous metaphor, *American Behavioral Scientist*, 35(2), 104–121. http://doi.org/10.1177/0002764291035002003.

Salehan, M. and Negahban, A. (2013) Computers in human behavior social networking on smartphones: When mobile phones become addictive. *Computers in Human Behavior*, 29(6), 2632–2639. http://doi.org/10.1016/j.chb.2013.07.003.

Schrock, A. (2015) Communicative affordances of mobile media: Portability, availability, locatability, and multimediality, *International Journal of Communication*, 9, 1229–1246.

Skoric, M. M., Teo, L. L. C. and Neo, R. L. (2009) Children and video games: Addiction, engagement, and scholastic achievement, *CyberPsychology & Behavior*, 12(5), 567–572. http://doi.org/10.1089/cpb.2009.0079.

Staksrud, E. and Livingstone, S. (2009) Children and online risk, *Information, Communication & Society*, 12(3), 364–387. http://doi.org/10.1080/13691180802635455.

Toffler, A. (1980) *The third wave*, London, Collins.

Turkle, S. (2008) Always-on/always-on-you: The tethered self, in Katz J. E. (ed.), *Handbook of mobile communication studies*, pp. 121–137, Cambridge MA, MIT Press. http://doi.org/10.7551/mitpress/9780262113120.001.0001.

Vandewater, E. A. (2006) Time well spent? Relating television use to children's free-time activities, *Pediatrics*, 117(2), e181–e191. http://doi.org/10.1542/peds.2005-0812.

Winn, M. (1977) *The plug-in drug*, Harmondsworth, Penguin.

10 Addiction or emancipation?

Children's attachment to smartphones as a cultural practice

Giovanna Mascheroni

Introduction

The appropriation of smartphones by children[1] has raised concerns among adults, preoccupied with excessive screen time and risks of withdrawal from co-present interaction. The fear of losing control over their relationships with smartphones is also shared by young users, who often report a 'compulsion' to check their phones frequently, or complain that smartphones have altered the context of face-to-face interactions with peers. In making such claims both adults and children adhere to the language and frame of 'internet addiction', which equates excessive internet use with other impulse-control disorders such as gambling or substance abuse. The medical approach to excessive internet use as a pathological condition has, however, been questioned in recent studies, which instead adopt 'a compensatory model' of internet use (Kardefeldt-Winther, 2014). In this view, the 'symptoms' of internet addiction may signal a new way of life characterised by the embeddedness of the internet in daily activities and routines, and novel modes of communication and entertainment. These symptoms, therefore, should not necessarily be assumed as an indicator of pathological behaviour. Only some individuals turn to the internet as a way of escaping from their problems and compensating for psychological difficulties, and develop a truly pathological relationship with digital media.

The extension of the 'internet addiction' framework to young people's relationships with smartphones is even more problematic in the light of the literature on mobile communication. This has actually emphasised the process through which mobile phones, and smartphones today, have become an integral and 'normal' part of our 'social ecology' (Ling, 2012). Being accessible to our friends and family by means of smartphones is not only part of the social expectations that we form of one another, but this accessibility also informs our sense of personal security. Moreover, being able to access the internet on the move helps us to manage a variety of daily tasks, including rearranging meetings 'on the fly', using maps, accessing information in real time, etc. When it comes to younger users, the literature on children's mobile communication does not exclude the possibility of excessive and compensatory uses of mobile devices as a means of escaping from psychological vulnerabilities. However, and similar to the 'compensatory model' of internet use described above, these approaches situate, and thus make sense of, young people's attachment to smartphones within the context of their everyday practices and relationships. More specifically, the use of mobile phones by teenagers and children has been viewed through the lens of the so-called 'emancipation approach' (Ling, 2004). This approach acknowledges that mobile communication plays into the parent-child relationship and, by fostering autonomous and continuous access to the peer group, accelerates teenagers' emancipation from the family sphere (Ling, 2004; Vanden Abeele, 2016). As a consequence, children develop an emotional attachment to the smartphone and the relationships it mediates, which can generate both positive (intimacy, proximity and belonging) and negative (anxiety, 'addiction') feelings (Mascheroni and Vincent, 2016).

Building on the 'circuit of culture' model (Du Gay *et al.*, 2013), this chapter argues for an approach that recognises children's attachment to their mobile devices as a cultural practice, which unfolds at the interplay of different moments. To illustrate the interplay between representations, identities, production, consumption and regulation, as well as the ambivalent meanings smartphones have in children's lives, the chapter draws on qualitative data collected across Europe as part of the Net Children Go Mobile project,[2] which examined the access and use of the internet from mobile devices among 9-to-16-year-olds. This material shows how children's communicative practices and their uses of smartphones (consumption and lived cultures) are embedded in specific communicative affordances of smartphones (production). It reveals how those practices are subject to social negotiations and expectations regarding appropriate uses (regulation). And it illustrates how those practices are shaped by, while in turn shaping, discourses, for example about the 'smartphone generation' (representations). In so doing, it acknowledges elements of both perspectives on youth's relationship with smartphones – as either 'addictive' or as a component of the peer group's role in the transition to adulthood.

Representations of children and smartphones: the 'smartphone generation' vs. the 'addicted child'

Two overarching and contrasting representations of children and digital technologies have dominated social and media discourses in the past decades, and have now been extended to the smartphone. The discursive construction of the 'digital native' (Prensky, 2001) represents children as media-savvy and sophisticated consumers, who are 'naturally' skilled and capable of using digital devices. When it comes to smartphones, this discourse is condensed in the iconic representation of children as the 'smartphone generation', for whom the smartphone is nothing but a 'natural' extension of their being and doing in the world. Here we see how children themselves draw upon that particular representation:

SARA: How much do I use it? I use it … basically I always have the smartphone in my hand.

(Girl, 15, Italy)

ISLEEN: I think our generation has just grown up to have the phone in our hand.

(Girl, 15, UK)

What Sara's and Isleen's words show is how meanings do not arise in cultural artefacts themselves, but rather from the interrelated practices of constructing meaning and making use of the devices (Du Gay *et al.*, 2013). Through the interacting processes of representation and consumption, then, the smartphone is rendered meaningful, is attributed a special place within youth cultures, and is incorporated in the very construction of identity in which pre-teens and teens are engaged. The general assumption in this representation is that young people develop distinctive practices and meanings around the smartphone, which are turned into a defining feature of a generation of users and their overall culture, represented as a 'mobile youth culture' (Vanden Abeele, 2016).

By contrast, the discursive construction of the 'child at risk' typical of 'media panics' (Drotner, 1999), emphasises the threats that smartphones pose to children and society at large, including health and behavioural issues (e.g. poor quality of sleep, attention deficit, sight and other physical problems, aggressive behaviour). Fears about 'addiction' and the breach of face-to-face sociality are a part of this broader negative representation. In sharing negative social commentaries on smartphones, interviewees draw upon such media representations (as Henning does below, referring to what he learned on TV), parents' discourses and concerns, and urban myths re-embedded in everyday life contexts and reinforced by first-hand experiences:

HENNING: There is also a new disease now which is called WhatsAppitis. It is really bad for the bones in your thumbs, you can hurt yourself very badly, when you type as hard and as long on WhatsApp.

(Boy, 10, Germany)

GIORGIA: My parents are worried about the extended use of these devices, for example if a person uses the smartphone too much.... They think that ... well, that you become anti-social, or you become addicted.

(Girl, 16, Italy)

KATRIEN: When I'm on my mobile all the time, my parents get mad and they tell me to do something else, like reading a book instead of being constantly looking at my mobile. Because it's also bad for your eyes.

TAMARA: True, I was really ill because of it. I was really feeling ... for a few weeks.... Just like if I was away from the world, and then I returned and then it was like I would fall down every second. I had this for a while, and I was talking to people about this. And they told me to go to the doctor. So eventually I went to the doctor, and they did a whole lot of tests on me, but they couldn't find it. So I stayed at home for a while.

Probably it's something with these radiations from the mobile that ruined my balance organs.

(Girls, 15–16, Belgium)

As the excerpts above show, children themselves actively participate in reproducing and enriching the discursive environment constructed by media representations and parental concerns (Mascheroni, Jorge and Farrugia, 2014). Moreover, in children's discourses, negative representations of smartphones are associated with specific age and gender identities, recognised as more vulnerable to developing an addictive relationship with their phones, the contents and the ties it mediates. Based on a 'third-person effect' (Davison, 1983), children tend to perceive others as more addicted than themselves. More specifically, boys and older children tend to overestimate girls' and younger children's addictive behaviour (and vice versa):

ADAM: Some of us, especially the girls, except not really me, but I see all these girls when they go to cafes they don't even pay attention to each other, everybody's on the phone.

(Boy, 14, Romania)

Negative representations of smartphones as 'addictive' and 'disruptive' technologies, though, are far from new. In part they reflect the 'mobile' origins of this device, as accounts of the mobile phones' potential to breach the etiquette and favour the abrupt and unwelcome entrance of mediated interactions in the context of co-present interaction are as old as the commercialisation of the mobile phone itself, and suggestive of the conflicting discourses that accompanied its domestication (Haddon, 2004; Ling, 2012; Silverstone and Hirsch, 1992). Added to this, as already noted, are the concerns about problematic health and behavioural consequences of smartphones that draw upon prior representations of videogames and the internet, within the medical framework on excessive use. The specific functionalities of the smartphone – first and foremost, its portability, its being 'always at hand' – are indeed believed to amplify the addictive nature of videogames and online communication. Therefore, both the 'smartphone generation' and 'addicted child' representations of children's relationship with smartphones are related to the communicative and entertainment practices that smartphones now enable. Representations are deeply interrelated with the processes of consumption but also with those of production, as discussed in the next section.

The influence of production: the affordances of smartphones

As the 'circuit of culture' model highlights, technologies are culturally produced, 'encoded' with meanings and 'imagined' uses/users that are translated into specific functions. These functionalities guide use, and so influence consumption, without fully determining it.

The notion of 'affordances' (Gibson, 1979) is particularly relevant here, in that it emphasises the interplay between production and consumption. Hutchby points to 'the constraining, as well as enabling materiality of the technology' (2001, p. 444) and acknowledges affordances as both 'functional' – in that they enable or hinder users' engagement – and 'relational' – shaping agency in different ways depending on context (Hutchby, 2014). Through their 'affordances' technologies provide material opportunities for and constraints on the user's agency that are always situated and contingent. In this perspective, affordances are not pre-given nor can they determine agency in a univocal manner. Instead, they only acquire meaning through the practice of use-in-context.

The way children talk about the changes that smartphones brought along in their everyday lives is illustrative of how affordances are both 'functional' and 'relational'. First, children's experiences and representations of the 'anywhere, anytime' social accessibility to peers and family are grounded in the communicative affordances of smartphones, that result from 'an interaction between subjective perceptions of utility and objective qualities of the technology that alters communicative practices or habits' (Schrock, 2015, p. 1232). Indeed, when discussing the 'always on' mode of interaction that smartphones afford, young people connect this opportunity to the main functionalities of smartphones, namely the very mobility or portability of the phones, on the one hand, and the availability of free instant messaging apps that enable group communication, on the other (see also Mascheroni and Vincent, 2016):

> LARS: That is because of WhatsApp, too. In the past you maybe watched a video when you arrived at home, and after that you turned the computer off or maybe looked up the railway timetable for the next day, if you planned to go somewhere. You didn't do anything else. But now it is this way, you arrive at home, have a short look and put it in a charging station, maybe on the desk and then always, when you're doing homework, see directly what's going on, on the smartphone.
>
> (Boy, 14, Germany)

> ANUJ: If you had normal text, people would only message you if they need to message you. And you can't really create groups on text message so I think that's why you might message more. So if you want to tell, let's just say, about your birthday party, or something, you could instead of sending it individually, and paying a lot on the text message, on the group you could send it one time for free and everyone would know about it on the group.
>
> (Boy, 11–13, UK)

As Anuj's words suggests, these affordances, though, are not only individually perceived and acted upon, as Schrock's (2015) definition of affordances emphasises. Rather, they become embedded in the communicative practices that tie a group together, thus informing group-based reciprocal expectations (Ling, 2012).

In other words, and as stated above, affordances are not only functional, but relational and, thus, social (Hutchby, 2014).

Therefore, how affordances are acted upon highlights the interrelations between production and consumption but also connects with another dimension of the circuit of culture, the interpersonal regulation of use that will be examined in more detail later in this chapter. Through consumption, production also shapes social regulation, insofar as affordances can turn into 'institutionalised' and 'normalised' social practices that acquire a normative character (Mascheroni and Vincent, 2016).

Consuming the smartphone: communicative practices and their meanings

We now focus in more detail on the consumption part of the circuit. Through the varied practices of consumption, technologies are appropriated and integrated into users' everyday lives, and in this way are attributed significance and value (Du Gay *et al.*, 2013). Looking at children's experience of smartphones as a cultural practice, consumption is the moment in the cultural circuit when the ambivalent meanings of smartphones emerge most vividly, and 'the tension between being connected and being stressed' (Ling, 2012, p. 111) is expressed. Children experience this ambiguity through the conflicting feelings of appreciating mediated proximity but being wary when they had less control over the own accessibility. In the Net Children Go Mobile survey, 81 per cent of the respondents reported feeling more connected to their friends since having a smartphone, but three out of four children (72 per cent) also felt they had to be always available to family and friends (Mascheroni and Ólafsson, 2014). Similarly, the following excerpts from focus groups show how increased sociability and intimacy are coupled by negative consequences, such as the urge to check the phone at school or while doing homework:

SOFIE: You see that, when you're outside, everybody is on his mobile.
ELIEN: I'm more social now with the internet. Towards people I know, because otherwise I wouldn't talk to them.
SOFIE: Also, less studying maybe [laughs]. Because it distracts me, and my smartphone is always with me when I'm doing my homework.

(Girls, 12–13, Belgium)

INTERVIEWER: When you say 'addicted' what do you mean?
SARAH: That you like....
PERNILLE: That you use it everyday.
SARAH: Yes, that you sort of need it.
SILLE MARIE: You know, share you everyday life.
KRISTINE: You need to be updated all the time.
SARAH: Well of course if it's. If you sit in school and if you notice you have received a Snapchat or something like that, then you really want to look at....

(Girls, 11–13, Denmark)

Interviewees and focus group participants associate smartphones and instant messaging apps with a rise in the volume of communication with peers, and, subsequently, an improved sociability. Children describe a continuous flow of communication with friends that creates a 24/7 communicative bubble which provides them with a sense of 'full-time intimate sphere' (Ling, 2008; Matsuda, 2005). On the positive side, the full-time access to one's social circles represents an opportunity to strengthen friendship ties, and is especially valued when face-to-face contacts with peers are reduced – either because one lives far from school or during summer holidays:

> HANNAH: I think it's the other way around, if someone I see them every day I tend to talk to them more, I texted to my friends more if I talked to them more, then we have more things to share and talk even more than that.... hmm, I feel more connected, as I have freedom to talk to them whenever I can.
>
> (Girl, 11–13, Ireland)

> TEEMA: Well I'm definitely closer to my friends because of that, because there's more opportunities to talk to them like through the summer. Without phones I'd have no way to talk to them and arrange to meet up with them and stuff.
>
> (Girl, 14, UK)

> GIORGIA: It has changed a lot because before we didn't keep in touch once back home. When we didn't have a smartphone.... And it is much better now because it strengthens relationships. I used to feel lonely before.
>
> (Girl, 16, Italy)

On the negative side, the 'full-time' access to peers it enables can become a source of tensions (Baron, 2008; Bond, 2014; Ling, 2012), such as when the volume of the messages is too large to manage and keeping up with the flow of messages is difficult due to temporary disconnections. The fear of missing out and the inability to conform to the imperatives of real-time communication generate discomfort, annoyance and even anxiety:

> MATTEO: Sometimes if the phone turns off, if you forget to recharge the batteries, I mean, if you recharge it over night, when you turn it on, WhatsApp doesn't work because you find over 300 messages.
> VALERIO: once I received 692 messages in a single group, and I couldn't read them all, I had to leave the group.
>
> (Boys, 12–13, Italy)

> ABDUR: Yes, also I had to delete my account. I've always had thoughts about it because half the groups I'm in I really don't want to be in them

but if I leave it they'll think 'he's not cool, he's uncool, blah-blah-blah'.
So what I do is, it says, 200 messages from this group and there'll be
five of us so I'll click it back, click it and go back. I wouldn't even read
the text because it just gets so annoying.

(Boys, 11–13, UK)

Feelings of anxiety are especially expressed in relation to new features of instant
messaging and chats, namely the ability for the sender to see if a message has
been received and read, and if the receiver is online. Waiting for a reply is particularly stressful in the context of romantic relationships, as a further confirma-
tion of the relational character of communicative affordances (Hutchby, 2014):

ALEXANDRA: Being able to see when someone was last online is problematic, because you keep on thinking that he was online but did not reply.
Now you can de-activate the 'seen at…' function and it is getting
better, but it is now possible to see everyone's last connection and this
creates problems within couples.

ANA: I have a boyfriend and often I spend 2 hours with my mobile, seeing
that he is online and hasn't replied to me. I don't take it to heart so
much anymore … if he is ignoring me he'll have a reason for it, or he'll
be doing something else. Maybe he has his mobile there, but he is using
his Play Station. But you can cause yourself mental and psychological
problems.

(Girls, 14–16, Spain)

Stress and fear of being 'out of the loop' are often accompanied by what the
medical framework might label as symptoms of 'addiction', such as checking
the phone frequently, even when it is not appropriate nor socially legitimated
(e.g. at school or when out with friends). However, investigating the meanings
and emotions through which children make sense of the affordances of smartphones helps us re-evaluate so-called addictive behaviour by situating it within
the context of peer relationships and within the very process of domestication of
smartphones. We cannot ignore the role the peer group plays in pre-teens' and
teens' lives, in a phase in which they are progressively negotiating their independence from the family sphere also by means of a stronger connection with
peers via mobile communication. The following exchange is indicative of the
symbolic meaning of smartphones in children's everyday lives, as the most personal, mobile and always available tool in which interactions with peers are re-
embedded. Not having a smartphone 'at hand' means to be temporarily out of
the loop, isolated and deprived of the sense of group belonging that mobile communication supports:

RALUCA: One day without the mobile phone … when I go out of the house
and I don't have the phone with me, it's like something of me is not
present. I feel lost without the phone. I cannot be called, I cannot call

anyone, I cannot send messages.... I don't know. And when I forget my phone at home when I come to school, I always call mom to bring it to me, can't do without it.

ALINA: If it were to be a day in which I cannot take my phone with me, then I should be surrounded by all the people I normally talk to, and to do a lot of stuff, in order to avoid going on Facebook or sending messages or other things.

(Girls, 14–16, Romania)

The relationship between children's daily experiences and practices with mobile communication, and the representations of smartphones is recursive and circular. On one side, it is true that the thorough incorporation of smartphones into the activities and contexts of everyday life contributes to its construction as an essential and defining component of youth cultures. On the other side, however, children's negative experiences with smartphones are grounded in and shaped by negative representations of smartphones as addictive tools that disrupt the etiquette of face-to-face encounters and interpersonal relationships:

VALERIA: When I am with someone and this person is always texting, as I am talking to her, this bothers me.

GAIA: Yes, you are right, there are many people that when in group, they are stuck on the phone and it really bothers ... me at least.

(Girls, 14–16, Italy)

UNAI: I used to hang out with a group of people who always had the smartphone in their hands ... it was exaggerated. Instead of moving from park to park [to play basketball] they used to move from a Wifi zone to the next.

(Boy, 14, Spain)

Comments as the ones above signal that young people are still working out the rules governing reciprocal availability and the 'texting etiquette', and that the domestication of the smartphone is still under way. Indeed, the domestication of technology approach shows that once individuals and groups have worked through the appropriation of a technological device, adapting it to their own needs and negotiating or resisting the 'imagined' users and uses inscribed in its design, technologies tend to become 'institutionalised' (Berger and Luckmann, 1966). Especially in the case of 'social mediation technologies' (Ling, 2012) – that support social interactions and, in so doing, the maintenance of social groups – the process of domestication becomes less and less open through time, and meanings and values attributed to technologies gain a normative character. Once the mobile phone became embedded in our daily practices of communication, work and learning, it gained social legitimation and became 'invisible', taken for granted, but at the same time normative, regulating behaviour and reciprocal expectations (Ling, 2012). So, while the process of domestication is never completed once and for all, practices, meanings and norms tend to become relatively crystallised. We now expect other people to use mobile phones and be accessible 'anywhere, anytime' by means of these devices (Mascheroni and Vincent, 2016).

Regulating smartphone use: negotiating social accessibility

The meanings we attribute to technologies – through representation, production and consumption – 'also regulate and organize our conduct and practices' (Hall, 1997, p. 4). More specifically, we have argued that the 'anywhere, anytime' social accessibility has become a socially legitimated cultural practice to which most children tend to conform and which shapes the relationship of young people with their smartphones, at times leading them to develop 'addictive' behaviour (e.g. constantly checking their phones).

Reciprocal expectations and in-group norms are just one side of the regulation of children's behaviour and use of smartphones. Indeed, the failure to reciprocate and reply in real time can also be caused by institutional and parental norms that prevent children from accessing their smartphones in certain places (e.g. at school) and times (e.g. dinner time) and are aimed at reducing their excessive use. Indeed, children experience a number of constraints on their smartphones' use both at home and at school (for parents' and teachers' mediation of children's use of smartphones see Haddon and Vincent, 2014 and Chapters 4, 6 and 11 in this volume). While these discourses are usually less morally charged than discussions on the disruptive nature of the Walkman in the Nineties (Du Gay *et al.*, 2013), adults' reactions to young people's 'always on' mode – perceived as anti-social and un-healthy – can still be heated.

Interestingly, though, children themselves engage in negotiations around their accessibility to others and their attachment to smartphones. As noted, some interviewees and focus group participants experience the compulsion to be always accessible as being particularly annoying and disruptive of certain activities and spaces. Accordingly, peers who are 'always on' are labelled as 'addicted':

> FABIO: I used to be very attached to Facebook, but after a while I understood that … I mean, I see all my friends that are always on Facebook. They hang out with friends and they are stuck on their phones. That is not real life. It is not good. On Saturday night you go out to have fun and he is with his phone in his hand all the time.
>
> (Boy, 16, Italy)

Setting common rules and agreeing on a shared 'texting etiquette' can be difficult, though, and takes time to be worked out. On such occasions, then, children develop defensive strategies to avoid being disturbed. These include setting the phone – and especially WhatsApp – to the silent mode while in class, switching to the 'do not disturb' mode at night and during homework, or leaving the smartphone in another room to avoid hearing or seeing the incoming messages, as in the following examples:

> STEFANIA: The negative side of smartphones is that they distract you, I know that many study with their smartphones turned on and, well, it is not a very efficient method because, indeed, you got distracted and it is for this reason that I leave my smartphone in the dining room
>
> (Girl, 13, Italy)

> ANDREA: And then I put it away. And then when I go to sleep, I turn it on the 'do not disturb' mode, such that stuff don't come up when I lie down to sleep. Because I think at some point I didn't do that and for example, you are just about to fall asleep, and the screen just lights up or something. It is quite annoying.
>
> (Girl, 14–16, Denmark)

However, there are occasions where self-defensive strategies cannot be adopted or are not effective, such as during face-to-face interactions. Most children agree that engaging in mediated communication while simultaneously interacting with co-present others is undesirable and a symptom of excessive attachment to smartphones. Nonetheless, a common etiquette that prevents the clash between two 'theres' of in-talk-interaction (Schegloff, 2002, p. 287) are still being negotiated:

> PILAR: It happened to me with people and often we end up, not having an argument, but commenting about whether we have to make a rule or something. A rule that says we can't use our mobiles, because you have arranged to be with your friends and if you are looking at your mobile the whole time then you can't be with them as well.
>
> (Girl, 14–16, Spain)

Finally, there are examples of self-regulation, through which young people resist the pressure towards an 'anywhere, anytime accessibility', by not logging in on Facebook too often, or turning notifications off, or even leaving WhatsApp groups in case of a communication overload as we have seen:

> EA: Well I'm quite relaxed about it. I have experienced sometimes people have said 'You are never on Facebook'. Yes, but I don't care. I use it when I like [giggling].
>
> (Girl, 11–13, Denmark)

> INTERVIEWER: Some of you just said you sometimes have the feeling that you are under pressure to be online, right?
>
> JOACHIM: You decide yourself whether you answer or not. It's like … with this push-messaging, which makes you receive things on your screen.

> You can also turn it off, if you don't want to be bothered by other people.
>
> (Boys, 15–16, Belgium)

Practices such as those above suggest that young people are not only able to self-regulate their use and limit their perceived 'addiction' to the technology, but also actively engaged in negotiating their accessibility to others.

Concluding remarks

The chapter has shown the heuristic validity of applying a 'circuit of culture' perspective to the issue of young people's perceived 'excessive' use of smart-phones. The chapter began with representations of children's relationships with smartphones and showed how those representations are influential, having a bearing also on practices of consumption and social regulation. Then, the account of children's relationship with their phones has more systematically focused on the different moments on the circuit of culture, including production, and their multiple interrelationships in order to provide a richer framework through which we can evaluate the 'addicted child' representation.

Understanding children's 'always on' mode as a cultural practice situated at the dynamic interplay of consumption, production, regulation and representation helps to avoid simplifications and labelling youth behaviour as either 'addictive' or 'emancipated'. Rather, what the empirical evidence here presented suggests is that children's relationships with their smartphone is a multifaceted phenomenon that unfolds at the intersection of the different moments on the circuit of culture, and which is attributed different, at times conflicting, meanings by the same actors. While children make sense of the affordances of smartphones (production) that enable full-time access to peers (consumption) through celebratory accounts, they simultaneously adhere to the 'addiction' framework when they share adults' representations and engage in practices of social regulation in order to manage potentially conflicting activities and demands. Similarly, parents appreciate being able to reach their children anywhere and anytime, but actively regulate their attachment to smartphones in the domestic context and engage in the circulation of the 'addiction' representation.

Indeed, addiction and social accessibility are two sides of the same coin, and constitute a cultural product that emerges out of the domestication of smart-phones. Instead of being passive victims of addictive technologies, young people are navigating their way through the conflicting demands of peer pressures, adults' regulation and communicative affordances; and the contrasting discourses of social desirability, whereby 'anywhere, anytime' accessibility is legitimate in some cases while it is negatively sanctioned in others.

Notes

1 In this chapter the term 'children' refers to 9-to-16-year-olds.

2 The Net Children Go Mobile project was co-funded by the EC's Safer Internet Programme, now renamed Better Internet for Kids (SI-2012-KEP-411201). In 2013–2014, Net Children Go Mobile conducted a face-to-face, in-home survey among 3,500 9–16 year-old internet users and their parents in Belgium, Denmark, Ireland, Italy, Portugal, Romania and the UK, using a stratified random sample and self-completion methods in the case of sensitive questions. Net Children Go Mobile also conducted 55 focus groups ($N=219$) and 107 interviews ($N=108$) with children, and 40 focus groups ($N=180$) and 44 interviews ($N=50$) with adults across nine countries (Belgium, Denmark, Germany, Ireland, Italy, Portugal, Romania, Spain and the UK). The interview and focus group schedules covered the following issues: perceptions and experiences around smartphones and tablets; changes in their everyday life associated with mobile devices; specific problems regarding communication, images, location (such as sexting, cyberbullying and geolocation); parental concerns; school rules. Drawing on the methodology developed by a previous comparative qualitative research conducted in Europe (Smahel and Wright, 2014), interviews and focus groups were thematically analysed through three levels of coding. To avoid translating all transcripts into English, in the first level of coding, national teams produced condensed descriptions of the conversation in English, providing information on the device (e.g. whether a smartphone, or a laptop or a shared desktop computer, etc.), the platform (Facebook, WhatsApp, gaming site, etc.), the practices (e.g. communication or entertainment) the actors involved, any emotions expressed, etc. First-level codes were then thematically analysed through a second level of coding based on a semantic coding guide defined in a network meeting inductively (based on the preliminary findings of the pilot focus groups and interviews) and theoretically (drawing on concepts and theories in mobile communication studies and children and media research). Finally, in the third phase data were analysed and interpreted by grouping second-level codes and interviews or focus groups extracts in key themes.

References

Baron, N. (2008) *Always on: Language in an online and mobile world.* New York, Oxford University Press.

Berger, P. and Luckmann, T. (1966) *The social construction of reality.* New York, Doubleday & Co.

Bond, E. (2014) *Childhood, mobile technologies and everyday experiences.* Basingstoke, Palgrave Macmillan.

Davison, W. P. (1993) The Third-Person effect in communication. *Public Opinion Quarterly*, 47(1), 1–15.

Drotner, K. (1999) Mediatized childhood, discourses, dilemmas directions, in Qvortrup, J. (ed.), *Studies in modern childhood*, pp. 35–58. London, Palgrave Macmillan.

Du Gay, P., Hall, S., Janes, L., Madsen, A. K., Mackay, H. and Negus, K. (2013) *Doing cultural studies: The story of the Sony Walkman*, London, Sage.

Gibson, J. J. (1979) *The ecological approach to visual perception*, Boston, Houghton Mifflin.

Haddon, L. (2004) *Information and communication technologies in everyday life: A concise introduction and research guide*, Oxford, Berg.

Haddon, L. and Vincent, J. (2014) *European children and their carers' understanding of use, risks and safety issues relating to convergent mobile media.* Milano, Educatt. Retrieved from: http://netchildrengomobile.eu/reports/ (accessed 21 July 2016).

Hall, S. (ed.). (1997) *Representation: Cultural representations and signifying practices.* London, Sage.

Hutchby, I. (2001) Technologies, texts and affordances. *Sociology*, 35(2), 441–456.

Hutchby, I. (2014) Communicative affordances and participation frameworks in mediated interaction. *Journal of Pragmatics*, 72, 86–89.

Kardefelt-Winther, D. (2014) A conceptual and methodological critique of internet addiction research: Towards a model of compensatory internet use. *Computers in Human Behavior*, 31, 351–354.

Ling, R. (2004) *The mobile connection. The cell phone's impact on society*, San Francisco, Morgan Kaufmann.

Ling, R. (2008) *New tech, new ties. How mobile communication is reshaping social cohesion*, Cambridge, MA, MIT Press.

Ling, R. (2012) *Taken for grantedness. The embedding of mobile communication into society*, Cambridge. MA, MIT Press.

Mascheroni, G., Jorge, A. and Farrugia, L. (2014) Media representations and children's discourses on online risks: Findings from qualitative research in nine European countries. *Cyberpsychology*, 8(2). Retrieved from: www.cyberpsychology.eu/view.php?cisloclanku=2014072101.

Mascheroni, G. and Ólafsson, K. (2014) *Net Children Go Mobile: Risks and opportunities. Second edition*. Milano, Educatt. Retrieved from: http://netchildrengomobile.eu/reports/ (accessed 21 July 2016).

Mascheroni, G. and Vincent, J. (2016) Perpetual contact as a communicative affordance: Opportunities, constraints and emotions. *Mobile Media & Communication* 4(3), 310–326.

Matsuda, M. (2005) Mobile communication and selective sociality, in Ito, M., Okabe, D. and Matsuda, M. (eds), *Personal, portable, pedestrian. Mobile phones in Japanese life*, pp. 123–142. Cambridge, MA, MIT Press.

Prensky, M. (2001) Digital natives, digital citizens. *On the Horizon* 9(5), 1–6.

Schegloff, E. A. (2002) Beginnings in the telephone, in Katz, J. and Aakhus, M (eds), *Perpetual contact: Mobile communication, private talk, public performance*, pp. 284–300. Cambridge, Cambridge University Press.

Schrock, A. (2015) Communicative affordances of mobile media: Portability, availability, locability, and multimediality, *International Journal of Communication*, 9, 1229–1246.

Silverstone, R. and Hirsch, E. (eds) (1992) *Consuming technologies: Media and information in domestic space*, London, Routledge.

Smahel, D. and Wright, M. F. (2014) *The meaning of online problematic situations for children: Results of qualitative cross-cultural investigation in nine European countries*. London, EU Kids Online, London School of Economics and Political Science.

Vanden Abeele, M. M. P. (2016) Mobile youth culture: A conceptual development. *Mobile Media & Communication*, 4(1), 85–101.

Part V
Regulating the smartphone

11 Smartphones in the classroom

Current practices and future visions. Perspectives from teachers and children

Sofie Vandoninck, Marije Nouwen and Bieke Zaman

Introduction

The portability and personalized nature of smartphones facilitates ubiquitous (mobile) being online and constant connectivity, even at school. These affordances extend children's online opportunities but also pose new challenges (Alper, 2013; Haddon and Vincent, 2014; Wartella *et al.*, 2014). This chapter investigates the practices and meanings associated with the presence of smartphones in a school environment. We can embed this within the circuit of culture (Johnson, 1986; Du Gay *et al.*, 2013), which identifies interconnected cultural processes that help us to understand the role and impact of smartphones in teachers' and children's lives. We will use the framework to structure the analysis of how smartphones are being used (*consumption*), mediated (*regulation*) and perceived (*representation*) within a school environment, taking into account the perspectives of both children and teachers.

We formulate three research goals. First, we aim to understand the current trends and practices concerning smartphone use and mediation in school environments. Second, we aim to uncover the opportunities and challenges teachers and children experience when dealing with the presence and integration of smartphones at school. Third, we look at the expectations of teachers and children as regards a successful integration of smartphones in a school environment.

To help us answer these questions, we designated two dichotomies that are visible throughout the various cultural processes we will discuss. First, there is the apparent opposition between the school context and the home context. Previously, these contexts have been studied separately. However, in a 'culture of convergence', some writers are enthusiastic about how the functions of media have shifted the boundaries between *home* and *school*, and between *learning* and *entertainment*. This, it is claimed, has created additional opportunities for consuming, sharing and creating online content (Ito *et al.*, 2008; Jenkins, 2006; Jenkins *et al.*, 2013). One of the overarching questions asked in this chapter is about perceptions of this in the school and the extent to which this is actually occurring.

The second theme is the tension between autonomy and control. Building autonomy or independence is an important developmental task for young people

(Fine, 2004; Ito *et al.*, 2008; Kowalski *et al.*, 2012). On the one hand, smartphones support the development of autonomy. They enable children to create their own spaces to interact with peers, without (much) interference from adults (Köhl *et al.*, 2014; Lenhart *et al.*, 2010). On the other hand, smartphones can also be employed as tools for control and supervision (Ling and Yttri, 2002; Ling, 2004; Campbell, 2006; Nelson, 2010; Blair and Fletcher, 2011). Parents can easily connect with their children to check up on them, even during school hours.

Last, although smartphones are the main focus of this chapter, the scope of the empirical studies we build on is wider as they take into account various kinds of mobile media or devices that share affordances such as portability and individual or personal usage. Participants do not always specify the type of device, platform or application, and often talk about 'mobile media' in general. Therefore, we also use the terms 'mobile media' and 'mobile devices' in this chapter, which mainly refer to (platforms and applications for) smartphones and tablets.

Literature review

One challenge when trying to regulate smartphones in the school context is that they are often beyond teacher surveillance. Although there are some examples of schools where children have to drop their smartphone in a box before classes start, most smartphones remain in the hands, pockets or bags of the children, and with smartphones being out of their sight and control. Therefore, it is challenging for them to find appropriate smartphone mediation practices (Wartella *et al.*, 2014). Research has suggested that although children sometimes complain about strict teachers, they accept that some rules and restrictions are necessary in a school context. Nevertheless, children would like their teachers to take up more active mediation strategies (e.g. talking about the benefits and risks of smartphones) rather than merely setting rules (Ito *et al.*, 2008).

One problem identified in previous research on mobile phones more generally is that teachers are sometimes worried that the use of phones might hinder class management and reduce their control over the class. The teachers' perceptions might create tensions between the rules laid down by the school and the children's (and sometimes even their parents') interests, who believe it is important to be available for peers and parents during school hours (Green, 2001; Horst and Miller, 2006; Nelson, 2010). Nevertheless, teachers can also recognize that smartphones are inherently part of children's daily routines and acknowledge the school's responsibility in preparing children for active citizenship in a digital society (Hobbs, 2011; Pereira, 2014).

Last, we have questions of identity, as identity construction is a very important developmental task during adolescence (Fine, 2004; Ito *et al.*, 2008; Kowalski *et al.*, 2012). Various writers have shown how smartphones allow young people to experiment with self-expression and gradually develop their own self-concept and identity (boyd, 2008; Livingstone, 2008; Ellison and boyd, 2013; Mazzarella, 2010; Smock *et al.*, 2011). Teachers are aware of the importance of identity construction as a developmental task for youth, and sometimes acknowledge the role of smartphones in this process (Prendes *et al.*, 2010; Nycyk, 2011). However, both teachers and children primarily associate smartphones with entertainment and communication activities that support young people's developmental needs and concerns, which aligns with the idea that smartphones are 'something for youth'.

Existing research suggests that some teachers feel they lack the skills and knowledge to discuss their pupils' use of mobile media or to teach them the necessary digital skills. Moreover, these teachers do not believe that smartphones are tools that are part of their equipment as a teacher to support learning activities in class. Hence, studies suggest that most of the unskilled teachers prefer not to use mobile media in class and resort to a restrictive approach towards smartphones (Prendes *et al.*, 2010; Nycyk, 2011; Haddon and Vincent, 2014).

Methodology

The Net Children Go Mobile (NCGM) data provide us with insights into the perspectives of children. For more methodological details about the procedures for data collection in the NCGM project, we refer to Mascheroni's chapter in this book. Because the two other studies we used for this chapter were conducted in Belgium, we believe it would be confusing to connect the results of NCGM on a European level with (qualitative) data from Belgium. As we want to eliminate the influences of the country's cultural context and educational system in the interpretation of outcomes, we decided to interpret only the Belgian NCGM data in the results section.

In the study of secondary school teachers in Flanders, we organized a focus group with six teachers, four males and two females. This focus group is part of a longitudinal fieldwork study in Flanders in which both teachers and children were involved. In this chapter, we only use data from the teachers. The teachers discussed several topics, i.e. perceptions about the consequences of children's mobile online activities and risky experiences, the implementation of mobile media at school, how to benefit from the opportunities of (mobile) devices in the school context, children's coping with online risks at school, experiences with various mediation practices and the role of parents in mediating children's online activities.

In a separate, specifically Flemish, study, semi-structured interviews and observations were carried out by Masters students to obtain insights into the current practices of the use of digital media in kindergarten in Flanders. The interview guide included the following conversation topics: the barriers to and facilitators of the use of digital media, the type of digital media that is used by teachers, the motivations to use or avoid using digital media, the role of school policy in the teachers' choices and the changes in teacher practices after the advent of digital media in the classroom.

The final, Flemish, study consisted of two semi-structured interviews conducted with music teachers in primary schools. The goal was to understand their education and current professional activities, their approach in music lessons and

Table 11.1 Overview of data collections

Study	Method	Target group (selected for this chapter)	Number of participants (in Belgium)	Age range
Net Children Go Mobile	Survey	Children	511	9–16
	Focus groups	Children	38	9–16
Flemish study 1	Focus group	Secondary school teachers	6	25–35
Flemish study 2	Observations/interviews	Kindergarten teachers	5/28	24–55
Flemish study 3	Interviews	Primary school (music) teachers	2	20–50

how they motivate their students. The interviews were part of an applied research project that aimed to design an educational music game. As such, some of the questions related to the use of digital media in the teachers' current teaching practices.

All the qualitative data have already been analysed in detail within previous studies (Vandoninck *et al.*, 2016a, 2016b). However, because the scope of this chapter required a different focus, we decided to conduct a secondary analysis, looking in particular at those codes or thematic labels that are associated with mobile media in the school context, mediation of their use by teachers and the consequences of information communication technology affordances for teacher practices and communication with students (Crabtree and Miller, 1999; Fereday and Muir-Cochrane, 2008). The coding scheme reflects the structure of a SWOT-analysis, uncovering the Strengths, Weaknesses, Opportunities and Threats that teachers and children experience regarding the use of mobile media at school. Based on this analysis, we acquired the necessary knowledge base to describe current trends and practices regarding smartphone use in schools, the opportunities and challenges for teachers and children, and the expectations concerning smartphone integration in school environments.

Regulation of smartphones in schools

In Belgium, smartphone use at school for educational purposes is still rare. According to the NCGM survey, only 4 per cent of Belgian nine to 16 year olds use a smartphone for assignments in class every school day. A further 11 per cent collaborate daily with other pupils over the internet and 14 per cent use the internet to do research for school on a daily basis. These low figures can be associated with limited Wi-Fi access at school, many schools restricting smartphone use and a strong focus on knowledge reproduction instead of actively encouraging children to search online information themselves. In Belgium, 51 per cent of the respondents say the school has a Wi-Fi connection. However, among those children where Wi-Fi is technically available at school, about half (52 per cent) are not allowed to access the network because the Wi-Fi connection is exclusively for school staff. Another 38 per cent says Wi-Fi is accessible for pupils but with some restrictions, for example only for use at particular times. Thus, unrestricted Wi-Fi access at school is a privilege for only 2 per cent of the children in Belgium.

That said, in the qualitative research some teachers in our studies have experimented with adopting smartphones (and tablets) in class, even though a clear policy or framework at the school level was missing. In secondary schools, these 'innovators' employed smartphones themselves and/or encouraged pupils to use their smartphones to search on an ad hoc basis for information in the event of unexpected questions or sudden discussions or disagreements. In kindergarten and primary school, teachers mainly used videos, images, song or games to illustrate certain topics or themes. Besides this, several teachers see it as an advantage to have a wide range of educational and illustrative materials in pocket size available to them, especially those who often change classroom or teach in more than one school. In contrast to earlier technologies, the effort required to grab and 'turn on' mobile media is minor compared to PCs or laptops. When using mobile media in class, most teachers prefer working with smaller groups. This helps them to avoid a chaotic or messy situation and facilitates involving all children simultaneously in a meaningful learning activity. In kindergartens in Belgium, a common approach is to create 'corners' or 'islands' in class, which allow children to be split in smaller groups and rotate from one activity to another. Teachers particularly encourage the use of mobile media to support equal opportunities for all children, regardless of the access they have at home. Even in kindergarten, teachers argue it is important for young children, whatever their background, to feel comfortable and confident in using mobile media.

CHRISTIANE (teacher in kindergarten): I have to say, a child living in a home where computers are totally not present, versus a child living in a home where computers are prevailing … you can easily reduce the difference between them. With regard to this issue, children are mostly very flexible and capable to adapt themselves quickly.

Nevertheless, not all teachers are convinced of the value of mobile media in class. They argue that the range of currently available apps does not encourage children to think or reflect about the exercises or assignments offered. In kindergarten, some teachers believe that children just swipe or touch randomly, taking a trial-and-error approach. In secondary school, teachers criticize what they perceive as young people's 'superficial' use of smartphones, showing little or no interest in using the device for searching for information or other educational purposes.

Our qualitative data reveal three reasons that explain why schools do not adopt mobile media for learning activities. First, the school's policy on digital media is either a key facilitator or an inhibitor. When schools struggle to obtain an agreement between all members of the staff on the school's mobile media policy, teachers are reluctant to implement mobile media across all classes and curricula. A second reason is the availability of infrastructure, technical support and appropriate content. Even if the school favours using mobile devices in class, the classrooms often lack a stable and fast Wi-Fi-connection. Many teachers express frustration when they lose time in class because of a technical failure and regret the lack of, or long delays in getting, technical support. If the problem persists, some teachers quickly lose their motivation to use mobile media and return to 'offline' teaching – sometimes for good. In addition, many teachers are critical of the shortage of appropriate and user-friendly learning material that meets their needs and fits within the prescribed curriculum and class routines. The final reason relates to the personalities and perceptions of the school's staff. Whereas some teachers feel comfortable about using mobile media in their teaching activities, others feel insecure. Confident teachers tend to emphasize the opportunities inherent to the use of mobile media in class and are more likely to experiment with digital teaching methods. Insecure teachers are often not inter-ested in using digital devices, and believing their own digital skills are limited. These inexperienced teachers are more likely to express the belief that using mobile media in class would cause chaos, and distract children from their learn-ing activities.

MARIE (teacher in kindergarten): Well, I notice among some older colleagues that they see the benefits, but because they have very limited knowledge themselves about digital devices, it is very complex for them. While for the younger teachers, yeah, we are used to this. We grew up with digital media, so for us it is a lot more self-evident.

As found in previous research, perhaps one of the main inhibitors is that although mobile media provide opportunities to support learning in a school context, both teachers and children perceive smartphones mainly as instruments for entertainment and communication

The small size and portability of the smartphone make it very convenient to bring it into school in a pocket or (small) bag. For children, bringing a smart-phone to school is self-evident. Although in most schools it is officially not allowed, many children admit they (secretly) use their smartphone during class for a quick moment of distraction. Very often, parents encourage the presence of smartphones at school. Children explain their parents feel less worried if their son or daughter is able to contact them in case of an emergency or problem on their way to and from school. With these practices, the home and school context now intersect and have become more intertwined. In the same vein, boundaries blur when children use their smartphones while doing homework at home. Many children use the smartphone to connect with classmates and give each other advice and assistance, especially when it concerns group assignments. This prac-tice is perceived as helpful, and children appreciate the support of their peers. However, it also creates scope for a certain amount of distraction.

IRIS (age 15): Yes, you are distracted more easily [because of the smartphone]. I'm always thinking 'actually I should study', but at the same time I also want to have a quick look, secretly, although I'm trying to stop myself doing that.

The boundary between learning and entertainment blurs even further outside of classic teaching activities, for instance during lunch breaks, field trips or project work. Most teachers agree that smartphones offer many opportunities to enrich these activities. Various apps allow children to document their experiences on a field trip and share them with others. For example, during breaks or trips chil-dren can take pictures or create other types of online content than can be used in courses, projects or creative activities at school. At the same time, in a less regu-lated setting, smartphones can easily be misused or lead to conflicts. Many teachers report on instances of ridiculing or bullying teachers online, often including pictures or videos taken with smartphones during (informal) school activities. Among classmates, teachers have seen how mobile communication can easily lead to misunderstandings and conflicts.

For many teachers, it is a challenge to find a good balance between giving the children sufficient autonomy to benefit from smartphone opportunities in a school context and at the same time keeping control over the situation in class. In this process, both teachers and children recognize the importance of good class management, with respect for each other's interests and concerns. Four issues illustrate how various elements in a school context facilitate and/or hinder the balance between autonomy and control.

First, parental interference during school hours can be very disturbing for teachers. Teachers complain particularly about parents who want to reach their children when they are at school and expect them to reply sooner rather than later. This undermines the teachers' sense of authority, since children usually consider requests or rules from both their teacher and parents. Ultimately, teachers feel disrespected by the parents that communicate with their children during school hours. Overall, teachers believe their position has changed, as they no longer have absolute control over the situation on class.

JOHAN (teacher in secondary school): Those parents, they call ... they call and send text messages. And, if they don't get a reply after some time, then they would go very quickly ... they would go to the police or something. The parents, they are so overprotective! These children, they are too available!

Second, it is challenging for teachers to deal with certain types of children and particular situations. The teachers interviewed feel that a common rule for all students at school, across all grades, does not make sense. According to the teachers, it is normal to be stricter in the lower grades, and to give the older students more autonomy and personal responsibility. Many teachers have ambivalent feelings about smartphone restrictions at school. On the one hand, teachers argue that (very) strict rules do not help young people to develop self-management skills and responsible smartphone use. On the other hand, clear and strict rules can be helpful to avoid endless discussions with the pupils or their parents.

JORIS (teacher in secondary school): I don't think you could install an absolute ban [on using smartphones at school].

PETER: True, but that makes it more complicated to install a consequent policy, because ... a school policy is always black-and-white, but in reality you have a lot of grey zones.

JORIS: A school policy is black-and-white, but you can make it more 'grey' and introduce the option for the individual teacher to decide under which conditions it would be useful to use smartphones in class.

JOHAN: On the other hand, a school policy that is black-and-white, then you can really say ... 'here it says so'! No further discussions! And in reality, I think teachers will always give a warning before actually giving a punishment according to the school's rules.

Third, our interview data show that a commonly used punishment for transgressing smartphone rules at school is confiscating the device. More recently, several teachers have raised objections about these strict practices. One is that students collectively break rules and confiscating hundreds of devices a week is simply not feasible. Another is that while the teachers see the smartphone as a tool that disturbs the class, for the children it is a tool that connects them with others and represents their personality or identity. Therefore, confiscating the device is a punishment that does not seem in proportion to the infringement, furthermore, a common practice in Flemish schools to punish children involves writing a negative comment or 'notification' in the children's school diaries, which the parents then have to sign.

JOACHIM (teacher in secondary school): Yes, it's a very severe punishment, confiscating their mobiles. Actually it hurts them more than what we intend to. Because if you confiscate the mobile ... those children ... it's really their instrument of their freedom and independence. So ... I believe some of them would rather have a note in their agenda than have their phones confiscated for the day.

Finally, looking at the perspectives of the children, many agree that some rules about smartphones are necessary in a school context. Children accept that in some situations smartphone use should be restricted, as it helps them to stay focused on learning activities. They are willing to discuss certain rules and agreements with their teachers.

RAFAEL (age 9): I think [some rules] are good. Otherwise children would only text during class, and they would become stupid.

Despite the policies, perceptions and challenges described above, many teachers anticipate a different future. Overall, the teachers in our studies expect mobile devices will be integrated in a wide range of teaching practices and school activities, from kindergarten to secondary school. Several teachers indicate that flexibility is paramount and it is more appropriate to take up the role of coach or facilitator in class, instead of merely transferring knowledge. Regardless of whether or not teachers currently implement mobile devices in class, they believe it is important to introduce children coming from all backgrounds to new media.

Several teachers identify opportunities to support personalized learning with mobile media, as well as to follow up children's personal efforts and progress. They need assistance to attend to all children's (special) needs and are particularly hopeful that mobile media will assist them in providing personal support for children with particular learning problems or certain deficiencies. Another opportunity lies within the exploration of alternative or creative use of smartphones. Teachers emphasize that the school is an appropriate environment to counter the current repetitive use of mobile devices. Instead, teachers can introduce children to apps or platforms that support the children's learning trajectory, apps that would otherwise not be spontaneously discovered by the children themselves.

> FILIP (ICT-coordinator in a primary school): Certainly when we are talking about differentiation at school. Digital media are wonderful tools for that. If you have good software that suits the capacities of the child, it will motivate the child. A child who just has to make exercises, it will stop. But a tool that feels what the child is able to do and what not, and adjusts to the child … for example, going a level lower with easier exercises, so the child feels motivated again to continue, and ultimately reaches a higher level at its own pace. And those children who need a more challenging task, well, they just go to a level higher. So that's how [mobile media] fit perfectly [to this challenge].

Some teachers remain reluctant to accept the introduction of mobile media in class, but identify this evolution as 'unavoidable'. Teachers with a lack of self-confidence often have a low estimation of their own digital literacy, particularly when it concerns informational, critical and strategic skills. Nevertheless, even moderate tech-savvy teachers can play a meaningful role in assisting children in how to search for and evaluate information online. Possible hurdles that need to be overcome before this evolution is made possible, relates to the facilitation of successful integration of apps and tools within the curriculum and class routines. Teachers that lack self-confidence need tools that support them to achieve a better class management. Willingness to engage with mobile media in class and acquire the necessary (digital) skills also depends on support and assistance of colleagues and the school board.

> HANNELORE (teacher in kindergarten): Well, some colleagues at first were reluctant to use it [mobile media]. But because the school obliged them to learn how to use it, well … I now often see them using games or videos in class.

Despite the expected increase of mobile media in class, most teachers point out that digital tools or apps should not replace current teaching methods. Instead, they envision an evolution towards blended learning, i.e. a mix between 'online' and 'offline' activities and assignments. As such, they believe smartphones should support learning activities, but their use should not be a goal in itself. Among the enthusiasts, a few teachers expect a move towards a bring-your-own device approach. Others do not support this idea because they believe that it would emphasize inequalities among children since not everyone can afford the most recent type of smartphone.

Conclusion

Many teachers themselves recognize that smartphones have indeed blurred boundaries between home and school, and between entertainment and learning, but this may also help to explain the ambivalent feelings teachers have about using and regulating smartphones in a school context. Several teachers question the restrictive approach of confiscating children's smartphones, and acknowledge that smartphones can offer valuable learning opportunities. At the same time, however, they feel uncomfortable about losing control over the class if there were to be no strict rules about when children are and are not allowed to use smartphones. Particularly those teachers who do not feel competent enough in using smartphones are reluctant and favour restrictive mediation.

While most children in Belgium take their smartphone to school, this research has shown the extent to which and reasons why the use of these devices is constrained in that location (see the chapter by Haddon in this book). Looking more closely, the main reason for taking their smartphones to school seems to be for entertainment purposes or for informal communication with friends or parents during school hours. In contrast to the claims about convergence, rather than 'creating additional (educational) opportunities', using smartphones for educational purposes is something that happens occasionally rather than being part of the daily routines in class.

Although some (young) teachers have experimented with using smartphones in a class context, the survey indicates that a restrictive approach still prevails in most schools in Belgium. Our research confirms that regulating smartphone use in a school environment is a serious challenge, as it should balance the various concerns of school staff, parents and children. The teachers in our studies agree that educational smartphone use mostly depends on initiatives from individual teachers instead of being a practice that is supported or coordinated at the school level. Nevertheless, they believe that a supportive school policy can motivate teachers to explore the benefits of smartphones in class. Besides this, smartphone use at school is also associated with the availability of infrastructure, technical support and appropriate content or materials.

Teachers recognize that not all their colleagues are enthusiastic about using smartphones in educational practices. In order to facilitate successful integration of smartphones in a school context, they believe that a combination of restrictive and active mediation makes most sense. Children agree that some regulation is necessary, as this helps them to deal with the difficulties of blurred boundaries and the downsides of being connected continuously. Although some teachers lack self-confidence, our study shows there is a willingness among many teachers to consult children when making rules about smartphone use. What is needed to motivate teachers to integrate smartphones in class are school policies favourable towards smartphones and extra efforts to support less confident colleagues.

References

Alper, M. (2013) Children and convergence culture. New perspectives on youth participation with media, in Lemish, D. (ed.) *The Routledge international handbook of children, adolescents and media*, pp. 148–155, New York, Routledge.

Blair, B. and Fletcher, A. (2011) The only 13-year-old on the planet Earth without a cell phone: Meanings of cell phones in early adolescents' everyday lives, *Journal of Adolescent Research, 26* (2), 155–177.

boyd, d. (2008) Why youth love social network sites: The role of networked publics in teenage social life, in Buckingham, D. (ed.) *Youth identity and digital media* (Vol. 6), pp. 119–142, Cambridge, MIT Press,

Campbell, R. (2006) Teenage girls and cellular phones: Discourses of independence, safety and 'rebellion', *Journal of Youth Studies, 9* (2), 195–212.

Crabtree, B. F. and Miller, W. L. (eds). (1999) *Doing qualitative research*, London, Sage Publications.

Du Gay, P., Hall, S., Janes, L., Koed Madsen, A., Mackay, H. and Negus, K. (2013) (Second edition) *Doing cultural studies: The story of the Sony Walkman*, London, Thousand Oaks, CA, Sage.

Ellison, N. B. and boyd, d. (2013) Sociality through social network sites, in Dutton, W. H. (ed.) *The Oxford handbook of internet studies*, pp. 151–172, Oxford, Oxford University Press.

Fereday, J. and Muir-Cochrane, E. (2008) Demonstrating rigor using thematic analysis: A hybrid approach of inductive and deductive coding and theme development, *International Journal of Qualitative Methods, 5* (1), 80–92.

Fine, G. A. (2004) Adolescence as cultural toolkit: High school debate and the repertoires of childhood and adulthood, *The Sociological Quarterly, 45* (1), 1–20.

Green, N. (2001) Who's watching whom? Monitoring and accountability in mobile relations, in Brown, B., Green, N. and Harper, R. (eds) *Wireless world: Social and interactional aspect of the mobile age*, pp. 32–45, London, Springer.

Haddon, L. and Vincent, J. (2014) *European children and their carers' understanding of use, risks and safety issues relating to convergent mobile media*, Milano, Educatt.

Hobbs, R. (2011) The state of media literacy: A response to Potter, *Journal of Broadcasting and Electronic Media, 55* (3), 419–430.

Horst, H. and Miller, D. (2006) *The cell phone: An anthropology of communication*, Oxford, New York, Berg.

Ito, M., Horst, H., Bittani, M., boyd, d., Herr-Stephenson, B., Lange, P. … Robinson, L. (2008) *Living and learning with new media: Summary of findings from the digital youth project*, Chicago, IL, The John D. and Catherine T. MacArthur Foundation.

Jenkins, H. (2006) *Convergence culture: Where old and new media collide*, New York, New York University Press.

Jenkins, H., Ford, S. and Green, J. (2013) *Spreadable media: Creating value and meaning in a networked culture*, New York, New York University Press.

Johnson, R. (1986) The story so far: And further transformations? in Punter, D. (ed.) *Introduction to contemporary cultural studies*, pp. 277–313, London, Longman Group.

Köhl, M., Gützenbrucker, G. and Herdin, T. (2014) *'Always on' – communication practices of mobile, networked youth in Europe and SE-Asia*, Paper presented at the 5th ECREA European Communication Conference on 12–15 November, Lisbon, Portugal.

Kowalski, R., Limber, S. and Agatston, P. (2012) *Cyberbullying: Bullying in the digital age*, Singapore, Wiley-Blackwell.

Lenhart, A., Ling, R., Campbell, S. and Purcell, K. (2010) *Teens and mobile phones*, Washington DC, Pew Research Center.

Ling, R. (2004) *The mobile connection: The cell phone's impact on society*, Amsterdam, Morgan.

Ling, R. and Yttri, B. (2002) Hyper-coordination via mobile phones in Norway, in Katz, J. E. and Aakhus, M. (eds) *Perpetual contact: Mobile communication, private talk, public performance*, pp. 139–169, Cambridge, Cambridge University Press.

Livingstone, S. (2008) Taking risky opportunities in youthful content creating: Teen-agers' use of social networking sites for intimacy, privacy and self-expression, *New Media & Society, 10* (3), 393–411.

Mazzarella, S. (2010) *Girl Wide Web 2.0: Revisiting girls, the internet and the negoti-ation of identity*, New York, Peter Lang.

Nelson, M. K. (2010) *Parenting out of control: Anxious parents in uncertain times*, New York, New York University Press.

Nycyk, M. (2011) Review of key competences in the knowledge society conference, 2010: E-learning and computer competency research in the age of social media, *Digital Culture & Education, 3* (2), 157–162.

Pereira, S. (2014) *Media education in schools and other educational institutions*. Paper presented at the ECREA pre-conference on 12 November, Lisbon, Portugal.

Prendes, P., Castaneda, L. and Gutierrez, I. (2010) ICT competences of future teachers, *Comunicar, 35* (XVIII), 175–181.

Smock, A. D., Ellison, N. B., Lampe, C. and Wohn, D. Y. (2011) Facebook as a toolkit: A uses and gratifications approach to unbundling feature use, *Computers in Human Behavior, 27*, 2322–2329.

Vandoninck, S., d'Haenens, L. and Roe, K. (2016a) *Dealing with online risks: How to develop adequate coping strategies and preventive measures with a focus on vulner-able children*, Leuven, KU Leuven Institute for Media Studies.

Vandoninck, S., Nouwen, M. and Zaman, B. (2016b) *Persona's, huidige scenario's en user requirements* [personas, actual scenarios and user requirements]. Deliverable 1.2. VLAIO-TETRA MeToDi, Leuven, Mintlab.

Wartella, E., Rideout, V., Lauricella, A. R. and Connell, S. L. (2014) *Parenting in the age of digital technology: A national survey*, Evanston, IL: Northwestern University.

12 Experiences of writing on smartphones, laptops and paper in the digital age

Sora Park and Naomi S. Baron

Introduction

With the growing prevalence of mobile media, the way people interact with digital devices has changed. People are not only always on but always with the device (Park, 2013). This physical proximity enables them to interact with the medium (and other people) at the time of their choosing, while ease of access makes mobile devices an approachable medium.

Several chapters in this book examine ways in which the ability to access information and communicate at any time via a smartphone has changed the ways in which people engage with the surrounding world. In this chapter we focus specifically on how they engage in written communication. One of the changes in writing practices that has resulted from using mobile devices, particularly smartphones, is that users are increasingly typing on screens, rather than writing by hand or using a traditional computer keyboard. In this chapter, three types of writing practices – handwriting, keyboard typing and touch screen typing – are compared with regard to how mobility, space and context shape writing practices. We explore how the affordances of paper, keyboards and screens affect the ways in which people engage in different forms of writing activities and their perceptions of these activities. As in Chapter 13, which looks at students reading and writing practices, our own research has a wider salience beyond discussing the relationship between (different) digital and paper media, helping us think critically about the overall place of smartphones in our everyday lives.

We begin by reviewing some of the literature on digital versus print literary practices. Taipale (2014) examined the affordances of electronic reading and writing in comparison to reading and writing on paper. The most prevalent affordances of writing on paper reported by the participants were immediacy and portability. People valued the personal imprint and its emotional meaning. Similarly, writing on paper was associated with creativity and preplanning, while editing on paper was seen as being not as easy as on computers. Writing on keyboards was associated with speed and easy editing – in Taipale's words, 'economic writing'.

Other studies suggest a lowering of mental barriers given the ease of access and editing afforded by digital writing. Children who blog, text or use social networking websites are reported to be more confident about their writing skills (Clark, 2014). Warschauer (2006) found that students felt it was easier to write on computers (as opposed to longhand on paper) because of the easy editing function. Casual digital writing can help young people develop the habit of writing. According to Rosen *et al.* (2010), 'super communicators' (those who use numerous tools – the internet, instant messaging, text messaging, mobile phones and social networking sites – to communicate with friends) also engaged in more journal writing (45 per cent) compared to non-multichannel teens (29 per cent). Lenhart *et al.* (2008) report that bloggers were also more active in other writing genres.

However, if studies such as those above indicate a positive outcome of electronic communication, other research indicates a more complex landscape. For example, there has been a concern about how textese often described as a hybrid of spoken and written language might impact literacy. Powell and Dixon (2011) conclude that exposure to textese had a positive effect on adults' spelling skills. Similarly, use of text abbreviations was reported to be positively related to literacy skills among nine to ten-year-old children (Wood *et al.*, 2011). On the other hand, other researchers noted that frequent users of texting made considerable numbers of spelling mistakes in academic writing (Shafie *et al.*, 2010).

Writing is mainly a cognitive activity used to communicate ideas using coherent language. Some studies suggest that the cognitive processes at issue may differ between modalities of writing, mainly because of how writing occurs physically. Mangen *et al.* (2015) compared three writing modalities – keyboard, screen and paper – in an experiment examining participants' recognition and recall of words. The study found there may be cognitive benefits regarding word recall to writing on paper – in other words, handwriting might have some benefits compared to electronic writing. Mangen (2013) argues that the sensorimotor aspect of writing is important in defining the experience of writing. She characterizes handwriting as a unified and contiguous cognitive activity, where visual attention and sensorimotor action occur simultaneously. By contrast, keyboard typing requires using both hands and, according to Mangen, is more abstract and physically detached in that the act of writing and its outcome are separated. Olive and Passerault (2012) emphasize the fact that although writing is intended to communicate intentions linguistically through coherent language, it also has an important visuospatial aspect. Earlier, Haas and Hayes (1986) argued the crucial role of the visuospatial dimension of handwriting.

One potential constraint associated with electronic writing is that when writing on screen, writers have limited access to the full page (compared with writing on paper) and engage in different revision behaviours. Piolat *et al.* (1997) have reported that because the screen does not show the upper and lower boundaries of the page, when revising, subjects identified fewer errors and their recall of text was poorer. Visibility of text gives the writer spatial information about where words are located (Hayes, 1996). When writing on screens, the scope of previous writing that is visible can be limited due to the screen size, particularly when writing on a small screen such as on a mobile device (Olive and Passerault, 2012).

Another physical difference between writing modalities is where the writing happens, which may have a bearing upon the nature of communication practices. Typically, handwriting occurs where a flat surface (such as a table) is available and (at least commonly) when there is ample time allotted for writing. By contrast, writing on mobile screens tends to be spontaneous, and conducted without spatial restriction. Screen writing frequently occurs as a response to a message that has been received. When writing on a laptop, the writer can either simulate desk-writing practice or capitalize on device portability.

Much of the focus of the existing literature has been on how using digital media impacts users' literacy, cognitive processes and communication styles. However, the questions of how users incorporate the affordances of different writing media into their daily context, how they switch between various contexts and what role digital writing plays in the overall digital environment have not been well explored. Furthermore, people's perception of writing may also be changing: How do these affordances influence the user's writing? In response to these lacunae, we undertook an in-depth analysis of a small cohort of writers to examine the following research questions:

Research Question 1: What are the different experiences of writing on paper, laptops and smartphones among young adults?

Research Question 2: What factors influence how people engage in and experience writing practices on paper, laptops and smartphones?

This exploratory study asked whether young adults, when writing on different media, experience the process and outcomes differently. While laptops and mobile devices are similar in that they are digital writing tools, the input method, mobility and portability were predicted to have different impacts on writers.

Methodology

Participants at a university in Australia were recruited in March and April 2016 via an email newsletter that is centrally distributed to enrolled students, an invitation to participate through a compulsory first year course, and through paper flyers on campus bulletin boards. The sample consisted of ten participants ($M=2$, $F=8$). The age range of participants was 18 to 34 (mean$=26$). Participants were asked to complete four writing tasks, divided over two sessions. An online survey and an interview were conducted after completing the writing tasks.

The first set of tasks was writing on an online forum via a smartphone after watching a short video clip and writing an opinion piece on a laptop after reading an article. The second set of tasks was writing on an online forum via a laptop after watching a short video clip and writing an opinion piece on paper after reading an article. Participants were asked to bring their own devices, thereby simulating their everyday writing practices. The video clips and articles were randomly assigned to participants. The two video clips were similar in length and characteristics. Likewise, the articles were similar in length and characteristics.

After the second session, interviews were conducted with the participants. The writing tasks served as prompts regarding how participants experienced writing on the three different platforms, i.e. smartphone, laptop and paper. However, the interview focused on the participant's overall writing patterns and perceptions. We also asked about both personal and academic writing. Personal writing includes writing for purposes of interpersonal communication (e.g. texting, email and letters) and personal record keeping (such as notes to oneself, diaries and journals).

The interviews were recorded and transcribed, with the participants' consent. The project was approved by the Human Ethics Committee of the first author's institution. A summary of participant characteristics appears in Table 12.1.

Results

Different modes and experiences

Participants in the study reported being tethered to their smartphones in their everyday lives. Eight out of ten participants said they had their smartphones with them all the time, including when they go to bed. Eight participants mentioned checking their phone first thing in the morning when they woke up. All remarked that they were mindful of charging the phone so that it would not run out of power. Six participants said they checked notifications on their phone immediately upon receiving them, and three said they often checked their phone during face-to-face conversations. Smartphones were central to participants' digital lives. The time reported spent on smartphones ranged from one hour to 14–16 hours a day. All participants used texting or messaging. Except for one participant, everyone engaged in daily social media activities such as posting or commenting online using their phones.

When participants referred to 'writing', they usually meant handwriting on paper. Writing on laptops was typically labelled as 'typing' rather than 'writing'. Writing on smartphones was described as 'messaging' or 'communicating'. These differences in terminology were reflected in reported behaviour patterns. Participants spent less time writing on their phone compared to writing on laptops. None preferred smartphones as a medium for writing. In most cases, participants preferred using laptops to write and spent more time writing on laptops than on any other medium. Six participants indicated spending more than an hour per day writing on their laptops, whereas four spent more than an hour on paper and four on smartphones. However, many participants did not think that texting or posting on social media on their smartphones constituted writing. This means that they may spend more time physically 'writing' on smartphones, without acknowledging it to be writing.

In the following section, the experiences of writing on laptops, paper and smartphones are described, along with how different media are used in varied writing practices.

Table 12.1 Participant characteristics

Pseudonym	Age	Gender	Laptop use	Smartphone use	Daily internet use	Daily smartphone use	First smartphone	First laptop	More comfortable writing
Alice	21	F	Several times a day	Several times a day	20 minutes	10 minutes	2016	4–5 years ago	Laptop
Jason	19	M	Several times a day	3–5 days a week	4 hours	30 minutes	2 years ago	8 years ago	Handwriting
Jasper	18	M	Several times a day	Several times a day	8 hours	3 hours	6 years ago	6 years ago	Laptop
Kate	34	F	About once a day	Several times a day	2 hours	4 hours	5 years ago	8–9 years ago	Handwriting
Kira	33	F	About once a day	Several times a day	1 hour	3 hours	6 years ago	6 years ago	Handwriting
Mandy	24	F	Several times a day	Several times a day	3 hours	5 hours	2 years ago	6 years ago	Laptop
Penelope	20	F	Several times a day	Several times a day	4–5 hours	1 hour	1 year ago	7 years ago	Laptop
Tanya	34	F	Several times a day	Several times a day	5 hours	1 hour	8–9 years ago	–	Laptop
Veronica	34	F	Several times a day	Several times a day	3–5 hours	2–3 hours	5–6 years ago	6–7 years ago	Laptop
Winona	24	F	Several times a day	Several times a day	10–12 hours	14–16 hours	–	4–5 years ago	Laptop

Laptops

Using a keyboard to type is a different experience from writing on paper. It also differs from typing on a mobile screen. Due to convenience, participants chose laptops as the most efficient medium on which to write. Participants reported being comfortable with writing on keyboards. Penelope, who is an active internet user, has been using a laptop for about seven years. In her words, 'Definitely writing on the laptop was by far the easiest just because it's something that I use every day'.

For most writers, the act of writing using a keyboard and a monitor does not require constantly concentrating on the written text on the screen. In some instances, participants reported that the act of typing can be separated from thinking and listening (e.g. taking notes during a class lecture) when writing on a computer.

Tanya, who is an older student (age 34), has lived through changes over the past decade in digital technologies and has taken advantage of the benefits. Tanya finds it useful to write on the computer (e.g. when taking notes during a lecture), because she can 'listen and type far more easily ... without really paying attention to what I'm [typing]'. However, she admits that 'it also probably means that I'm not really registering anything ... while I'm typing'. In the same vein, Kira notes that 'when I'm just typing I just feel ... almost like a zombie. You're just typing and you're just going through the motions'.

Writing on a laptop is perceived to be useful where the text at issue does not involve emotions or sentiments. Kira observes:

> It's just fixing, editing.... There's no emotion behind it. It's just I have to do a task ... when I'm doing my research I will handwrite my ideas or my points because I feel like I'm engaging with the material.

Efficiency and flexibility were rationales given for preferring to write on laptops. This kind of writing is perceived as 'more efficient and it's better ... to draft the whole thing on the computer' (Tanya), and therefore an 'efficient way of writing' (Winona). Writing with a computer increases the volume of text as well, because it's easier to pick up where you left off and therefore create more text in a given time. As Alice notes, the digital writer can multitask, which can be distracting:

> It's easier to get distracted ... my mind doesn't register what I'm typing. When I'm writing [on paper], I have to constantly think if that makes sense.

Ease of writing can make the writing experience enjoyable. When asked which medium they enjoyed writing on, many participants replied that they liked the laptop writing the most. Their main reason involved convenience:

> [I] enjoy writing on a laptop the most.... It's just a lot easier and a lot quicker to do. It looks neater as well. You can change it up whereas writing

[by hand] it's – pen writing, it's messy. It's not the best … iPhone I just don't find it as good because it's harder to [edit].

(Penelope)

I think a laptop I enjoy the most. It's basically a phone and a book put into a device which is much more convenient … it's less distracting than the phone, you can write down ideas quicker.

(Jasper)

Writers know they can go back to revise and edit. The laptop has given Mandy confidence in writing because, as she says, 'if you don't get it right, that's all right, you can go back and change it'.

Handwriting

In contrast to writing on laptops, writing on paper was perceived to require full engagement of the writer, as well as careful planning of what is to be written. This mental engagement enabled writers to be less distracted. Participants reported that writing on paper is an act that engages the brain. Kira reports that it requires focus of the writer in contrast to digital writing:

It helps my brain to think. When I'm writing in class [on paper] it helps me to actually take in the information more, where when I'm sitting in front of a computer I just feel like – I … blank out. So that's why I [think that with] handwriting you have to actually engage more. You have to concentrate on what you're actually writing, where typing, you can just blank out.

Mandy expressed similar sentiments:

When you're doing the handwriting, you have to stop and think, now I've got to have a clear picture in my mind of what I'm going to talk about and how it can flow through and like I said you're sort of thinking as you're going what's coming next all the time.

In the same vein, Veronica describes her handwriting experience to be more difficult compared to the other modes:

When you do writing on paper you have to be very careful with what you put in. If it happens I have to do writing on paper I try to come up with some plan first in my mind how it's supposed to look.… It's not always easy because, as I say, paper doesn't give you much chances to fix your work, you just have to write down and that's it.

Kira judges writing on paper, smartphones and laptops to be different in the degree of effort required in each mode:

> When you [are] handwriting on pen and paper … I've got to think about what I'm going to write because otherwise you're sitting there and you've got lines and things scribbled out.

The constant thought process involved with handwriting was regarded as an interaction between the writer and the written text. In contrast, digital writing was described as a one-way flow from the writer to text. In Kate's words:

> So if I type it as it's coming out of my head, type-type-type-type, I go and I read it and I go, oh yep that sounds alright. But if I handwrite it, because I'll be half way through a sentence and go, oh no that's not what I – this actually sounds a little bit better in my head so I'll write it down.

Kate has been using a laptop for about nine years. However, she still spends more time writing on paper, more than two hours a day, than on her laptop, on which she spends less than an hour to write. She values handwriting and exerts more effort when writing on paper.

However, to some participants, the perception of a free flow differed. For example, Mandy thinks that there is more of a flow when she writes on paper because she pours out thoughts and emotions:

> It really does flow a lot more on the paper. You're sort of you're writing and as you're writing you're thinking about what's coming next and what you can put after that and it was quite consistent … I was writing it as it came out.

According to Kira, when writing on paper, she needs to 'focus on this, block everything else out'. Mandy notes that the focus needed when handwriting makes is less distracting compared to other modes of writing:

> Handwriting's a little bit of a harder one to think of distractions because I don't do it very much I guess. I can't really think of a time when I sat down to write something by hand and been distracted.

The sources of distraction when writing on paper are different from those when engaged in digital writing. With handwriting the source could be exhaustion, passers-by, a knock on the door – generally something external to the writing activity.

Jason said when he writes on paper, he feels it's coming more 'directly from' him. That is why, he reports, he spends more time writing on paper than on any other medium. The physical output makes the experience more 'real' (Jason). In Jason's words, 'I think it's because it's something I can touch, that I own. Whereas with the document that is saved on my computer, in the cloud, it doesn't really feel as real'. Handwriting is a physically engaging act, where the writer has to simultaneously engage the brain, the hand, and the pen and paper. Several participants commented on the issue of physicality:

> Handwriting something to pen and paper is an extension of you. Because you physically can touch it, you can physically run your hands over the words, because there's indentation from the pen and the force that you've used on the paper.
>
> (Kira)

> When you're [hand] writing, you've actually got to physically look at the paper and make sure you've got it correct.
>
> (Kate)

For a number of participants, handwriting was an emotional experience with sentimental value. Tanya chooses to write by hand when keeping her journal because 'what I'm writing is very emotional and it would feel strange to have that false separation'. Similarly, Kira experiences a 'release' when handwriting. Participants described handwriting as having a cathartic effect. Once written down, the thoughts or emotions leave the writer. From Tanya:

> I'm a thinker and I tend to get stuck in my own head. I have always found that it's quite useful to get those thoughts literally out of my head and onto paper … you write things down to process information, to help you through a difficult time and if you get to a point where you're like well actually I'm past that.

However, increasingly handwriting is replaced by digital writing, and some of the participants were no longer used to writing by hand. As Penelope comments,

> I definitely think handwriting is more chaotic. I don't really think about what I'm supposed to be writing. I sort of just write massive chunks and things.... It's not very planned out. Laptop I find a lot easier. I can write it out and then I can write things underneath that and get it looking good.... Then iPhone I just don't enjoy that at all … I'll write something and if it's not as good I … ignore it because it's just too difficult to … change it.
>
> (Penelope)

Smartphones

Smartphones were the most problematic medium for most participants when they were writing. Often times, they did not regard composition on smartphones as writing at all. Writing on smartphones is 'more like talking' (Alice), a 'conversation' (Jasper) or a 'short response to something' (Tanya). Smartphones were regarded to be ineffective for 'writing' because participants were not comfortable with 'writing' on mobile screens. Participants differentiated communicative activities such as texting or social media engagement from writing activities.

Winona, who reports spending the majority of her day on her phone, estimates doing more than two hours of texting or messaging daily. However, she does not think of this activity as writing but rather, 'communicating with another person'. Penelope claims she never writes on her smartphone. Yet she spends time on messaging, posting texts on social media, taking notes, keeping a to-do list and blogging using her smartphone.

Despite the significant amount of time participants spent on their phones, they did not enjoy writing on them. The medium has technical inconveniences that make it a poor interface for writing. Phones were described as 'frustrating' (Mandy) because of autocorrect or predictive texts functions. The small screen also meant it was hard to track and read back what the writer had written (Mandy). Simply put, 'the interface doesn't really work very well' (Tanya).

Many participants commented on the small screen size and the difficulties of editing text on the phone. This challenge led participants to think through what they were going to write before they started to type on the screen. They reported being more careful when writing on mobile devices, knowing that it would be hard to go back and edit, similar to when they were writing on paper. Tanya, for instance, reported:

> I'd say that the handwriting was actually more like the mobile writing because going back and editing it is harder in handwriting and it takes more time so I would be certainly thinking more before I wrote.

One consequence, at least for Jasper, was tending to write less on a smartphone than on other media:

> [When writing on the smartphone] I was thinking about what I was writing but I was writing significantly less. I was trying to paraphrase most things so it would be slightly less time to type everything, just like I do for most, like my Facebook posts.

Digital writing and mode-switching

Writing on diverse media offered differing experiences to the participants. Most of them engaged in all three modes of writing at some point in their everyday context. The majority preferred writing on laptops, mainly because of the ease of access and convenience of editing. Writing on paper was a familiar task, but participants expressed mixed feelings about it. Smartphones were used frequently for sending text messages. Participants were aware of these different experiences and described utilizing each medium for particular purposes in the course of their daily routine. New media for writing such as smartphones add to the mix of available writing practices. For participants in our study, one technology does not supplant the others.

Those who have been immersed in digital technologies acquire skills to adapt to and switch between different modes of writing, depending on the medium. Most participants did not experience any difficulties in switching modes, finding the process has become habitual. Veronica engages in messaging, shares links, writes comments on posts, and 'likes' things on social media. With her phone, she also emails, takes notes and keeps a 'to do' list. However, she distinguishes between different modes of writing and finds it easy to switch back and forth:

> I can separate those two styles, yeah. I don't feel any difficulties and, as I said, I'd already done something similar, I mean just in Facebook, for my studies and that's why it was a good help to focus and sort of switch mode.

In fact, being an adept user of smartphones and laptops, Veronica sometimes uses multiple modes to complete one writing task:

> It's kind of convenient to do it with two or even three devices sometimes because I actually can use iPad as well, so I have some things open on the phone, some things open [on the] iPad and actually do typing on laptop. It saves a lot of time.

Jason switches modes of writing depending on whom he writes to. In Jason's words, 'who I write to is linked to the medium I write with'. Writing is largely an activity with an audience. Tanya gets the sense that when she is writing on her laptop, even if it is not for a specific audience (like an assignment), she still writes for others, and tries to make the text formal. The potential audience sets the tone and style of writing:

> My style of writing wildly depends on whoever I'm talking to. If I'm talking to some of my friends who are more academically based who are going to see my writing I'll be a lot more intellectual and formal.
>
> (Jasper)

Conclusions

In this chapter, we posed two research questions. The first asked what the different experiences were that young adults had when writing on paper, laptops and smartphones. The second asked what factors influence how people engage in and experience writing practices with these three media. The Results section above presents details of our answers to these questions for the participant sample we studied.

In many cases, the choice of writing on paper, laptop or smartphones was a matter of the individual's preference. Personal experiences were tied to these preferences. However, some common elements of writing on paper versus on digital devices were suggested from the interviews.

A narrow definition of 'writing' was commonly applied to writing on paper, and was sometimes specifically linked to concentrated thinking. Writing on paper was reported to be used for sentimental purposes, for focusing on ideas and for mapping out new ideas. Writing on digital devices entailed a looser definition of 'writing'. For example, initially in the interviews, many participants did not think that social media posts counted as 'writing'. However, on reflection, some of them did acknowledge that this type of communicative practices was indeed a type of writing. Much of the writing on small mobile screens constitutes short messages rather than longer text. Most of that writing is not intended to be 'writing' in a traditional sense. Users frequently text, comment, take notes or record some aspect of their lives on the screen without perceiving they are engaging in a 'writing' activity. As found in a previous study, these activities are not merely a replica of spoken communication (Baron, 2015).

A second theme was that different media were more suitable to different types of writing. Writing on laptops was judged useful for structuring pieces systematically and for revising. Writing on smartphones offered the opportunity to quickly jot down thoughts, as well as communicate efficiently with others through written text.

Third, participants in this study grew up in an environment where they had access to and learned to use a multiplicity of digital devices and writing media, including pen and paper. Habit, social context and the requirements of academic work shape their uses of the writing medium. The interviews indicated they have adopted effective ways of engaging in writing by shifting between media, functionally separating the media of choice depending on the situation. In fact, the ability to switch seamlessly from one writing medium to another has become a necessary skill in the digital age. In the process, our understanding of what is meant by 'writing' needs to expand to take into account the new range of media and contexts in which such textual production may take place.

Finally, and looking beyond the detailed considerations affecting writing choices, 'older' digital devices like laptops and recently more mobile ones like smartphones had far from eliminated traditional practices like handwriting. In the case of writing we see one more example from our everyday practices where newer and older media have different affordances and different roles in our lives, which provide a more nuanced assessment of the impact of the digital.

Writing is an activity that transcends time and space. With or without digital technologies, it is an important task that people engage in. The aspect of digital writing adds to the lived culture of the digital era, where people can experience different modes and contexts of writing in various contexts. This study is a snapshot of the changes that are occurring in writing practices in the digital age.

References

Baron, N. (2015). *Words Onscreen: The Fate of Reading in a Digital World.* Oxford, UK: Oxford University Press.

Clark, C. (2014). *Children's and Young People's Writing 2013: Findings from the National Literacy Trust's Annual Literacy Survey.* Retrieved from London National Literary Trust: http://files.eric.ed.gov/fulltext/ED521656.pdf (accessed 25 August 2016).

Haas, C. and Hayes, J. R. (1986). What did I just say? Reading problems in writing with the machine. *Research in the Teaching of English, 20*(1), 22–35.

Hayes, J. R. (1996). A new framework for understanding cognition and affect in writing. In Levy, C. M. and Ransdell, S. E. (Eds), *The Science of Writing: Theories, Methods, Individual Differences and Applications* (pp. 1–27). Mahwah, NJ: Erlbaum.

Lenhart, A., Arafeh, S., Smith, A. and Macgill, A. (2008). *Writing, Technology and Teens*. Retrieved from Washington, DC: www.pewinternet.org/files/old-media/Files/Reports/2008/PIP_Writing_Report_FINAL3.pdf.pdf (accessed 25 August 2016).

Mangen, A. (2013). '... scripta manent'? The disappearing trace and the abstraction of inscription in digital writing. In Pytash, K. and Ferdig, R. (Eds), *Exploring Technology for Writing and Writing Instruction* (pp. 100–114). Hershey, PA: IGI Global.

Mangen, A., Anda, L. G., Oxborough, G. H. and Brønnick, K. (2015). Handwriting versus keyboard writing: Effect on word recall. *Journal of Writing Research, 7*(2), 227–247. doi:10.17239/jowr-2015.07.02.1.

Olive, T. and Passerault, J.-M. (2012). The visuospatial dimension of writing. *Written Communication, 29*(3), 326–344. doi:10.1177/0741088312451111.

Park, S. (2013). Always on and always with mobile tablet devices: A qualitative study on how young adults negotiate with continuous connected presence. *Bulletin of Science, Technology & Society, 33*(5–6), 182–190. doi:10.1177/0270467614528900.

Piolat, A., Roussey, J. Y. and Thunin, O. (1997). Effects of screen presentation on text reading and revising. *International Journal of Human-Computer Studies, 47*, 565–589.

Powell, D. and Dixon, M. (2011). Does SMS text messaging help or harm adults' knowledge of standard spelling? *Journal of Computer Assisted Learning, 27*(1), 58–66.

Rosen, L. D., Chang, J., Erwin, L., Carrier, L. M. and Cheever, N. A. (2010). The relationship between 'textisms' and formal and informal writing among young adults. *Communication Research, 37*(3), 420–440. doi:10.1177/0093650210362465.

Shafie, L., Azida, N. and Osman, N. (2010). SMS language and college writing: The languages of the college texters. *International Journal of Emerging Technologies In Learning, 5*(1), 26–31.

Taipale, S. (2014). The affordances of reading/writing on paper and digitally in Finland. *Telematics and Informatics, 31*(4), 532–542. doi:http://dx.doi.org/10.1016/j.tele.2013.11.003.

Warschauer, M. (2006). *Laptops and Literacy: Learning in the Wireless Classroom*. New York: Teachers College Press.

Wood, C., Jackson, E., Hart, L., Plester, B. and Wilde, L. (2011). The effect of text messaging on 9- and 10-year-old children's reading, spelling and phonological processing skills. *Journal of Computer Assisted Learning, 27*(1), 28–36. doi:10.1111/j.1365-2729.2010.00398.x.

13 Students' preferences for smartphones versus other media within their academic study

Jane Vincent, John O'Sullivan, Christopher Lim and Manuela Farinosi

Introduction

Technological transformation is often celebrated, indeed sometimes deemed to be revolutionary, entailing an inevitable and radical break with previous generations (e.g. Tapscott, 1998; Prensky, 2001). A more measured examination of change and continuity can be found in writings in response to early enthusiasm for the information society (Lyon, 1988; Winner, 1989; Winston, 1989; Silverstone, 1995) and more recently in relation to the internet and social media (Turkle, 2011; Fuchs, 2014; Curran, 2016; Wu, 2016). Digital technologies, including smartphones, the internet and all the devices used to access it, are changing people's everyday lives at numerous levels, including how we organise communicating, learning, teaching and many more social practices. At a time of widespread digital adoption (European Commission, 2016), disruption, which occurs with the introduction of each new technological innovation, including the smartphone, provides increasing challenges in the academic environment. Indeed, in societies in which established practices and modes of organisation are seen to be subverted by innovation, disruption has emerged as a central theme not only in business but in other key aspects of society, such as health and education (Christensen, 1997), and, most visibly in recent times, news (Franklin and Eldridge, 2017). At the individual level, the rise of social media has brought users into a culture founded on connectivity and participation (Gardner and Davis, 2013; van Dijck, 2013). In this context of disruptive technological change, not only in academia but across all aspects of daily life, we aim to take forward this questioning by investigating in this chapter one mundane area, our preferences for reading and writing with pen and paper compared to doing so with digital media. In particular we explore students' preferences in this regard, especially for smartphones.

Literature and theoretical stance

The smartphone is sometimes singled out as itself representing a singular convergence of elements of the digital world. Applications range from photography (Halpern and Humphreys, 2016), to dating (Sumter *et al.*, 2017) and medicine

(Khanna *et al.*, 2016). However, no technology simply represents the culmination of all the benefits of previous innovations, superseding them all. To use concepts from different theoretical frameworks, each technology, including the smartphone, has its own affordances (Bijker *et al.*, 1987; Bolter and Grusin, 1999), meaning it is good for some purposes, less good for others, and is domesticated (Silverstone *et al.*, 1992) in particular ways.[1] How smartphones are appropriated, adapted and repurposed by their users and the intertwining of information and communication technologies (ICT) with paper and pen is a continual personal journey that can also be articulated following the circuit of culture (Johnson 1986) as an aspect of 'lived culture'. This represents recognition of the constant iterations of social, technological and cultural influences of the mundane use of the smartphone. Thus, rather than celebrating the smartphone as a new revolutionary platform, we need to appreciate where its roles might be more limited in order to develop a rounded picture of its overall place in daily life.

The use of the smartphone in teaching is part of a familiar drive towards the adoption of digital education technologies, sometimes referred to as 'edtech'. Official and industry narratives strongly promote ICT, or 'ICT-enabled learning innovations' (ICT-ELI) as the solution to the problem of maintaining the competitiveness of societies in the challenging new era which itself has been delivered of such technologies (Brečko *et al.*, 2014; European Commission, 2014). The language deployed at an official level in this regard is of a piece with the templated form of language it created and echoed in European, national education and skills policies more generally, in which the message of digitally-enabled progress and reform is re-rehearsed (Holborow, 2015). Elsewhere, digital dissident Kentaro Toyama has described America's frenzied rush to video instruction, massive open online courses (MOOCs) from elite university brands and iPads as 'an orgy of educational technologies despite scarce evidence that they improve learning' (2015a, p. 11)

The evangelising of technology is now a loud drumbeat on the ground within higher-level educational institutions. In addition to familiar solicitations from technology offices for staff and students to adopt innovative digital teaching and learning methods, in the research, many narrowly instrumental accounts emphasise student-centred pedagogical improvement, sometimes assumed and therefore unmeasured, or else narrowly assessed by way of user satisfaction and engagement. Here, a linear relationship between technology use and learning is uncritically proposed, with, consequently, an imperative, 'must-do-better' tone often directed ultimately towards teaching practice (Kivunja, 2014; Santamarta *et al.*, 2015; Urh *et al.*, 2015). This approach circumvents more basic pedagogical and philosophical questions as to whether capitulating to students' deficit of interest should be at the expense of teaching that rewards intrinsic motivation (Toyama, 2015b). Strategic initiatives towards ICT adoption are shaped not only by public authorities or by the burgeoning of technology functions to be found within institutions, but also by commercial interests in the edtech sector, whose products, 'platforms', 'solutions' and outsourced services provide an increasingly familiar share of the infrastructure of teaching. External actors are manifest plainly through their marketing activities using familiar global brands, including their funding of research as well as their sponsorship of events diffusing their message. But, deploying software theory (Manovich, 2013), an emerging field of study of the active role of code in social and cultural processes, Williamson (2015) shows how in the UK such actors are more deeply embedded, via networks including foundations and think tanks, in the social-algorithmic governance of public education. In the US, this political, social and cultural shift has been more contentiously mapped by Media Matters, detailing links between the education reform movement and privatising advocaters, edtech entities and media interests (Vogel, 2016).

In the discussion on smartphones, representative of contributions confined to elucidating the technology is Bowen and Pistilli's 2012 US study that reports students' general preferences for apps over mobile-friendly browser systems, urging closer alignment of systems to user needs. Others focus on pragmatic applications in which smartphones are shown to improve engagement and participation, as with multiple choice questions for graduate medical students (Shaw and Tan, 2015).

A slightly more critical edge has emerged in relation to reading, with a particular focus on distraction and the perceived fragmented nature of the smartphone experience. In their survey of students, Tossel *et al.* (2015) find unambiguously that participants, contrary to the authors' expectations at the outset of the study, thought smartphones detrimental to learning. However, the authors add a speculative, ICT-friendly twist to argue that this apparent failure of technology may instead mean that the traditional 'classroom-centric' model of education needs to adapt to facilitate the development of m-learning. In a broadly similar study, students were found to suffer from distraction, from 'reading avoidance' stemming from a habit of consuming short texts, and from the dislocation of reading in unfamiliar contexts, such as in transit. Again, rather than questioning the relevance of the technology, the authors emphasise the need to make adjustments in implementation in order to improve engagement (Liu *et al.*, 2015). Distraction (Beasley *et al.*, 2016) and addiction (Hawi and Samaha, 2016) continue to garner attention. However, Cohn (2016) addresses such concerns from a digital literacy perspective, claiming, following a non-anonymous coursework study, to have registered the emergence of an 'addiction' trope among students. Such an interpretation, in which negative sentiment towards the smartphone is attributed to teachers' influence, facilitates a return to the familiar theme of a mostly ICT-resistant, laggard academic community comprising mostly digital immigrants.

Notwithstanding this critical perspective, since claims about how the digital world (or the smartphone) is changing lives tend to be universalistic, the default position one could derive from this literature is that we would expect few national differences. Hence, the country comparative element of the chapter, in which we explore students in three countries, the UK, Italy and Ireland, aims to explore the extent to which this is the case. If there are some differences we may not be able to explain from this evidence why they exist, but it would provide a basis for questioning universalistic claims and provoke further potential research questions we might explore in order to investigate why culture might make a difference.

The student preferences study

In the context of this growing 'edtech' academic culture members of the collaborative European project EU COST Action FP1104 exploring new possibilities for print and media (Frohlich and Mills, 2016),[2] carried out a study of students' preferences for paper or digital alternatives in 12 countries to ascertain whether paper for reading and writing still had a place in students' lives and to learn more about their digital and paper reading and writing practices. The first stage of the research, reported in Vincent (2016), asked undergraduate and graduate students to write freely in response to open ended questions about the differences they encountered, and their preferences when using pen, paper, keyboard and screen (see also Fortunati and Vincent, 2013; Isaias *et al.*, 2014; Taipale, 2014). The responses to these surveys were examined through content analysis and quotations rather than statistical analysis thus, although not directly comparable for coding purposes, the body of rich data obtained from this first stage was used to design a questionnaire consisting of closed questions that could be coded and analysed in accordance with a quantitative analysis. This chapter reports the results of three national studies that used this same online questionnaire in each country, conducted in the native language (five more countries, Hungary, Serbia, Slovakia, Russia and Bulgaria also conducted this survey but are not reported here). The quantitative questionnaire aimed to generate comparative data about the types of devices owned and used, preferences for hard copy (paper) or digital texts for writing and reading, for university work or for pleasure. Students were asked to respond to questions in ten sections: Part I Background information including which digital devices they owned; Part II Reading and Writing – which devices they used for university work and for pleasure; Part III, Amount of Reading for university work and for pleasure; Part IV Reading in Hard Copy or on Digital Screens if costs for both are the same and recorded as a percentage of preference for each; Part V Text Length to see if this influences students' choice between hard copy or digital device; Part VI Reading and Multi-Tasking, which explored frequency and most common way of multitasking; Part VII Reading and Concentration, examining what was easiest and hardest – using hardcopy or digital devices when reading; Part VIII Writing and Concentration, investigating what was easiest and hardest: using hardcopy or digital devices for writing; Part IX Learning to read and write, and in Part X the respondents were invited to add any comments about reading and writing on paper versus doing so digitally. The questions aimed to focus on academic experiences but also asked about reading and writing for pleasure in order to determine whether these were the same as for academic practices. The categorisation of the devices reflected the user experience, for example, students were asked if they owned a mobile phone with internet access (smartphone) or without internet access.

The questionnaires were completed by volunteer students. In Italy (149 respondents) they belonged to a communication or a social science programme and were mostly undergraduates. In the UK (134 respondents) the majority were full time graduate and undergraduate students in the final year of their studies, including the design and media disciplines. The Irish study (88 respondents) drew on students from across journalism, multimedia and communication programmes, primarily from taught undergraduate and masters courses, but including some research postgraduates. Respondents in each country were expected to have some familiarity with technical and wider communication and media platform issues. Students at universities in these countries are directed to lecture notes and other learning materials online. Paper handouts are a rarity.

The study was unfunded and this imposed a few limitations. Obtaining representative samples from each country was not possible, and as the respondents were mostly self-selected the surveys may have attracted students with stronger opinions on the topic. The gender balance and courses studied varied by country as did the length of undergraduate (3–4 years) and graduate (1–3 years) courses. Furthermore, there are nuances not explored in the survey such as the difference between screen or page size (this is explored by Park and Baron in their complementary study reported in the previous chapter), the size of the text or whether it was hand written or typed.

Results

The students' responses in the three countries reported here were mostly similar, especially regarding their smartphone use, the exceptions being that in Italy there was a much stronger preference for using paper for writing and reading throughout and in Ireland there was a greater use of the laptop for reading especially. An illustrative summary of the results is shown in Table 13.1 which contains extracts from the quantitative survey of students from the UK, Italy and Ireland.

More than 91 per cent of the students in the study owned a smartphone, reflecting the higher smartphone use generally in these countries as shown in European comparisons in the most recent Google Consumer Barometer (2016). Fewer than 9 per cent owned mobiles without internet access but these students also owned laptops or tablets so had access to the mobile internet via another device. The number of students using a laptop was higher (94 per cent – 100 per cent) and although far fewer owned a desktop PC (60 per cent in Italy, 26 per cent and 29 per cent respectively in UK and Ireland), given the number of internet-enabled mobile devices owned by students it is perhaps notable that desktop computers are still part of their digital portfolio, and especially so for Italy.

Smartphone use for academic reading was minimal at less than 2 per cent, although digital devices (laptop/tablet) were favoured by British and Irish students more than hard copy, in contrast to the Italians. When it comes to writing none of the students used their smartphones for academic work and 5 per cent or less used them for pleasure. The number of students using paper and pen for

Table 13.1 Illustrative coded results from the student questionnaire from Italy, UK and Ireland expressed as percentage of respondents

	UK	*Italy*	*Ireland*
Female undergraduate	72	91	39
Male undergraduate	34	40	26
Female graduate	21	7	18
Male graduate	7	11	5
Total number of students	**134**	**149**	**88**

Extracts from Quantitative Survey expressed as rounded % of total students per country

Q4 Devices owned include	Devices owned by students		
Mobile phone with mobile internet	91	97	92
Laptop	100	94	94
Laptop and tablet	49	46	34
Desktop	26	60	29
Q5 Prefer to read on	When you read for University work what do you most often use to read? Check one answer. Hard copy means printed work including material you have printed yourself		
Hard copy	42	69	34
Laptop/tablet	46	25	53
Mobile phone	<1	<1	2
Q7 Prefer to write at university using	When you write for university work what do you most often use for writing? Check one answer		
Paper and pen	22	62	8
Desktop	12	5	14
Laptop/tablet	63	33	76
Mobile phone	0	0	0
Q8 Prefer to write for pleasure using	When you write for pleasure what do you most often use for writing? Check one answer		
Paper and pen	47	63	42
Desktop	6	4	7
Laptop/tablet	34	19	39
Mobile phone	<1	5	2
Q14 If costs identical which medium preferred?			
Hard copy	77	91	64
Digital screen	23	9	35
Q18 Would rather read short text (<3 pages)			
Hard copy	31	42	23
Digital screen	34	32	60
No preference	35	26	17
Q19 Would rather read long text (>3 pages)			
Hard copy	69	89	67
Digital screen	25	10	27
No preference	6	1	6
Q23 Multitasking while reading hardcopy	What is the most common way you multitask? Check one answer		
With mobile phone	16	35	32
With computers	16	5	11
Talking with someone	14	11	9

	UK	Italy	Ireland
Q24 Multitasking while reading on digital screen	What is the most common way you multitask? Check one answer		
With mobile phone	11	28	18
With computers	60	52	57
Talking with someone	12	7	8
Q25 Easiest to concentrate on for reading	Which device is the easiest to concentrate on for reading i.e. not get distracted or multitask?		
Hard copy	90	93	85
Desktop/laptop	4	4	8
Mobile phone	1	1	3
Q26 Hardest to concentrate on for reading	Which device is the hardest to concentrate on for reading i.e. not get distracted or multitask?		
Hard copy	3	9	8
Desktop/laptop	65	52	43
Mobile phone	44	33	44
Q27 Easiest to concentrate on for writing	Which device is the easiest to concentrate on for writing i.e. not get distracted or multitask?		
Paper	68	76	66
Desktop/laptop	30	21	32
Mobile phone	<1	1	1
Tablet	<1	1	1
Q28 Hardest to concentrate on for writing	Which device is the hardest to concentrate on for writing i.e. not get distracted or multitask?		
Paper	5	15	14
Desktop/laptop	43	34	33
Mobile phone	45	38	41
Tablet	7	13	13

writing was highest as regards writing for pleasure, whereas their responses as regards writing for academic work showed the most national differences of all the questions: the UK was 22 per cent, Italy was 62 per cent and Ireland was only 8 per cent. Again, the Irish students preferred using their laptops for academic writing the most, and although a third of the Italian students used their laptops far fewer used their desktops. Indeed, despite the fact that the Italian students have by the far the most desktop computers the fact that they owned one did not mean they used it.

The vast majority of Italian students (91 per cent) said that if the cost of hard and digital copy was identical, they would prefer the paper version, their written comments indicated this was because of less eye-strain and it was better for highlighting and taking notes; this was borne out by the UK (77 per cent) and Irish (64 per cent) responses. The choice also depended on the length of the text: students were amenable to reading shorter text (less than three pages) on digital screen although British students had no strong preference either way, whereas 60 per cent of Irish students preferred digital screens and 42 per cent of Italian respondents did so. On the other hand, if the text was long, 89 per cent of Italian students and 69 per cent of British and 67 per cent of Irish students would rather read long text in hard copy. Furthermore, as less than 6 per cent of the respondents responded 'no preference' to this question they clearly felt strongly on the matter. Thus, not only are smartphones not used for academic work but when it comes to reading long text digital devices overall are also preferred less.

Multitasking activity showed national variation, with the Italian and Irish students using their smartphones more when reading hard copy than British students and fewer still mentioned using computers. This changed considerably while reading on digital screens as between 52 per cent (Italy) and 60 per cent (UK) use computers but between 11 per cent (UK) and 28 per cent (Italy) used smartphones when also reading hard copy. Overall the smartphone was the device used most in tandem with hard copy.

Looking now at concentration, the smartphone was reported as the least easy media for reading and writing (less than 3 per cent) whereas paper was strongly in favour for both – over 85 per cent for reading and over 66 per cent for writing. When considering what is the hardest to concentrate on for reading, 33 per cent (Italy) and 44 per cent (UK and Ireland) said it was the smartphone with comparable figures for writing and also for desktops and laptops. This would appear to show that although the students, especially in Ireland, reported they did use laptops for reading and writing they nevertheless found it easier to concentrate when using hard copy.

Discussion

Empirically, this chapter has reported on findings from a study of how university students value pen and paper compared to digital options, and in relation to what purposes. There are two reasons why this is a strategic group for examining how much the digital world has been embraced, and how much non-digital formats (here pen and paper) have retained a place in people's lives. First, whatever reservations one may have about claims about 'digital natives' (Stern, 2008; Selwyn, 2009), contemporary university students, certainly in European countries, have grown up with digital technologies and have years of experiencing the smartphone. Furthermore they are at an age when we might expect them to be more skilled and have developed more digital practices, than younger children who have also grown up in a digital world. That said, one caveat is that some critics have a suggested that we often overestimate the competencies of even this group (Herold, 2012). Second, they are studying in a university environment that, as observed, is increasing digital. Apart from in examinations, they are expected to submit word-processed assignments and, although teachers still may encourage them to look at books, more and more material can be used digitally, either directly or via their virtual learning environments (VLEs), such as Blackboard or Moodle, which lately have introduced smartphone apps. If they really want to read paper, students nowadays often must print files, potentially at a financial cost. So, this cohort constitutes a 'critical case', not a group representative of the population but a leading edge group (Patton, 2015). As has been shown, there are some significant preferences for paper within even this group, and thus we might assume that preference is still widespread in the population at large.

We have already observed from the literature the growth of interest in the use of smartphones by students. Once again, if we then find some reservations about using smartphones for reading or writing, as indeed we have done even among this sample, we might assume that this would apply to others beyond their universities. Furthermore there was no immediately obvious reason why one should expect there to be differences by country and while this was in the most part correct, there were certainly some stronger preferences for paper being expressed by the Italian respondents, and by the Irish students for their laptops. It was notable that such a small role was played by smartphones in the academic learning regime of this cohort, despite the fact that nearly every student owned one.

Our research finds that these students combined their use of multiple digital devices, especially mobile or portable computers including the smartphone, with their use of pen and paper and paper books and articles. Most students owned a smartphone but few reported using them for study although they are integral to their day to day lives: it is this juxtaposition of smartphone with the everyday and academia that we need to study more. Smartphones are apparently compelling devices combining multiple applications for communication and content, but our research shows they have not wholly replaced the use of paper for writing, or indeed other digital devices. Furthermore, students are able to concentrate more using pen and paper and they say smartphones are not conducive to reading more than short sections of academic text, if any.

In all three countries examined here, it appears that most students do have a smartphone (less than 9 per cent of respondents did not have a smartphone) but they do not use it for university study, nor do many students use it for reading or writing for pleasure. Whatever they do use their smartphone for it is not as an edtech device. The students instead use digital devices in the form of tablets, laptops and desktop computers for university study, they also use books and would prefer to use them more than they were able to.

Conclusions

In this chapter we have explored students' preferences for reading and writing with pen and paper compared to doing so with digital media and within the university setting. The smartphone may well be integral to the student's everyday university life but it is complemented by a portfolio of digital ICTs comprising mostly laptops and shared desktop computers in libraries or labs, as well as access to learning material via paper and online articles, borrowed library books and a few purchased texts. We have seen for some purposes other digital ICTs are preferred, while for others the more traditional medium of paper is preferred to all ICTs, smartphone included.

Overall the results highlight that while smartphones appear to be a vital part of students' digital and paper-based information and communications portfolio they are not yet ready to dispense with the paper-based methods or other mobile internet-enabled digital devices in favour of their smartphone. This suggests the process of learning is not necessarily inextricably linked to the technological transformation proposed by the edtech culture and nor to the omnipresence of the smartphone in the hands of nearly every student. Instead, the students' preferences lean towards what helps them learn best and if this unattainable due to cost or availability, as in the case of books and paper articles, they chose the next portable alternative – their tablet or laptop but not (yet) their smartphones. We do not make the claim that our findings pertain to all students in all countries. However, in Italy, for example, the students surveyed clearly had a stronger preference for reading and writing using hard copy and pen and paper, in the UK the students were more ambivalent about their preferences and in Ireland they preferred their laptops for reading and writing. Thus, we do recognise that there may be some nuanced country differences with regard to student preferences and this needs more study. We cannot be certain from this study if the lived culture of our student cohort and the adoption and consumption of smartphones and edtech culture in their particular country setting may have impacted on their daily life. However, there is more than a hint from our work that we should be questioning universalistic claims that universities should be moving towards wholly digitalised governance and teaching methods. Our study shows that for our cohort of students a move away completely from paper-based learning is not the preferred course of action, and further that there may be cultural differences emerging in the use of smartphones in the students' social and academic practices.

Notes

1 The authors thank Leslie Haddon for his helpful editorial comments given in the review process.
2 COST Action FP1104 New Possibilities for Print, Media and Packaging – combining print with digital www.cost.eu/COST_Actions/fps/FP1104.

References

Beasley, R. E., Mcmain, J. T., Millard, M. D., Pasley, D. A. and Western, M. J. (2016) The effects of college student smartphone use on academic distraction and dishonesty, *Journal of Computing Sciences in Colleges* 31 (1), 17–26.

Bijker, W. E., Hughes, T. P. and Pinch, T. J. (eds), (1987) *The social construction of technological systems: new directions in the sociology and history of technology*, Cambridge, Mass, MIT Press.

Bolter, J. D. and Grusin, R. (1999) *Remediation: understanding new media*, Grusin, R. A. (ed.), Cambridge, Mass, London, MIT Press.

Bowen, K. and Pistilli, M.D. (2012) *Student preferences for mobile app usage*, pp. 1–13, Educause, Center for Applied Research.

Brečko, B. N., Kampylis, P. and Punie, Y. (2014) *Mainstreaming ICT-enabled innovation in education and training in Europe*, Luxembourg. Available at: http://ftp.jrc.es/EURdoc/JRC83502.pdf [accessed 20 March 2017].

Christensen, C. M. (1997) *The innovator's dilemma: when new technologies cause great firms to fail*, Boston, Mass, Harvard Business School Press.

Cohn, J. (2016) 'Devilish Smartphones' and the 'Stone-Cold' internet: implications of the technology addiction trope in college student digital literacy narratives, *Computers and Composition* 42, 80–94.

Curran, J. (2016) The internet of dreams, in Curran, J., Fenton, N. and Freedman, D. (eds) *Misunderstanding the internet* (Second Edition), pp. 1–47, London, Routledge.

European Commission, (2014) *Report to the European Commission on new modes of learning and teaching in higher education.* Available at: http://bookshop.europa.eu/en/report-to-the-european-commission-on-new-modes-of-learning-and-teaching-in-higher-education-pbNC0214899/;pgid=GSPefJMEtXBSR0dT6jbGakZD0000ODpsu_s C;sid=ixMbNi1YgIEbAnX1KBeFkU99jMAd5SqLjcA=?CatalogCategoryID=AGwK ABstsBgAAAEjpJEY4e5L [accessed 12 December 2016].

European Commission, (2016) Digital economy and society statistics – households and individuals. *Eurostat.* Available at: http://ec.europa.eu/eurostat/statistics-explained/index.php/Digital_economy_and_society_statistics_-_households_and_individuals. [Accessed February 22, 2017].

Fortunati L. and Vincent J. (2013) Sociological insights into writing/reading on paper and writing/reading digitally, *Telematics and Informatics* 31 (1), 39–51.

Franklin, B. and Eldridge II, S. A., 2017. *The Routledge companion to digital journalism studies*, London, Routledge.

Frohlich D. and Mills J. (2016) Introduction to special issue: audience, design, technology and business factors in new media innovation, *Journal of Print and Media Technology Research* 2 (2), 93–93.

Fuchs, C. (2014) *Social media: a critical introduction*, Los Angeles, Sage.

Gardner, H. and Davis, K. (2013) *The app generation: how today's youth navigate identity, intimacy, and imagination in a digital world*, New Haven, Yale University Press.

Google. (2016) The online and multiscreen world. *Consumer Barometer.* www.consumer-barometer.com/en/insights/?countryCode=GL [accessed 12 December 2016].

Halpern, M. and Humphreys, L. (2016) Iphoneography as an emergent art world, *New Media and Society* 18 (1), 62–81.

Hawi, N. S. and Samaha M. (2016) To excel or not to excel: strong evidence on the adverse effect of smartphone addiction on academic performance, *Computers and Education* 9 (July), 98–89.

Herold, D. (2012) Digital natives: discourses of exclusion in an inclusive society, in Loos, E., Haddon, L. and Mante-Meijer, E. (eds) *Generational use of new media*, Aldershot, Ashgate.

Holborow, M. (2015) *Language and neoliberalism*, Routledge, Oxford.

Isaias, P., Miranda, P. and Pifano, S. (2014) An empirical study on computer and paper based resources: are they competitive or complimentary means?, *IADIS International Journal on Computer Science and Information Systems* 10 (2), 129–144.

Johnson, R. (1986) The story so far: and further transformations, in Punter, D. (ed.) *Introduction to contemporary cultural studies*, pp. 277–313, Essex, Longman Group.

Khanna, R. R., Wachter, R. M. and Blum, M. (2016) Reimagining electronic clinical communication in the post-pager, smartphone era, *JAMA* 315 (1), 21–22.

Kivunja, C. (2014) Theoretical perspectives of how digital natives learn. *International Journal of Higher Education* 3 (1), 94–109.

Liu, Z., Huang, X. and Fu, Y., 2015. Information behavior in the mobile environment : a study of undergraduate smartphone users in China, *Library and Information Science Research* 38 (3), 1–2.

Lyon, D. (1988) *The information society: issues and illusions*, pp. 1–21, 123–129, Oxford, Polity Press.

Manovich, L. (2013) *Software takes command*, London, Bloomsbury.

Patton, M.Q. (2015) *Qualitative research & evaluation methods: integrating theory and practice*. 4th edition, Thousand Oaks, CA, Sage.

Prensky, M. (2001) Digital natives, digital immigrants, *On the Horizon* 9 (5), 1–6.

Santamarta, J. C., Hernández-Gutiérrez, L. E. , Tomás, R., Cano, M., Rodríguez-Martín, J. and Paz Arraiza, M. (2015) Use of tablet PCs in higher education: a new strategy for training engineers in European bachelors and masters programmes, *Procedia – Social and Behavioral Sciences* 191 (June), 2753–2757.

Selwyn, N. (2009) The digital native – myth and reality, *Aslib Proceedings: New Information Perspective* 61 (4), 364–378.

Shaw, C. M. and Tan, S. A. (2015) Integration of mobile technology in educational materials improves participation: creation of a novel smartphone application for resident education, *Journal of Surgical Education* 72 (4), 670–673.

Silverstone, R. (1995) Media, communication, information and the 'revolution' of everyday life', in Emmott, S. (ed.) *Information superhighways: multimedia users and futures*, pp. 61–78, London, Academic Press.

Silverstone, R., Hirsch, E. and Morley, D. (1992) Information and communication technologies and the moral economy of the household, in Silverstone, R. and Hirsch, E. (eds) *Consuming technologies*, pp. 15–31, London, Routledge.

Stern, S. (2008) Questioning the generational divide: technological exoticism and adult constructions of online youth identity, in Buckingham, D. (ed.) *Youth, identity and digital media*, pp. 95–118, Cambridge, MIT Press.

Sumter, S. R., Vandenbosch, L. and Ligtenberg, L. (2017) Love me Tinder: untangling emerging adults' motivations for using the dating application Tinder, *Telematics and Informatics* 34 (1), 67–78.

Taipale, S. (2014) The affordances of reading/writing on paper and digitally in Finland, *Telematics and Informatics* 31 (4), 532–542.

Tapscott, D. (1998) *Growing up digital: the rise of the net generation*, New York, McGraw-Hill.

Tossell, C. C., Tossell, A., Kortum, P., Shepard, C., Rahmati, A. and Zhong, L. (2015) You can lead a horse to water but you cannot make him learn: smartphone use in higher education, *British Journal of Educational Technology* 46 (4), 713–724.

Toyama, K. (2015a) *Geek heresy: rescuing social change from the cult of technology*, New York, Public Affairs.

Toyama, K. (2015b) The looming gamification of higher education, *The Chronicle of Higher Education*. Available at: www.chronicle.com/article/The-Looming-Gamification-of/233992 [accessed 22 February 2017].

Turkle, S. (2011) *Alone together: why we expect more from technology and less from each other*, New York, Basic Books.

Urh, M., Vukovic G., Jereb, E. and Pintar, R. (2015) The model for introduction of gamification into E-learning in higher education. *Procedia – Social and Behavioral Sciences*, 197 (February), 388–397. Available at: http://dx.doi.org/10.1016/j.sbspro.2015.07.154 [accessed 28 February 2017].

Van Dijck, J. (2013) *The culture of connectivity: a critical history of social media*, Oxford, Oxford University Press.

Vincent, J. (2016) Students' use of paper and pen versus digital media in university environments for writing and reading – a cross-cultural exploration, *Journal of Print and Media Technology* 5 (2), 97–106.

Vogel, P. (2016) *Here are the corporations and right-wing funders backing the education reform movement: a guide to the funders behind a tangled network of advocacy, research, media, and profiteering that's taking over public education*, Washington, DC. Available at: http://mediamatters.org/research/2016/04/27/here-are-corporations-and-right-wing-funders-backing-education-reform-movement/210054 [accessed 28 February 2017].

Williamson, B. (2015) Governing software: networks, databases and algorithmic power in the digital governance of public education, *Learning, Media and Technology* 40 (1), 83–105.

Winner, L. (1989) Mythinformation in the high-tech era, in Forester, T. (ed.) *Computers in human context: information technology, productivity and people*, pp. 82–96, Oxford, Basil Blackwell.

Winston, B. (1989) The illusion of revolution, in Forester, T. (ed.) *Computers in human context: information technology, productivity and people*, pp. 71–81, Oxford, Basil Blackwell.

Wu, T. (2016) *The attention merchants: the epic scramble to get inside our heads*, New York, Atlantic Books.

Conclusion

14 Concluding smartphone cultures

Leslie Haddon and Jane Vincent

In this conclusion, we do three things. First, we summarise the chapters, picking out the specific ways in which the authors have addressed the circuit of culture, but also more generally clarifying what each chapter has added to our understanding of smartphones. Second, we specifically focus on that circuit, to reflect upon the contribution this book makes to that framework. Last, we look across the chapters to say a little more about the smartphone cultures that have been explored in this volume.

Chapter summaries

In the first section of the book on infrastructure and applications both chapter authors reflect more extensively on the circuit of culture. Smartphones provide quite a good example for thinking about the importance of infrastructure, here the electricity supply, in everyday life, given they are increasingly power hungry and we depend more and more on their multiple functionalities. Originally the editors thought that Maren Hartmann's discussion of infrastructure could provide an opportunity to discuss production processes, expanding them beyond design decisions and the affordances of media devices and software. However, she argues that infrastructuring can be considered a process in its own right, an addition to the circuit of culture. Hartmann observes how the relatively small literature on infrastructure rarely covers media and communications, and hence an object such as the smartphone. Yet infrastructure is itself socially shaped and in turn has the power to both enable and constrain the use of devices. Hartmann goes beyond existing writing on infrastructures to illustrate how that constraint is made manifest, how it is reflected in the policies of institutions such as cafes and in the experiences, feelings and subsequent actions of users. Du Gay *et al.* (1997) note that rather than viewing the different process or moments in isolation it is important to see how they interrelate, and in this chapter we see how infrastructure issues affect consumption and also regulation (where an intentionally limited number of plugs in a café is one means to regulate use). This shows how trying to work within a broader framework, in this case the circuit of culture, can inspire further lines of reflection. Finally, Hartmann suggests ideas for a research agenda on infrastructure and ICTs, including smartphones.

César Albarrán-Torres and Gerard Goggin also note the merits of the circuit of culture, more so the Du Gay *et al.* version. Their historical section on the development of mobile gambling and specifically social mobile gambling on the smartphone draws attention to several of those processes in that circuit, in order to provide a more holistic view of the gaming phenomenon. Regulation is referred to more briefly, but we see discussions of representations, in terms of how the social element of new forms of gambling are emphasised in the marketing of these products. The authors also point out how, more generally, social, casual gambling is changing the image of gambling in general, by normalising the practice in the face of history of negative discourses verging on moral panics. That same chapter reminds us how production is itself multifaceted. One aspect is how social elements are designed into apps, such as messaging capabilities to allow communication between gambling parties or the facility to allow spectators. We also see the various business models underlying different apps, which has a bearing on how a critical analyst might evaluate the social betting phenomenon (e.g. if users are providing marketable information about themselves). Last, we have the changing industry structure and players, with both start-up companies and established gambling companies moving into new areas. Although not in itself a study of users of apps, the chapter provides reflections pertinent to lived culture, by noting how social gambling builds on existing consumption practices – for example, by basing social gambling features on social gaming ones. Mobile gambling and social gambling may be just one type of app, where the arrival of smartphones enabled this whole field of mobile gambling to develop. But the study of this single type of app reminds us how we can talk of smartphone cultures in the plural, suggesting the scope for investigating myriad different possibilities opened by this technology.

In the next section, Cristina Ponte, Anca Velicu, José Alberto Simões and Claudia Lampert examine parental mediation of children's use of the smartphone. As might be anticipated, some of the motivations behind parental mediation and mediation strategies are a mixture of the old and the new. Some carry over from the experience of mobile phone technology more generally – for example, many of the concerns parents have about smartphones and the rules they develop for limiting children's use (e.g. in terms of the time children are allowed to spend using the devices). Other elements are more specific to the smartphone, especially when discussing some type of mobile internet access, for example what children can upload and download, parental control of the Wi-Fi system, and the parental strategy of checking the smartphone browser history. The authors note that in relation to the circuit of culture, the particular set of practices they address, i.e. parental mediation, is a dimension of lived culture. But the chapter shows what aspects this can entail. One element is perceptions, be that in the form of parental concerns, more positive views about the benefits of smartphones, an appreciation of the ubiquity of this technology in general or ideas about what it means to be a good parent. Some of these perceptions presumably draw on wider public representations, ranging from advice on parenting to fears about the 'problems' of addiction. Such perceptions are important because they influence parental actions, among other factors (e.g. parental technical skills, observations of how older siblings experienced smartphones). The other important area covered in this chapter is the complexity of rules, looking beyond children's use to see the regulation of that use to varying degrees in various guises – a theme developed further in later chapters.

Mireia Fernández-Ardèvol and Andrea Rosales report on Spanish studies that explore older people's experience of the smartphone, a group often neglected given the association of youth with new technologies. Although this is mainly a study of consumption practices, we see very early in the chapter how representations of the elderly as 'laggards' in technology adoption can even affect the buying experience. Fernández-Ardèvol and Rosales note that although this consumption experience may not be unique to this age group, the elderly exhibit forms of access to smartphones not necessarily anticipated by industry: borrowing them, getting others to use them on their behalf and sharing devices as a couple. As the most common use, the chapter then focuses on WhatsApp, an application that rose to prominence during the course of the studies. It shows how these older users can be as ambivalent and critical as the youth discussed in other chapters, indicating where the app has a positive role to play, but also where voice communication is preferred and where some are concerned that voice is in decline because of the increase in textual contact. One of the important uses of WhatsApp is the group function, which differs from the equivalent on platforms like *Facebook*, by virtue of providing a more detailed awareness of the audiences for messages – a fact appreciated by elderly participants in this study who appear not to be *Facebook* enthusiasts. On these *Facebook* groups we also see the circuit of culture's regulation processes as norms about appropriate ways to communicate in the group emerge, albeit varying from group to group. Finally, Fernández-Ardèvol and Rosales observe that older people's conversations and reflections about this app themselves contribute to an on-going process of constructing a representation of the WhatsApp service.

Leslie Haddon's chapter is the first of two that deals more specifically with the domestication framework. Like many domestication studies, the main attention is on factors affecting the process of consumption, in this case one major consideration being how children's use is regulated by adults and how children react to that regulation in their practices. The earlier chapter by Ponte *et al.* emphasised the parental perspective behind the constraints imposed on children's use, but Haddon notes the negative discourses about ICTs, the representations that may affect parental perceptions. The chapter focuses on how the financial, temporal and spatial constraints – largely imposed by parents, but also other adults – are experienced by children and how they deal with them, how it not only limits but also changes their consumption practices. That said, children also have agency not only in terms of reacting to adult influences, but in their own reflections on their priorities in the face of competing time demands and on appropriate behaviour in certain spaces (on certain occasions) that also influence their smartphone use. There is a general academic interest in consequences for children of their experiences of technologies, and here the smartphone may be somewhat iconic. Sometimes that interest is framed in terms of risks to children, sometimes in more celebratory accounts of how technologies are improving their lives. But either way, it is important to appreciate the factors that limit what they do with technologies in the first place.

The chapter by Troels Fibæk Bertel also acknowledges that while the focus of domestication may be on consumption, the other process in the circuit of culture are pertinent. Using the smartphone scenarios as illustrations, Bertel deals with several strands that he argues are less well developed in the domestication frame-work, more so in its original form and still with a frequent focus on households. One strand involves how domestication handles the mobility of technologies like the smartphone as the device moves across spaces and hence social contexts. Although first examined when the mobile phone was mainly used for communi-cation (Haddon, 2003), smartphone-enabled mobile media, and especially the mobile internet, mean that we now have to think about how even apps are them-selves domesticated through experiences outside the home and bearing in mind audiences other than family members. Second, the stress on social negotiation in much of domestication analysis appears to underplay individualised use of devices. But the picture is more complicated as smartphone scenarios are used by Bertel to demonstrate how apparently individualised practices such a using the map app or finding ways to store information can still be seen in the wider context of interacting with social networks and pursing collectivist goals. Third, although not unique to this device, the high degree of malleability of the smart-phone, its extreme multifunctionality, raises questions about what should be the object of any domestication analysis: whether it is a material object (the device), an app (and its symbolic environment) or even the texts made available through it (symbolic content). Finally, domestication needs to take into account increas-ingly cross-media use. Not only do smartphones need to be seen within a wider ecology of devices, platforms and services, but the choice to use or not use any particular app on the smartphone takes place bearing in mind the affordances of other apps that could achieve related goals. Apart from providing some guidance about how to think about approaching a domestication analysis that considers a whole array of elements associated with smartphones, the chapter shows how this new technology can provoke us to revise and refine theoretical frameworks.

The chapter by Carla Barros brings an anthropological perspective on cultural differences, reflecting on how particular consumption practices to be found in the Global South differ from expectations at the moment of production in Europe and North America. When discussing the history of smartphones in Brazil, Barros notes that when illegally imported cheap devices first entered the country one uncommon development unanticipated by technology developers was that the consumption of TV on these smartphones was pioneered by lower classes. This in turn had an effect of production, as companies sought to develop this type of phone legally for the Brazilian market. The chapter then moves on to focus on the consumption of ICTs of Brazil, especially among poorer groups. Elements of this consumption are shared in other countries, as shown in African studies. In various ways, Barros argues that consumption is more collective, as illustrated by older ICTs like TV sets being watched in the street. This ethno-graphy then focuses on interactions on long distance train commutes, where passengers share various technologies, one practice being the collective viewing and discussing by maids and cleaners of a telenovela shown on their smartphones. Reflecting the Johnson version of circuit of culture, here the reading of this content is informed by the lived experiences of these maids and cleaners, who in turn use those texts to form the basis for discussion of their (lived) employment experiences. Barros goes on to explore collective consumption more generally, covering forms of orality and sociability in public, as illustrated by newspaper consumption in publics spaces and learning to play massively multiplayer online games (MMORPG) in internet cafes. Through reflection on some African studies, the chapter comes back to the more general point that at the moment of production in parts of the Global North there are various assumptions about indi-vidualised consumption of ICTs, and hence the importance of privacy, that are reflected in design decisions. But these assumptions are at odds with many col-lectivist consumption practices in the Global South, and may actually hinder usage there. In fact, there are a variety of assumptions about how smartphones will be consumed (e.g. associations with geographic and social mobility) that do not do justice to how they are experienced in these parts of the world.

Maialen Garmendia, Miguel Casado del Río and Estefanía Jimenez examine the issue of communication overload on the smartphone, exacerbated by mul-tiple communication options, and by the fact that it is more 'at hand' compared to a PC. Hence, they shed more light on the complexity of consumption within the circuit of culture. The first part of the chapter shows the ambiguity about being 'always on': the positives of being connected to peers and the feeling that this can enhance friendships and the negatives of peer pressure, having to be available and being aware that the constant messages can be a distraction. Yet, worries about social exclusion, a sense of being obliged to respond to others and the practicalities of dealing with a backlog of messages if they do not keep up all help to explain the tendency to check smartphones constantly, even when being caught doing so involves sanctions, as in school. Garmendia *et al.* then focus on how young people cope with this overload problem, turning their smartphones off or leaving them out of sight, or prioritising some communications over others. In fact, some of the study's participants indicate they would welcome more rules about use, not only to reduce their own overload problems but because of what they perceive to be inappropriate use. This involves those peers who are always with their smartphone in hand and dealing with communication at times when the participants feel that face-to-face interaction should take pri-ority. In general, this chapter shows the social complexity of the situations in which these young people have to make consumption decisions and how their 'use' (very broadly understood to include turning off the device, placing it out of sight and choosing not to check messages) can also be seen as attempting to cope with those situations.

Framing the chapter in terms of critical commentary on notions of smart-phone addictiveness and excessive use, Giovanna Mascheroni locates this whole experience systematically within the Du Gay *et al.*'s version of the circuit of culture, stressing especially the interplay between processes such as representation and consumption. For example, she observes how in their accounts of their smartphone experiences children draw upon both the positive representation of the 'digital native', indeed it forms part of their identity, but also upon various representations of the 'child at risk', both in describing their parents' concerns and their own. Not only do they participate in reproducing these discourses, which pre-date the smartphone, but they do so specifically referring to the smartphone's potential to amplify some behaviours. Mascheroni goes on to explore the relationship between production and consumption, by looking at how children refer to and build upon the affordances of the technology, when accounting for their practices. Although with a different emphasis because of its engagement with claims about excessive use, the chapter lastly touches upon some of the same themes as the previous chapter, noting young people's ambiguity about the smartphone and how they are active agents in coping with various issues. But Mascheroni explicitly ties this in with issues of regulation, as the young people seek or try to create rules about appropriate and inappropriate smartphone-related behaviour (such as using the smartphone too much in the co-presence of others). Making links to the domestication framework discussed earlier, as the use of smartphones becomes normalised or 'institutionalised', that use takes on a normative character as we develop expectations about use, giving young people less freedom in how they can domesticate the technology in their own lives.

The chapter by Sofie Vandoninck, Marije Nouwen and Bieke Zaman draws on Belgian studies to examine different facets of the process of regulation of smartphones in schools. The authors frame this by critically noting claims about the 'convergence of culture', including those about the blurring of boundaries between home and school, learning and entertainment, then demonstrating that for the most part this is not happening. Quantitative data are first used to show how school rules, and restrictions on Wi-Fi access in school generally serve to inhibit the use of smartphones in schools. Behind the broad figures, the interviews reveal that there are actually some innovative teachers who use mobile media (smartphone and tablets) in their general practices, or else allow children to use them on more exceptional occasions (e.g. field trips and project work). In fact many teachers see some educational potential for the devices in the future. However, there are, first, some more practical barriers to teachers either using or allowing use of these technologies – the school rules noted above, the lack of technical support and fast Wi-Fi infrastructure and a lack of technological skills, and hence confidence, among teachers. Perhaps more important for the convergence claim is a widespread perception among both teachers and pupils that smartphones are mainly devices for entertainment and communication, not education – i.e. this representation of the smartphone dominates, for the most part those categories have not 'blurred'. In addition, some of the concerns that teachers have about the potential disruptive consequences of smartphones for learning are justified, as parents are willing to break school rules and contact their children in school time, expecting a reply, and children break rules as they check their phones. In this context, the main response of classroom teachers is to not allow smartphone use at all, even if they show more latitude to older students because they appreciate how important phones can be for their developing autonomy. And despite some reservations about the severity of the most common form of sanction, the other response to rule breaking is to confiscate the device. In sum, the chapter shows the complexity of a specific example of regulation: there are a wide range of considerations that ultimately having a bearing upon teacher decisions to regulate smartphones – including the fact that potential positive learning outcomes are often not appreciated. Meanwhile, implementing such regulation remains a challenge.

Sora Park and Naomi S. Baron focus on one very specific practice, writing, comparing laptop typing, traditional handwriting on paper and writing with smartphones. This chapter was a study of consumption by virtue of looking at the choice of when and how to use different media. The empirical evidence in this Australian study points to the affordances of the different media, but also emphasises the experiential dimension: the ease of use, the thought process and indeed the emotions associated with each mode of writing – as well as the context of writing. In fact, writing on the smartphone was the most problematic, less preferred, mode, and although the participants communicated via texts written on this device, sent social media posts or used it to jot down notes, they often did not even consider that this counted as being 'writing' – at least initially. That said, in different circumstances and for different purposes people were willing to use all three modes, and for the most part found it easy to switch between them. In this sense, the smartphone had added to the writing mix, rather than displacing other forms of textual production, and perhaps helped reshape our ideas about what it means to write in general.

Jane Vincent, John O'Sullivan, Christopher Lim and Manuela Farinosi first frame their chapter at the most general level by pointing out how claims about how ICTs are revolutionising all aspects of everyday life have been criticised. Here they examine the practices of reading and writing, to explore just how much difference smartphones make in this mundane area of life. Within the circuit of culture, this constitutes a study of lived culture in Johnson's version. More specifically, they are critical of the enthusiasm for technology in the field of education, pointing to ways in which vested interests promote edtech, and its uncritical acceptance in some policy discourse. While some studies claim that students embrace the smartphone as the latest edtech, others cast doubts on this, showing the various negative experiences of this technology that have been noted by this particular audience. To engage in this debate, the chapter reports on a study of how students evaluate and use smartphones, laptops/desktops and pen and paper for reading and writing. Part of a wider study, the chapter reports on the results from three countries, the UK, Italy and Ireland, to provide a comparative element in a field of discussion where universalistic statements are often made. While the study involved a range of different questions, producing more detailed observations (e.g. about how length of text makes a difference) and some national variation, the main and clear finding was a preference for pen and paper, with even laptops/desktops faring better than smartphones. Despite the celebration of smartphones more generally, they had made little headway into this area of life. Moreover, students are arguably a strategic case – given they have grown up with digital technologies and are increasing immersed in them in universities, if they still value more traditional media for reading and writing, we might expect this to be true for the wider population.

Circuit of culture

We introduced this volume by describing the circuit of culture and how we aimed to use this approach to frame the contributions. In doing so we not only drew on Johnson's original approach, with his example of the mini-metro, but also the subsequent and influential work of Du Gay *et al.* (1997) on the Walkman, brought up to date in 2013 with the inclusion of the smartphone. One of our contributors Goggin (2006) also used this approach for his volume on cell phone culture and now we see that Johnson's approach still pertains today in our new exploration of smartphone cultures, albeit over 30 years since he first presented his new idea of the circuit of culture to summarise the work of the then emerging discipline of cultural studies.

When discussing why it is important to be aware of the whole circuit, Johnson noted: 'If we are practically preoccupied with one moment and familiar with its forms, the other moments may not exist for us' (1986: 284). In other words, if the researcher is focusing on the production of an artefact, perhaps its social shaping, the question of how it is then used or 'consumed', maybe in ways unintended by the developer, may not be foremost in mind. Or to use Johnson's framework, if researchers are conducting a critical reading of the semiological processes operating within a text (e.g. recently both editors of this book attended a seminar that looked at messages implicit in the record covers of vinyl records in 1950s America), they may not focus on people's actual readings (how buyers of those records in practice 'read' those texts).

However, neither Johnson nor Du Gay *et al.* were unique in making these connections – there are other examples where researchers are sensitive to other moments in the circuit. The 'encoding-decoding' model (Hall, 1980) in cultural studies that preceded Johnson's circuit explicitly draws attention to how those vinyl record buyers might 'read' (decode) the covers in different ways from those intended by the designers (who had encoded it with certain meanings). In relation to the first example of researchers looking at production, there is work in technology studies that examines how producers monitor consumption practices and modify their products accordingly (Sotamaa, 2005). Both the editors of this book have recently been involved in the Net Children Go Mobile project studying children's use of smartphones and tablets – but, as is clear in some of the chapters in this volume, those children have to deal with the affordances of the technology (shaped in production), they act under constraints (regulation) and in the light of public discourses about how children should behave and a history of specific concerns about the effects of those technologies on their lives (representations). While they manage this situation, children exercise agency, they do so against the backdrop of these other moments.

But if the insights from Johnson and Du Gay *et al.* are not unique, one merit of both contributions is that they are systematic when inviting us to think about the nature of cultural processes, which is why they have been used in teaching over the years. As in the case of domestication, these scholars provide sensitising frameworks, that also invite researchers to ask certain questions, ones they might not otherwise have asked – in this case prompting analysts to think through the relation to other processes in the circuit beyond the focus of their own studies. Of course, the circuits of Johnson and Du Gay *et al.*, have over-lapping but different elements: production, texts, readings and lived cultures on the one hand and production, consumption, regulation, representation and iden-tity on the other. But they share the principle of asking researchers to reflect across moments, to explore the connections. Hence, in this volume we asked the contributors to at least locate their own work in relation to either one of these circuits and if possible to consider the relation to other moments.

Many of the contributors developed those connections. For example, Hart-mann considered the regulation and consumption implications of infrastructural decisions. Albarrán-Torres and Goggin drew attention to issues relating to the representations of mobile social gambling, and how in the production process elements incorporated in the app draw on gaming practices from lived culture. Indeed, the latter authors argued that seeing the whole circuit is useful for getting a grasp, an overview, of this new mobile gambling phenomenon. Meanwhile, Barros had a whole range of different observations about the circuit in her study of viewing TV on smartphones in Brazil. We see how this unanticipated practice stirred companies to produce legal smartphones for this market. Readings of the content of these phones were informed by these users' experiences and fed into further reflection on their lives. And then we have the key theme about collectiv-ist consumption in parts of the Global South being at odds with anticipated con-sumption when these devices as produced in parts of the Global North.

Other chapters also explored how the various moments in the circuit inter-acted, or, as some authors might prefer, articulated (Du Gay *et al.*, 1997, p. 3). When exploring claims about excessive use, Mascheroni described how user accounts drew upon public representations, the role of the affordances of the smartphone arising from the production moment and the normative regulation of use. In their discussion of older users, Fernández-Ardèvol and Rosales drew attention to the emerging regulation of WhatsApp in different user groups, and argued that these discussions contribute to the over representation of this service. While Vandoninck *et al.* focused on the processes of regulating the smartphone in school, they also examined how a dominant, though contested, representation of the devices as being 'non-educational' served to justify that regulation. Last, on a more general level, in a chapter that assesses ways in which another frame-work, domestication, can be developed, Bertel observed how even though this analytical approach is chiefly concerned with lived culture, these other moments in the circuit were nevertheless relevant and needed to be borne in mind when appreciating how we make technologies part of our lives.

Apart from looking across the moments of the circuit, various authors elaborated what these processes at different moments entailed. For example, Hartmann drew attention to the role of infrastructure in relation to production, an aspect often neglected in production studies. Albarrán-Torres and Goggin outlined a variety of dimensions that can count as constituting production. Both Ponte *et al.* and Haddon examined the different ways in which children's consumption of smartphones is regulated by parents (and others) and hence influences smartphone use, while Haddon also draws attention to the motives behind children's own self-regulation. Vandoninck *et al.* explored the myriad considerations at work in the process of trying to regulate the use of the smartphone specifically in the school context. And several of the authors examined different aspects of lived culture, such as Garmendia *et al.* exploring how communication overload is experienced and managed, Park and Baron looking at the factors influencing choices about the mode of writing in a digital age, and Vincent *et al.* reporting students' evaluations of different media for reading and writing – both the latter chapters including whether and when to use a smartphone for these purposes. In general, these contributions explored what these rather abstract labels such as production, regulation, consumption and lived culture might entail and hence what future researchers might consider studying.

As Goggin notes, the circuit of culture approach has over the years been used by a variety of researchers, such as when Green compared narratives used in the marketing of mobile phone with narratives employed by mobile users (cited in Goggin, 2006, p. 7). Arguably, each time this framework is used it adds to a literature that in turn shows how this approach can be insightful – in relation to what objects of study, what research questions, and at what levels (e.g. what aspects of production, or consumption, or lived culture). In that sense, over and above any insights related to smartphones, the authors of this book have contributed to that body of writing, suggesting ways of thinking about how we might deploy the circuit of culture as an analytical tool.

Smartphone cultures

In the early literature on mobile phones Cooper *et al.* (2000) argued that the mobile was a device for the cultural mediation in everyday life. When focusing on technologies, even if only to exemplify a broader argument, one key reason why Johnson and Du Gay *et al.* refer to cultural processes in their respective circuits is because of the many symbolic meanings at play. This includes those constructed in the processes of production, added to in further representations of technological objects (e.g. concerns about their implications) that it turn underlie regulation, but also those generated through experience of the device, through practices, through what Goggin (2006, p. 3) has called 'little cultures of consumption'. This is one reason why the book refers to 'smartphone cultures' in the plural, but it is plural too because of the nature of the device. The social gambling case of Albarrán-Torres and Goggin and the WhatsApp groups described by Fernández-Ardèvol and Rosales demonstrate we are also dealing with the meanings of specific apps, specific parts of the smartphones' functionality – and as Bertel argues, these can be objects of analysis in their own right.

If that is the rational for the book to talk about cultures, why the focus on smartphones? What is exceptional, given some continuities with mobiles? The multifunctionality of the smartphone is one of the key factors that differentiates it from early mobile phones, although of course, this is not a totally sharp break between the two devices as the latter itself evolved over time, for example, adding camera and music playing facilities. The fact that you can now have arguments over whether the first Blackberry counted as a smartphone, or whether the history of smartphones has to start with Symbian or with the iPhone shows the potential for blurred boundaries between the two devices. But as we look across the contents of these chapters, although often 'about' smartphones, they pick up on concerns and practices that also related to mobile phones in the past. For example, there were issues about recharging the mobile in public spaces that touched on the infrastructure themes discussed by Hartmann – although more power hungry smartphones arguably make these more acute (and thus much less accessible in many locations globally). Many of the parental concerns described by Ponte *et al.* and the regulation of use in the home (Haddon) and school (Vandoninck *et al.*) have precursors relating to mobile phones. But there are also new elements within these: parental rules about mobile internet use or regulation of children's use of particular activities such as watching video on 3G because of the cost. And then there are some smartphone uses that simply had no equivalent on the mobile phone, such as the social mobile gambling app discussed by Albarrán-Torres and Goggin, the map app example provided by Bertel, watching television on the device, as discussed by Barros, and writing on screens noted by Park and Baron.

However, one other difference between the experience of the two devices is perhaps one of scale, that certain experiences are amplified on the smartphone, akin to the point made by boyd when comparing face-to-face interaction with that on social networking sites (2014). For example, when Garmendia *et al.* discuss communication overload, the greater number of communication channels through the smartphone appears to be increasing that traffic compared to the mobile. Or when Mascheroni discusses the norms emerging about when it is inappropriate to be absorbed in smartphones, this may in part reflect the fact there is more to be absorbed in – such as checking social networking posts – compared to the days of the mobile. Often the smartphone is celebrated for what it can do, but this may also mean more things to socially manage, new tasks for users.

That celebration of smartphones is also challenged by chapters of this book, as in various ways they each introduce critical reflections. Albarrán-Torres and Goggin remind us that for some gambling apps, users are providing marketable information about themselves. Barros raises questions about the assumptions about individual use built into design and in the representations of the device.

Both Haddon and Vandoninck *et al.* note the constraints on children's use of smartphone in the home, school and public spaces, meaning that they clearly are not devices that can be used 'anytime, anywhere'. Garmendia *et al.* show how those young people have certain negative feelings about the communication overload arising from smartphones, and both they and Mascheroni reflect upon what peers perceive as anti-social use of these devices. Last, both Park and Baron and Vincent *et al.* reflect on aspects of life, reading and writing, where smartphones have had a limited impact. In other words, while the chapters illustrate the multifaceted nature of smartphone experiences and, indeed, some of the diverse ways in which we can research smartphone cultures, they also show how we can ask critical questions in this domain.

We suggested when introducing this volume that smartphones might have more significant roles in the future with regard to influencing and shaping user experience and industry developments. While there is some evidence of this in our volume such as the development of social mobile betting, the watching of television, and the ways children and the elderly appropriate smartphones for their everyday use, there is also evidence in the mundane aspects of use showing that the smartphone is far from being at the centre of user experience, as in reading and writing. This is due both to limitations of communications infrastructure and to the portfolio of alternative and complementary technologies often preferred. There is little to indicate that the smartphone will simply subsume other technologies and become the heart and focus of future information and communication technologies. However, it would appear it is the versatility of the smartphone device, its mobility and range of capabilities, that is its strength. Each chapter in this volume has explored different scenarios in which the smartphones figure, some more than others, but all showing how people, acting within constraints and influenced by representations, have chosen certain affordances that suit their daily life. These modes of appropriation, by children, students, adults, the very old, and in business, education and everyday situations explored in this volume show us very diverse ways in which the smartphone is impacting on social relations. We have learned that there are many different forms of cultural representations of smartphones in the society and every chance that there will be many more. We anticipate, then, that smartphone cultures will dynamically and constantly form and reform as new consumption practices and lived experiences create new 'readings' and meanings for this apparently dependable device.

References

boyd, d. (2014) *It's complicated: the social lives of networked teens*, Yale University Press, New Haven, CT.

Cooper, G., Green, N. and Moore, K. (2000) Mobile culture: the symbolic meanings of a technical artefact, Paper for '*Culture, Psychology and New Technologies' Symposium* BPS London Conference, 20 December 2000.

Du Gay, P., Hall, S., Janes, L., Mackay, H. and Negus, K. (1997) *Doing cultural studies. The story of the Sony Walkman*, Sage, London.

Goggin, G. (2006) *Cell phone culture: mobile technology in everyday life*, Routledge, Abingdon.

Haddon, L. (2003) Domestication and mobile telephony, in Katz, J. (ed.) *Machines that become us: the social context of personal communication technology*, pp. 43–56, Transaction Publishers, New Brunswick, New Jersey.

Hall, S. (1980) Encoding-decoding, in Hall, S., Hobson, D., Lowe, A. and Willis, P. (eds) *Culture, media, language*, pp. 128–138, Hutchinson, London.

Johnson, R. (1986) The story so far: and further transformations, in Punter, D. (ed.) *Introduction to contemporary cultural studies*, pp. 277–313, Longman, Harlow.

Sotamaa, O. (2005) Creative user-centred design practices: lessons from game cultures, in Haddon, L, Mante, E., Sapio, B., Kommonen, K.-H., Fortunati, L. and Kant, A. (eds) *Everyday innovators, researching the role of users in shaping ICTs*, pp. 104–116, Springer, Dordrecht.

Index

Page numbers in *italics* denote figures, those in **bold** denote tables.

 # Taylor & Francis eBooks

Helping you to choose the right eBooks for your Library

Add Routledge titles to your library's digital collection today. Taylor and Francis ebooks contains over 50,000 titles in the Humanities, Social Sciences, Behavioural Sciences, Built Environment and Law.

Choose from a range of subject packages or create your own!

Benefits for you

» Free MARC records
» COUNTER-compliant usage statistics
» Flexible purchase and pricing options
» All titles DRM-free.

Free Trials Available
We offer free trials to qualifying academic, corporate and government customers.

Benefits for your user

» Off-site, anytime access via Athens or referring URL
» Print or copy pages or chapters
» Full content search
» Bookmark, highlight and annotate text
» Access to thousands of pages of quality research at the click of a button.

eCollections – Choose from over 30 subject eCollections, including:

Archaeology	Language Learning
Architecture	Law
Asian Studies	Literature
Business & Management	Media & Communication
Classical Studies	Middle East Studies
Construction	Music
Creative & Media Arts	Philosophy
Criminology & Criminal Justice	Planning
Economics	Politics
Education	Psychology & Mental Health
Energy	Religion
Engineering	Security
English Language & Linguistics	Social Work
Environment & Sustainability	Sociology
Geography	Sport
Health Studies	Theatre & Performance
History	Tourism, Hospitality & Events

For more information, pricing enquiries or to order a free trial, please contact your local sales team: www.tandfebooks.com/page/sales

 **Routledge**
Taylor & Francis Group

The home of
Routledge books

www.tandfebooks.com